9.95

D0171581

From Folk Psychology to Cognitive Science

⌐Ŀ Bradford Books

Edward C. T. Walker, Editor. EXPLORATIONS IN THE BIOLOGY OF LANGUAGE. 1979. The MIT Work Group in Biology of Language: Noam Chomsky, Salvador Luria, et alia.

Daniel C. Dennett. BRAINSTORMS. 1979.

Charles Marks. COMMISSUROTOMY, CONSCIOUSNESS AND UNITY OF MIND. 1980.

John Haugeland, Editor. MIND DESIGN. 1981.

Fred I. Dretske. KNOWLEDGE AND THE FLOW OF INFORMATION. 1981.

Jerry A. Fodor. REPRESENTATIONS. 1981.

Ned Block, Editor. IMAGERY. 1981.

Roger N. Shepard and Lynn A. Cooper. MENTAL IMAGES AND THEIR TRANS-FORMATIONS. 1982.

Hubert L. Dreyfus, Editor, in collaboration with Harrison Hall. HUSSERL, INTEN-TIONALITY AND COGNITIVE SCIENCE. 1983.

John Macnamara. NAMES FOR THINGS. 1982.

Natalie Abrams and Michael D. Buckner, Editors. MEDICAL ETHICS. 1983.

Morris Halle and G. N. Clements. PROBLEM BOOK IN PHONOLOGY. 1983.

Irvin Rock. THE LOGIC OF PERCEPTION. 1983.

Jon Barwise and John Perry. SITUATIONS AND ATTITUDES. 1983.

Jerry A. Fodor. MODULARITY OF MIND. 1983.

George D. Romanos. QUINE AND ANALYTIC PHILOSOPHY. 1983.

Robert Cummins. THE NATURE OF PSYCHOLOGICAL EXPLANATION. 1983.

Elliott Sober, Editor. ISSUES IN EVOLUTION. 1983.

Stephen P. Stich. FROM FOLK PSYCHOLOGY TO COGNITIVE SCIENCE. 1983.

Norbert Hornstein. LOGIC AS GRAMMAR. 1983.

From Folk Psychology to Cognitive Science

The Case Against Belief

Stephen P. Stich

A Bradford Book
The MIT Press
Cambridge, Massachusetts
London, England

Second printing, 1986

First paperback printing, 1985

Copyright © 1983 by

The Massachusetts Institute of Technology

Book design by Mary Mendell.

Jacket design by Irene Elios.

Set in Palatino by The MIT Press Computergraphics Department.

Printed and bound by The Murray Printing Company in the United States of
America.

Library of Congress Cataloging in Publication Data

Stich, Stephen P.

From folk psychology to cognitive science.

"A Bradford book."

Bibliography: p.

Includes index.

1. Belief and doubt. 2. Psychology—Philosophy.
3. Cognition. I. Title.

BF773.S75   1983   153′.01   82–25883

ISBN 0-262-19215-2 (h)

     0-262-69092-6 (p)

For my mother
Sylvia L. Stich

Contents

Acknowledgments

It is often no easy matter to say just when a project began. My best guess is that this one started about ten years ago in a discussion group at the University of Michigan. In that group Brian Loar and I were often at loggerheads over commonsense psychology, and before the group disbanded I resolved to write a book setting out my side of the story. During the 1978–1979 academic year, a Fulbright Fellowship, a grant from the American Council of Learned Societies, and the hospitality of the University of Bristol made it possible for me to devote the better part of a year to the project. While in Bristol I had the benefit of almost daily discussions with Daniel Dennett and Andrew Woodfield. During that year I wrote a long paper called "On the Ascription of Content," which has been reworked into chapters 4 and 5 of this volume. Chapter 6 evolved from an unpublished paper written with Dennett and presented to a conference at the University of Bristol. The bulk of the manuscript was written during the 1981–1982 academic year, when a grant from the National Science Foundation and an award from the University of Maryland provided a year largely free of teaching responsibilities.

While work was in progress, bits and pieces of the book were presented to conferences and colloquia at Stirling University, Warwick University, St. David's University College, Tel Aviv University, the University of Haifa, Stanford University, the University of Virginia, Yale University, the University of North Carolina at Chapel Hill, the City University of New York, Tufts University, the University of Manitoba, and the University of Arizona. I have benefited in countless ways from the varying reactions of these various audiences. I have benefited also from the advice and criticism of numerous friends and colleagues, including Ned Block, James Cargile, Patricia Churchland, Paul Churchland, Bo Dahlbom, Daniel Dennett, Jerry Fodor, Gilbert Harman, Mike Harnish, William Lycan, Richard Nisbett, Zenon Pylyshyn, Joseph Tolliver, and Meredith Williams. Harry and Betty Stanton of The MIT Press have been helpful in all sorts of ways that are above and beyond the call of duty. My thanks to all.

My deepest debts are to my wife, Jude, and my children, Jonah and Rebecca. Jude has patiently proofread the final draft of the manuscript. And all three of them have endured with good cheer my long, solitary sessions staring at the word processor. For the children, my preoccupation with the book has been a double burden, since it deprived them of both paternal attention and time on the computer.

From Folk Psychology to Cognitive Science

Chapter 1

Two Cultures and the Promise of Cognitive Science

In our everyday dealings with one another we invoke a variety of commonsense psychological terms including 'believe', 'remember', 'feel', 'think', 'desire', 'prefer', 'imagine', 'fear', and many others. The use of these terms is governed by a loose knit network of largely tacit principles, platitudes, and paradigms which constitute a sort of folk theory. Following recent practice, I will call this network *folk psychology*. From antiquity to the beginning of the twentieth century, such systematic psychology as there was employed the vocabulary of folk psychology. Those who theorized about the mind shared the bulk of their terminology and their conceptual apparatus with poets, critics, historians, economists, and indeed with their own grandmothers. The nonspecialist reader in 1910 would be in equally familiar territory in William James's *Principles of Psychology* and in the novels of James's brother Henry. By the middle of the twentieth century all this had changed. With Thorndike, Pavlov, Watson, and the birth of experimental learning theory, the vocabulary of folk psychology was quite self-consciously renounced. The founders of modern "behavioristic" psychology proposed to devise new terms and concepts to suit the purposes of their fledgling science, while renouncing the "mentalistic" vocabulary of folk psychology as prescientific mumbo jumbo. Watson, for example, derided folk psychological concepts as "heritages of a timid savage past," of a piece with "superstition," "magic," and "voodoo," and he urged the behaviorist to begin "his own formulation of the problem of psychology by sweeping aside all medieval conceptions."[1] By midcentury the battle had been won. Behaviorism was in full flower in the leading universities, and its claim to be *the* scientific way to study "the mind" (now pointedly spelled with scare quotes) was widely acknowledged.

As behaviorism flourished, a chasm began to open in our culture. The picture of the mind shared by the historian, the poet, the political theorist, and the man in the street was being rejected by the vanguard of scientific psychology. It was not simply that the new science of behavior described people in terms not shared by common sense. The two were flat out incompatible. Common sense offers *explanations*: people act as they do because they have certain beliefs or wants or fears or desires. But if behavioristic psychology was on the right track, then these explanations were mistaken. People act as they do because they have been subjected to certain histories of reinforcement, and the beliefs and desires, hopes and fears of commonsense psychology have nothing to do with their behavior. These mental states of folk psychology are, on the behaviorists' view, no more than myths conjured by primitive theory. Like the deities, humors, and vital forces of other primitive theories, they simply do not exist. Our readiness to describe ourselves in these mythical terms indicates only that we are still wedded to a wrong-headed prescientific theory, just as in earlier centuries people under the spell of other primitive theories described themselves and their fellows as bewitched or phlegmatic. The "manifest image" of common sense was not merely different from the emerging "scientific image"; one or the other had to be wrong.[2]

The enormity of this conflict and its implications are worth pondering. Consider history: Did Henry VIII believe that Pope Clement would allow the annulment of his marriage to Catherine of Aragon, or did he expect the Pope to resist? If the behaviorists are right, then the question has no answer. Beliefs are myths, and it is no more sensible to inquire about Henry's beliefs than to investigate whether he had an excess of phlegm or a deficiency of yellow bile. Consider literary criticism: What motivates Raskolnikov's brutal crime in Dostoevsky's *Crime and Punishment*? Was it anger and frustration, or did he want to prove something to himself, or, perhaps, did he subconsciously want to be caught and punished? For the behaviorist, again, the question is absurd. None of these putative states, singly or collectively, could be responsible for Raskolnikov's deed, for no such states exist. Consider philosophy: A central concern of epistemology is to articulate a normative theory of belief formation which tells us what we rationally ought to believe and which of our beliefs are justified. But this is a project embedded in the manifest image of folk psychology. If we adopt the scientific image as behaviorism presents it, then the classical project of epistemology is misconceived. We can no more determine which beliefs we ought to hold than which deities we ought to propitiate.

A pair of factors served to mask the magnitude of the divide between folk psychology and the avant garde of experimental psychology. The first was the ambiguous role of "philosophical behaviorism." This was the doctrine, inspired by the verificationist theory of meaning, which held that "mental" or folk psychological locutions must be definable in terms of observable behavior. Verificationism, in its earlier and more virulent forms, held that *all* meaningful empirical terms must be definable in terms of *observables*. And philosophical behaviorism drew the conclusion that if the terms in question were folk psychological terms, then the only observables likely to be relevant were behavioral events. Verificationists took delight in wielding their criterion of meaningfulness as a weapon directed against established fixtures on the intellectual landscape. Religion, ethics, aesthetics, metaphysics and even some putative sciences were accused of couching their claims in vocabulary that could not be cashed out in terms of observables, and thus of being, quite literally, meaningless.[3] But philosophical behaviorism never inherited the village atheist temperament of its parent doctrine. It was, apparently, simply unthinkable to these philosophers that the folk psychological vocabulary we all use to describe and plan our lives should prove to be meaningless jibberish. Indeed one of the motives of philosophical behaviorism was to defend verificationism by showing that it need not classify the bulk of folk psychology's mentalistic terminology as nonsense. Presumably that result would have seemed absurd enough to constitute a reductio ad absurdum of verificationism. So the chore for the philosophical behaviorist was to explain how commonsense mental terms could be defined within a verificationist framework. In the tradition of philosophical behaviorism, numerous attempts were made to produce definitions which captured the meaning of various folk psychological terms by invoking behavior and behavioral dispositions.[4] In contrast to practitioners of philosophical behaviorism, behaviorist *psychologists* need have no concern with defining or redefining folk locutions. Their central project is to elaborate and defend a paradigm for explaining behavior in terms of stimuli, histories of conditioning, and the like, along with relatively simple psychological laws relating these variables to behavior. Folk psychological theories, for them, are just bad theories, medieval superstitions populated by states and processes that do not exist. Whether these myths are meaningful but false, or not even meaningful (thus neither true nor false), is a technical semantic issue on which the behaviorist psychologist need have no professional opinion.

Unfortunately however, this neat division between philosophical behaviorism and psychological behaviorism does not mirror the rather messy historical reality. Psychological behaviorism was a shocking doctrine, radically at odds with our commonsense conception of the world. To lessen the shock and thus reduce resistance to this radical view, some behaviorist psychologists, most notably Skinner, took it upon themselves to demonstrate that we could live with behaviorism. His strategy was to borrow a page from the *philosophical* behaviorist's book and argue that many of the notions of folk psychology could be defined or reinterpreted in terms drawn from the lexicon of behavioristic psychology.[5] But as philosophical behaviorists had already come to realize, it just ain't so! Definitions of <u>folk psychological locutions in behavioristic terms capture neither the sense nor the extension of the expressions being defined.</u>[6] Behavioristic margarine is no substitute for folk psychological butter. Still, such definitions—and Skinner offers them by the dozens—often had their desired effect. The casual reader might be convinced that the manifest image and the scientific image were indeed compatible and that in history or poetry or in the law the vocabulary of folk psychology was both serviceable and susceptible to scientifically respectable definition.

A second factor deflecting attention from the conflict between science and folk theory in psychology was the disciplinary specialization so characteristic of the twentieth century. Behaviorist psychologists and scholars in the humanistic disciplines each "did their own thing" paying little attention to what was going on across campus. There were occasional exceptions, of course, perhaps the most notable being the controversy that erupted when Skinner's *Beyond Freedom and Dignity* encroached on the humanists' territory in a way that was impossible to ignore.[7] Despite these occasional clashes, the intellectual world—or that part of it concerned with human thought and action—gradually drifted apart into two separate cultures, one taking folk psychology more or less for granted, the other rejecting it and everything built upon it as a primitive superstition.

It is against this background that the emergence of cognitive science, in the mid 1960s, must be viewed. In the early 1960s a number of psychologists who had grown up in the behaviorist tradition came to suspect that in its thoroughgoing rejection of the conceptual scheme of folk psychology experimental psychology had thrown out the baby with the bath water. Some of the reasons for their disenchantment are, in retrospect, fairly obvious. Much of the most interesting behavior, particularly in humans, just cannot be described comfortably in the behaviorist newspeak that had come to dominate experimental psychology. Moreover folk psychological explanations of complex, intelligent, or innovative behavior in terms of such folk notions as *beliefs, desires, knowledge, plans, goals,* and the like seemed to provide a new starting point for scientific theories aimed at explaining such behavior, a starting point more promising than the behavioristic theories which were so awkward in dealing with problem solving, planning, and linguistic behavior. Gradually and tentatively, terms like 'plan', 'belief', 'knowledge', 'image', and 'memory', began to reappear in the theorizing of hard-nosed experimental psychologists. During the 1970s, this flirtation with the notions of folk psychology blossomed into a fecund marriage. We now have theories of reasoning, problem solving, inference, perception, imagery, memory and more, all cast in the commonsense idiom of folk psychology.[8] The use of this workaday "mentalistic" folk vocabulary has become one of the hallmarks of the burgeoning field of cognitive science.

The cognitivist "revolution" has been greeted with enthusiasm by a growing number of philosophers. In part, no doubt, this is traceable to the intrinsic interest of an intriguing and important new development in science. But there is another motive behind the philosophical fascination with cognitivism. For in cognitivism philosophers have seen the promise of an intellectual world made whole once again. Cognitivism, now clearly the ascendant paradigm in the scientific study of the mind, invokes the very same concepts, or seems to, that are invoked by historians, poets, and jurisprudents. To be sure, cognitive scientists may know more about memory, imagery, belief, inference, and so on than do laypeople or humanistic scholars. But what they know more about are the familiar states and processes of folk psychology. In short, with the advent of cognitivism, both philosophers and psychologists have concluded that the scientific image of mind and the manifest image have been reunited. A thinly veiled conflict has been replaced by the prospect of active collaboration.

That Panglossian prospect is what this book is about. And, like Candide's, my own position is one of reluctant skepticism. Much as I would like the story to be true, I simply cannot get it to square with the facts. In the pages that follow my focus will be on the folk psychological concept of belief, and my central thesis will be that this concept *ought not* to play any significant role in a science aimed at explaining human cognition and behavior. I shall also argue that, despite appearances to the contrary, the folk psychological notion of belief *does not* play a role in the best and most sophisticated theories put forward by contemporary cognitive scientists. What is more, the problem is not localized to the folk notion of belief. Although my focus is on belief, the problems I pose apply, mutatis mutandis, to the whole range of "intentional" folk notions or "propositional attitudes"—to any folk psychological state characteristically attributed by invoking a sentence with an embedded "content sentence." Thus it is not simply sentences like

S believes that Ouagadougou is the capital of Upper Volta.

that I would banish from cognitive science, but also

S hopes that Ouagadougou is the capital of Upper Volta.
S fears that Ouagadougou is the capital of Upper Volta.
S desires that Ouagadougou be the capital of Upper Volta.

and all of their intentional kin. As I see it, the notion of "content" or the folk psychological strategy of identifying a mental state by appeal to a "content sentence," despite all its utility in the workaday business of dealing with our fellow creatures, is simply out of place when our goal is the construction of a scientific theory about the mechanisms underlying behavior. The chapters that follow constitute an extended argument for this vision. The path I will follow is rather a long one, I am afraid, and on more than one occasion I have given in to temptation and taken a detour to survey some of the nearby sights. So perhaps the first order of business should be to sketch a road map indicating the general direction the route will take.

Since my thesis is that cognitive science and the intentional notions of folk psychology are ill suited to each other, my argument falls naturally into two parts. In part I of the book I take a careful analytical look at the workings of the folk psychological notion of belief, noting problems with earlier portraits of the notion and developing a detailed account of just what we are saying of a person when we ascribe a belief to him. In part II I set out the case against invoking the folk psychological notion of belief in cognitive science and present a critical survey of the arguments offered by those who think cognitive science and folk psychology are well matched.

Among the earlier accounts of belief which I reject, two feature prominently. In chapter 2 I sketch the dominant "functionalist" account of mental state terms, which takes them to be terms of a folk theory whose meaning is specified by detailing the causal links among mental states, stimuli, and behavior. This story has been a popular one for mental states like pains and sensations, which are not ascribed with the aid of a content sentence. But whatever its virtues may be for these cases, formidable obstacles must be overcome when we try to fit belief and other "contentful" states into the functionalist paradigm.[9] Some of these obstacles are explored in the last section of chapter 2.

In chapter 3 the "mental sentence" view of beliefs will be center stage. On this account beliefs are relations between the believer and a sentence or formula suitably stored in the believer's mind or brain. There are some impressive reasons to take this view seriously. When pushed, however, the mental sentence account divides into two quite different stories, the difference turning on how mental sentences are to be typed or individuated. On one version, a pair of mental state tokens count as type identical when they have the same "content" or truth conditions; on the other version—the one I call the "narrow causal account"—tokens are type identical when their pattern of causal connections with other tokens, other mental states, stimuli and behavior are the same.

The burden of chapter 4 is that the narrow causal version of the mental sentence theory will not do as an account of our folk psychological notion of belief. Though many examples are marshaled to make the case, they fall into two categories. Some illustrate the fact that the distinctions allowed by a narrow causal account of individuation are too coarse, forcing us to ignore differences between mental states that folk psychological intuition takes to be salient and important. Others make exactly the opposite point. Sometimes the distinctions mandated by narrow causal individuation are too fine grained, forcing us to draw distinctions where folk psychology recognizes none. The arguments in chapter 4 undermine the narrow causal version of the mental sentence theory and reinforce the case against functionalist accounts of belief. The reason is that functionalist accounts individuate mental states along much the same narrow causal lines. Thus arguments against the narrow causal version of the mental sentence theory also apply, mutatis mutandis, to functionalist accounts of belief.

In chapter 5, finally, I develop what I take to be the correct account of our folk psychological notion of belief. The story I have to tell is a relative of the mental sentence view with tokens individuated by content. What is central and novel in my account is its explanation of just what "sameness of content" comes to. Two themes predominate. The first is that *sameness* of content plays no role in our folk conception of belief. Rather, what we invoke in making judgments about how a belief is to be characterized is a tacit notion of *similarity*. Thus cases range in a gradual and multidimensional continuum from clear instances of the belief that p, through a swamp of intermediate cases where folk psychology provides no clear judgment, and ending up with clear instances of cognitive states which do not count as the belief that p. Common sense, buttressed by some sophisticated psychological experimentation, suggests that similarity judgments are acutely sensitive to context. Thus if my similarity account of belief ascription is correct, we should expect that judgments about the propriety of a content sentence in characterizing a belief will also be sensitive to context. And indeed they are, as we shall see. The second central theme in my account is that in ascribing content to a belief we are, in effect, comparing the believer to ourselves. We are saying that the believer is in a cognitive state that would underlie our own normal assertion of the content sentence. It follows that we should have increasing difficulty in ascribing content to the cognitive states of subjects, as those subjects become increasingly different *from us*. And once again this expectation is borne out. A sort of Protagorean parochialism is thus built into intentional folk psychological concepts, since when it comes to ascribing content, men and women *like us* are the measure of all things.

Chapter 6 turns attention to the most conspicuous lump swept under the carpet throughout part I. Just about all recent philosophical writing about belief assumes that ordinary language belief ascriptions are systematically ambiguous. On this view, belief sentences generally admit of either a *de dicto* or *de re* reading. If this is right, it bodes ill for my account, since on my view there is but one commonsense concept of belief and belief sentences are univocal. In chapter 6 I take the bull by the horns and argue that the putative systematic ambiguity of belief sentences is a myth. Like most myths, to be sure, it is based on some undeniable facts. But, I shall argue, these facts are better explained by a theory postulating no systematic ambiguity.

Part II and my brief against the marriage of folk psychology with cognitive science begin in chapter 7. The first question to be addressed is what a cognitive theory would be like which made serious use of the language and concepts of folk psychology. Two rather different answers to this question are abroad, though they are generally not clearly distinguished. The first is what I shall call the *Strong Representational Theory of the Mind*. The Strong RTM is a model or a paradigm for cognitive theories. As the Strong RTM views them, cognitive theories postulate mental states which are relations to tokens of mental sentences. The generalizations of a Strong RTM theory detail the causal interactions among mental states by adverting to their contents. Chapter 7 begins by elaborating on this idea and ends by arguing that it is a bad idea. The core of my argument is the claim that the theorist who seeks to couch the generalizations of cognitive science in the content-ascribing language of folk psychology will be plagued by problems that can readily be avoided. The fact that similarity assessments underlie the ascription of content entails that generalizations which attempt to detail the way beliefs interact with each other, and with other cognitive states in terms of the content of these states, will be beset by the *vagueness* and *context sensitivity* which similarity assessments engender. The Protagorean parochialism of content ascription, with its built-in comparison to our own cognitive network, makes it intractable to characterize in the language of folk psychology the cognitive states of relatively exotic subjects such as young children, "primitive" folk, and people suffering from various brain injuries and mental illnesses. Thus the regularities to be found in the cognitive processes of these subjects and the commonalities that they share with us will be beyond the reach of a cognitive science which casts its generalizations in the restrictive language of folk psychology.

Of course, we might learn to live with these difficulties if there were no alternative. But that is not the case. In chapter 8 I shall sketch an alternative paradigm for cognitive theories which avoids the problems engendered by appeals to content in Strong RTM theories. The alternative is what I will call the *Syntactic Theory of the Mind*. Cognitive theories which cleave to the STM pattern treat mental states as relations to purely syntactic mental sentence tokens, and they detail the interactions among mental states in terms of the formal or syntactic properties of these tokens. Though STM theories have evident advantages over theories in the strong RTM mold, some philosophers and psychologists have suggested that STM theories will miss important generalizations that can be captured by Strong RTM theories. Three arguments for this view are considered in chapter 8, and all of them are found wanting.

In chapter 9 attention is turned to the other view of cognitive theories advocated by those who think folk psychology and cognitive science are well matched. This view, the *Weak Representational Theory of the Mind*, is positioned midway between the Strong RTM and the Syntactic Theory. It shares with the STM the claims that mental states are relations to syntactic tokens and that the generalizations of cognitive psychology detail the interactions among mental states in terms of their formal properties. In agreement with the strong RTM, it insists that mental states (or their associated syntactic objects) have content or truth conditions. The more interesting version of the Weak RTM goes on to claim that the semantic properties of mental state tokens are correlated with their syntactic types. Various arguments have been offered purporting to show either that cognitive psychology does adopt the Weak RTM or that it should since there would be something to be gained by insisting that syntactic mental state tokens have semantic properties. However, I shall try to show that these arguments are defective. Ultimately the Weak RTM fails for much the same reason as the Strong RTM. By insisting that mental states have content or truth conditions, it imposes pointless limits on cognitive theorizing, limits which hamper efforts to understand the mental processes of children, brain damaged people, "primitive" folk, and others whose beliefs or cognitive processes are significantly different from our own.

There are various other arguments in the literature aimed at showing that folk psychology and cognitive science make strained bedfellows. Chapter 10 is devoted to reviewing three of these.

The concluding chapter is devoted to pondering the argument that has preceded. If it is granted that folk concepts have no role to play in an empirical science aimed at explaining the mental processes underlying behavior, then we must confront anew the problem with which this introduction began. If folk locutions are scientifically otiose, does it follow that they denote nothing? Or, to put the issue more vividly, are we to conclude that the behaviorists were right after all, albeit for the wrong reasons, and that the states and processes spoken of in folk psychology are mythical posits of a bad theory? The answer, I will urge, is that it is still too early to tell. If it turns out that the best theory about cognition and behavior is an STM closely paralleling the skeleton of folk psychology, then no such disastrous results follow. For in this case folk psychology, though not perhaps reducible to scientific psychology in any strong sense, would be vindicated by scientific theory. The states postulated by scientific psychology could be described in intentional folk psychological terms and thus many of the claims cast in the vocabulary of folk psychology would turn out to be unproblematically true. But if it turns out that the best theory is an STM theory which diverges radically from the folk psychological paradigm, or that the best theory is not an STM theory at all, then the prospects are poor for a reconciliation between the manifest and scientific images of the human mind. This last outcome is more than a mere logical possibility, for some impressive recent work suggests that the scientific study of cognition will lead in directions undreamed of in folk psychology.

Having glimpsed this vision of a scientific psychology cut loose from its folk forebear, one writer, Dennett, has proposed to salvage folk theory by treating it as an "instrumentalistic calculus." Others, it would seem, urge that we learn to love a world view in conflict against itself. But as I see it, neither of these strategies will do. If our science is inconsistent with the folk precepts that define who and what we are, then we are in for rough times. One or the other will have to go.

PART I
Folk Psychology

Chapter 2
The Theory-Theory

What may well be the most widely accepted theory about the nature of commonsense mental states is the view Morton has labeled *the theory-theory*.[1] 'Functionalism' and the 'causal' theory are more common labels for the doctrine.[2] But each of those terms has acquired such a daunting array of senses and subcategories that we do better to adopt Morton's less encrusted name. In explaining the view, it proves useful to show how it grew out of earlier discussions in the philosophy of mind, and to this end I will do a bit of historical reconstruction. But let the reader beware! The historical approach, for me, is no more than an expository convenience, and my historical sketch is more caricature than portrait.

1. From Descartes to David Lewis

The central problem in the philosophy of mind is to explain what mental states *are*, to say how they fit into our broader conception of nature and its categories. Since Descartes a common answer has been that mental states are, quite literally, *sui generis*. The Cartesian view divides reality into two quite distinct though causally interacting domains. My thoughts, perceptions and the like take place in my mind, a "substance" which has no location in physical space, though it does have a special and intimate relation to my body. This special connection between the mental and the physical proved to be Descartes' Achilles' heel. On the one hand it seems undeniable (though not undenied!) that what I think and feel can have a causal effect on the way my body behaves. If I feel a pain in my toe and decide to move it, it moves. Yet with the advance of the physical and biological sciences, it has become increasingly plausible that the physical world is a closed system. The spectacularly successful physicalist paradigm leaves no room for causal intervention from another domain. The textbook version of the problem this poses for Descartes' dualism is often cast in terms of the neurological events intervening between stimulus and behavior: Step on my toe and some nerves will fire; these will cause others to fire; these still others. Finally, though the firing pattern will be staggeringly complex, efferent nerves will fire, muscles will contract, and my toe will move out from under your foot. All this happens without the assistance or intervention of anything nonphysical. So either pains, decisions, and the like are not located in a nonphysical domain, or they are superfluous in the causation of behavior.

Of course this story about neural firings is for the moment no more than hopeful science fiction, since we have no serious idea about the details. Our confidence that the details can eventually be filled in derives from the success of physicalistic theories in other domains. I confess to a nagging suspicion that our confidence may be misplaced. But that is a long story and a different one.

With the decline of Cartesian dualism, philosophers began looking for a way to locate the mental *within* the physical, identifying mental events with some category of events in the physical world. A natural suggestion, in light of the intimate connection between our mental lives and the goings-on in our brains would be to identify mental events as brain events. But under the influence of the verificationist theory of meaning, that view was passed over for the prima facie less plausible view that mental events are (or are definable in terms of, or are logical constructs out of) behavorial events. This, of course, was the central theme of philosophical behaviorism.

It is worth pondering why theorists touched by the verificationist theory of meaning insisted on the primacy of *behavior* in their account of the mental. Granting, for the sake of argument, that all meaningful expressions must be defined in terms of observables, why not attempt to define mental vocabulary in *neurological* terms? My brain states are, after all, just as observable (in principle) as my behavior. The verificationists' preference for behavior was motivated by two closely related lines of argument. First, mental concepts are common coin, shared by the learned and the unlettered. The simplest of souls knows what it means to say 'the injured man is in pain,' or 'Hitler believed he could conquer the world.' But the meaning of these claims for persons of little learning cannot be cashed out in terms of neurological events, since they may be quite ignorant of the fact that they have a nervous system. The second line of argument focuses on language learning. Whether or not we know we have nervous systems, this information surely played no role in our learning to apply mental vocabulary to ourselves and others. The only observable indications of mental states that were available for use in teaching mentalistic vocabulary were behavorial events. So, it was argued, it must be in terms of these that our mental concepts were constructed.

With the growth of philosophical behaviorism, the problem addressed by philosophers of mind underwent a subtle but significant change. For Descartes, Locke, or Berkeley the questions of interest were ontological ones: What sort of thing (or stuff, or process, or substance) is the mind? What sort of thing is matter? How are they interrelated? The philosophical behaviorist, by contrast, is asking not about the nature of the mind, but rather about the *concept* of mind: What is the *meaning* of our mental terms? What is the correct *analysis* of our mental concepts? The shift from ontological questions to questions of conceptual analysis can easily go unremarked when, as was the case with philosophical behaviorism, an answer to the conceptual question trivially entails an answer to the ontological one. If 'S is in pain' means 'S is disposed to behave in certain ways', then, trivially, pain is a behavorial disposition. But, as we shall soon see, there are ways of answering the conceptual question without saying much of interest about the ontological status of mental states and processes.

Before proceeding with our historical reconstruction, it will be useful to have before us some examples of the sort of analyses attempted by philosophical behaviorists. Here are two.

(1) Hempel, in the widely reprinted essay, "The Logical Analysis of Psychology," urges that the meaning or content of any nonobservational empirical statement is given by the various physical tests we would use to determine whether the statement is true. "The statement itself clearly affirms nothing other than this: all these physical test sentences obtain. . . . The statement, therefore, is nothing but an abbreviated formulation of all these test sentences."[3] For the statement 'Paul has a toothache', Hempel offers the following partial unpacking of the abbreviation:

a. Paul weeps and makes gestures of such and such kinds.
b. At the question "What is the matter?" Paul utters the words "I have a toothache."*

---

*Not all who followed in the tradition of philosophical behaviorism took themselves to be offering analyses of commonsense concepts or everyday locutions. Some took their job to be the analysis of scientific concepts or perhaps the development of new concepts that pass behavioristic muster and might be used in some current or future science. Hempel must have had this latter project in mind, since he completed his list with

c. Closer examination reveals a decayed tooth with exposed pulp. . . .
d. Paul's blood pressure, digestive processes, the speed of his reactions, show such and such changes.
e. Such and such processes occur in Paul's central nervous system.

It seems, however, that the distinction between analyzing ordinary concepts and constructing new ones was often ignored. Hempel gives no hint that the locution he is analyzing is not part of our ordinary vocabulary.

(2) Carnap, offering an account of belief sentences that will cast a substantial shadow in the pages that follow, suggests this as a first pass:

> John believes that snow is white

can be analyzed as

> John is disposed to respond affirmatively to 'Snow is white' or to some sentence which is L-equivalent to 'Snow is white.'[4]

These behavioristic analyses are typical in both their flavor and their difficulties. Most salient among the latter is that the analyses are just plain *false*. The proposed definition or analysis does not capture the meaning or even the extension of the commonsense locution with which it is paired. To see this, consider Paul and his aching tooth. If the analysis is intended to provide necessary and sufficient conditions for 'Paul has a toothache', it fails miserably, for surely Paul may weep, gesture, and respond as indicated while feeling no pain at all; he is just practicing for his role in a dramatization of Mann's *Buddenbrooks*. Conversely Paul may be in utter agony, though as a matter of pride he does not allow himself to give the least indication of his suffering. John, for his part, may believe that snow is white while having not the least disposition to respond affirmatively to 'Snow is white.' He may, for example, believe that such a response would provoke his interlocuter to mayhem; or he may simply wish to deceive others about his beliefs.

These are, to be sure, specific complaints about specific behavioristic definitions, but they augur a more general problem. It is now widely conceded that it is impossible to define psychological expressions in terms of behavior, unless some further psychological terms occur in the definition. John's belief that snow is white will dispose him to respond affirmatively to 'Snow is white' only if he *understands* English, is paying *attention*, *wants* to let you know what he thinks, *believes* that this can be done by responding affirmatively, and has no other *desire* stronger than his desire to let you know what he thinks and incompatible with it. Put simply, the trouble with behavioristic definitions is that when they are not patently inadequate, they are inevitably circular.[5] As awareness of the difficulty sharpened, a number of writers in the philosophical behaviorist tradition explored ways of weakening the central behaviorist claim. Psychological terms were not to be *defined* in terms of behavior; rather, they were to be related to behavior in some less stringent way.[6] But these attempts at rescue generally foundered on one or the other of a pair of perils. Either the new weakened relationship between psychological terms and behavorial terms was too obscure to be understood, or, when the alleged relationship was clear enough, the circularity problem arose anew. Gradually philosophical behaviorism suffered the death of a thousand failures.

While philosophical behaviorism was struggling with the problem of circularity, similar problems were being uncovered by "operationalists" who were attempting to apply the verificationist doctrine to scientific concepts. There too, the doctrine insisted that to be meaningful an expression must be definable in terms of observables. But once again circularity loomed. Consider gravitational mass. We might try something like the following for an operational definition:

Two objects are equal in gravitational mass = df
The objects would balance each other on an analytical balance.

However, like the behavoristic definitions considered earlier, this definition is just mistaken; it fails to capture the concept it is trying to define. The test for equal mass will work only if the objects being tested are not being subjected to differential forces. (Imagine that one is wood, the other iron, and the test is being conducted in a strong magnetic field.) But an operational definition of 'subject to equal force' would in turn require some mention of mass in the definiens.

The reaction to this problem in the philosophy of science was to explore a quite different line for explaining how theoretical terms get their meaning. Rather than being *defined* in terms of observables, it was proposed that theoretical terms might get their meaning simply in virtue of being embedded within an empirical theory. The meaning of the theoretical term lies, so to speak, in its theory specified interconnections with other terms, both observational and theoretical. There is nothing mysterious about a term acquiring meaning by being embedded in a theory. Indeed, as a little tale by David Lewis makes clear, it is the sort of thing that happens all the time. Lewis asks that we imagine ourselves

assembled in the drawing room of the country house; the detective reconstructs the crime. That is, he proposes a *theory* designed to be the best explanation of the phenomena we have observed: the death of Mr. Body, the blood on the wallpaper, the silence of the dog in the night, . . . and so on. He launches into his story:

X, Y, and Z conspired to murder Mr. Body. Seventeen years ago in the gold fields of Uganda, X was Mr. Body's partner . . . Last week, X and Z confered in a bar in Reading . . . Tuesday night at 11:17, Y went to the attic to set a time bomb . . . Seventeen minutes later, X met Z in the billiard room and gave him a lead pipe . . . Just when the bomb went off in the attic, X fired three shots into the study through the French windows . . .

And so it goes: a long story.

The story contains the three names, 'X', 'Y', and 'Z'. The detective uses these new names without explanation, as though we knew what they meant. But we do not. We never used them before, at least not in the senses they bear in the present context. All we know about their meaning is what we gradually gather from the story itself.[7]

Yet by the time the detective is finished with his reconstruction, we know the meaning of 'X', 'Y', and 'Z' as well as the detective himself. We may discuss X's motives, debate whether Y was a drug addict, perhaps even disagree about the plausibility of the alleged meeting in the bar. Lewis gives the label *implicit functional definition* to this process of introducing terms by recounting a theory in which they play a role.

Before we see how all this ties up with mental concepts, four observations about implicit functional definitions are in order. First, as Lewis notes, the story the detective tells about X, Y, and Z would be essentially unchanged if, instead of simply plunging into his narrative, he had prefaced his remarks by saying: "There exist three people whom I shall call 'X', 'Y', and 'Z'." The "theoretical terms" 'X', 'Y', and 'Z' in the story would then function as variables bound by an existential quantifier.

Second, it is possible for an implicit functional definition of a set of terms to be quite noncommittal about various facts concerning the "theoretical entities" it introduces, including facts that may be of considerable importance. In the story at hand the detective did not tell us what we probably most wanted to know: the *names* of the persons involved. Perhaps when the tale is told our background knowledge will enable us to name the perpetrators ourselves. But perhaps not. The detective himself may have no idea of the bomber's (as they say) true identity. It is also possible, though this does not emerge in Lewis's tale, for an implicit functional definition to be noncommittal about the *ontological status* of the theoretical objects defined. Suppose, for example, that our detective is something of a spiritualist. He theorizes that there was something, call it 'W', which caused the French windows to slam shut at the crucial moment. That something, W, witnessed a scene between X and Y, and W became infuriated by what he (it?) saw. In short, W enters into a variety of causal relations with other characters in the story, with various physical objects, and so on. Now you may be convinced that W is a person, since you are convinced that only a person could fill that role. But the detective is not convinced. He is willing to entertain the possibility that W is not a physical object at all. Perhaps W is a spirit, a disembodied Cartesian mind. Note that nothing in his theory—which, recall, *is* the implicit functional definition of 'W'—commits him one way or the other on this matter. The theory simply claims that there is *something* which had various causal interactions, and it is neutral on the issue of the ontological status of that something.

The third observation is a corollary to the second. Since implicit functional definitions leave much unsaid about the theoretical entities denoted by theoretical terms, they leave ample room for further elaboration. We might discover a great deal about X that is unknown to the detective and unmentioned in his theory: that X was born in Rhodesia, perhaps, or that he lost a toe due to frostbite. The point is that by further investigation we might come to know more about the detective's theoretical entities than does the detective himself. In the extreme, though it raises some ticklish questions, we might even come to know that the detective was wrong in some of his beliefs about X. This in any event would be the natural conclusion if we were to discover a man who fit the detective's characterization to a tee, save for the bit about meeting Z in the billiard room. (Actually, it was in the adjacent pantry; but X walked through the billiard room to get to the pantry, and it was while walking throught the billiard room that he lost his cufflink.)

The fourth point is that *various* kinds of relations may play a role in implicit functional definitions. In Lewis's story characters are described in terms of their conversations, their business relations, their spatial locations at certain times, and so forth. One sort of relation that does not enter into Lewis's story but well might is what could be called the relation of _typically causing_: Fido is a placid beast, kind to cats, children, even postmen. But for some reason X typically sets Fido off on a howling fit. Not always, and not only X; occasionally Fido will greet X with a wagging tail, and once in a while just about anything will set Fido off. Yet it is the sight of X which typically causes Fido's fits.[8]

So much for implicit functional definition. Now let us turn to what I am calling the theory-theory, which is an attempt to apply the idea of implicit functional definition in the philosophy of mind. The basic thought is that commonsense mental terms gain their meaning just as 'X', 'Y', and 'Z' did in Lewis's detective story. They are "theoretical terms" embedded in a folk theory which provides an explanation of people's behavior. The folk theory hypothesizes the existence of a number of mental states and specifies some of the causal relations into which mental states enter—relations with other mental states, with environmental stimuli, and with behavior. Of course the theory implicitly defining mental terms is rough and incomplete. It may make ample use of the notion of typical causing, allowing for exceptions to causal regularities which are neither explained nor enumerated by the theory. Lewis suggests that we could assemble the relevant folk theory by simply collecting platitudes:

> Collect all the platitudes you can think of regarding the causal relations of mental states, sensory stimuli, and motor responses. . . . Add also all the platitudes to the effect that one mental state falls under another—'toothache is a kind of pain', and the like. . . . Include only platitudes which are common knowledge among us— everyone knows them, everyone knows that everyone else knows them, and so on. For the meanings of our words are common knowledge, and the names of mental states derive their meaning from these platitudes.[9]

Let us try to make this proposal a bit more precise. A fragment of folk theory about mental states might include a dozen mental predicates (like 'has a toothache', 'is afraid,' 'is thinking of Vienna') which we may abbreviate $M_1, M_2, \ldots, M_{12}$. It will also include some predicates characterizing environmental stimuli, say $S_1, S_2, \ldots$, and some predicates characterizing behavior, say $B_1, B_2, \ldots$. (The predicates may take any number of arguments, though for simplicity of exposition I will assume they are all monadic.) Some of the generalizations of folk psychology specify typical causal relations among mental states. If we let the arrow '$\rightarrow$' mean 'typically causes', then one of these generalizations might be represented as follows:

(1) $(x) M_1x \& M_2x \rightarrow M_5x \& M_8x.$

Other folk platitudes tell of causal relations between stimuli and mental states, thus:

(2) $(x) S_2x \& S_7x \rightarrow M_{12}x.$

Still others detail causal relations between mental states and behavior:

(3) $(x) M_8x \& M_4x \rightarrow B_6x.$

Finally, still others may detail complex relations with a stimulus and a mental state causing both some behavior *and* some subsequent mental states:

(4) $(x) S_3x \& M_4x \rightarrow M_7x \& B_{12}x.$

The whole of our folk psychological theory might be represented as a conjunction of principles similar in form to (1)–(4). Or, paralleling a move mentioned in the discussion of Lewis's detective story, we might replace all of the mental *predicates* with variables and preface the long conjunction of folk principles with a string of existential quantifiers. The result would be a Ramsey sentence of the form

(5) $(\exists m_1)(\exists m_2) \ldots (\exists m_k) \, (x) \, T,$

where 'T' is the conjunction of (1)–(4) and similar principles, with variables suitably substituted for mental state terms.

A number of points should be stressed about the theory-theory account of the meaning of commonsense mental terms. First, if the account is correct, then the ordinary use of mental state terms carries a commitment to the *truth* of our folk theory. If the folk theory expressed in a sentence like (5) turns out to be false, then the mental state predicates the theory implicitly defines will be true of nothing. We needn't be purists on the point, insisting that every detail of our folk theory turn out to be true. Various strategies are available for sidestepping this unwelcome implication.[10] But there is no escaping the fact that for a theory-theorist, most of our folk platitudes must be true if any attribution of a mental state is true. As Lewis notes, if the theory-theory is true, then "mental terms stand or fall together. If common-sense psychology fails, all of them alike are denotationless."[11]

My second point is that the theory-theory is ontologically noncommittal. Mental states are characterized by the role they play in a complex causal network purporting to explain behavior. But just as the detective's story may be noncommittal on whether the thing filling the role of W is a person or a disembodied spirit, so too the folk theory which implicitly defines mental state terms remains neutral on whether the fillers of the various causal roles are physical states, Cartesian mental states, or what have you. For the advocate of the theory-theory, this "topic neutrality" is a singular virtue, since it allows what seems prima facie obvious, viz., that a Cartesian and his materialist neurologist can communicate quite successfully using the vocabulary of folk psychology. If, as the theory-theory insists, mental terms are defined by topic neutral folk theory, then despite the differences in their further beliefs, the Cartesian and the neurologist mean the same when they invoke commonsense mental terms.

On the theory-theorist's view, it is a matter for science to determine just what fills the causal roles specified by folk theory. Though there is an important ambiguity in putting the matter this way. Assuming that folk psychology is true (or near true) of both you and me, we may ask exactly what it is that fills the causal role which folk platitudes specify for my current backache or for your current perception of a printed page. And surely the best scientific bet in both cases is that the causal roles are filled by current physical states of our brains—very different states, no doubt, for my backache and your perception. So the theory-theory along with some timid scientific speculation entails the *token identity theory*. Specific, individual, dated occurrences of mental states are to be identified with specific, dated occurrences in the brain of the person having the mental state. But what about mental state *types*? What, in general, are toothaches or thoughts of Vienna? If it were the case that for all toothaches the platitude-characterized causal role is filled by neurologically identical brain states, then it might be plausible to say that a toothache (the type now, not a token) simply *is* a type of neurological event. This is the doctrine known as the *type identity theory*. However, the premise on which the type identity theory rests, viz., that all individual toothaches (tokens) are identical with brain states of the same neurological type, may well turn out to be false. It is a good bet that different humans, or humans and sharks, or humans and Martians, typically have *different* sorts of brain states playing the causal role that folk psychology assigns to a toothache. Considerations of this sort have led most theory-theorists[12] to conclude that a state type like having a toothache is best viewed not as a physical state type, but rather as a "functional" state. On this view, the state (type) of having a toothache (for anyone, or anything, at any time) is the complex state an organism is in when it (1) satisfies the precepts of folk psychology (i.e., is truly described by folk psychology), and (2) is in some (presumably but not necessarily physical) state which, in the person or organism in question, fills the causal role assigned to toothaches by folk theory.

The third point to stress about the theory-theory is one which will take on great importance in subsequent chapters. Theory-theorists typically hold that commonsense psychology is a theory aimed at explaining behavior *in terms of the causal relations among stimuli, hypothesized mental states, and behavior.*[13] To adopt this view of folk psychology is to exclude any reference to noncausal relations in folk psychology. There can be no mention of a subject's social setting, natural environment, or personal history, nor of the psychological characteristics of other people. And since for the theory-theorist mental terms are implicitly defined by commonsense psychological theory, none of these factors can be conceptually tied to commonsense mental terms or concepts.[14] Thus the theory-theory is committed to what I will call the *narrow causal individuation* of mental states. Perhaps the best way to explain this terminology is to focus on the question of what must be true of a pair of subjects if they are to be in mental or psychological states of the same type. What, for example, must be true of Fido and me if we both have a toothache?[15] The answer provided by the theory-

theory goes like this: First, both of us must be truly described by folk theory. Second, each of us must be in a state which fills the role assigned to toothaches by folk theory. Note that for these two conditions to obtain, it is not necessary for Fido and me to be at all similar in our chemical or physiological makeup. Fido could perfectly well be a robot whose brain is made of silicon chips. But it is necessary that some state of Fido's be *causally isomorphic* with a state of mine. That is, his token and mine must exhibit parallel patterns of potential causal interactions as these are characterized by folk theory. When an account of mental states holds that only their respective patterns of causal interactions count in determining whether a pair of states are of the same mental or psychological type, I will say that the account is committed to a *causal individuation* of mental states. Now what about the "narrow"? Well, causal links can extend well beyond the boundary of an organism. There are, no doubt, causal principles of various sorts linking some of my current psychological states to events that occurred long before I was born. But on the theory-theory account of mental states, none of these causal links are relevant in determining the mental or psychological type of the state. The only potential causal links recognized by the theory-theory are those that obtain between mental states and other mental states, those that obtain between mental states and *stimuli* and those that obtain between mental states and *behavior*. Accounts of causal individuation which restrict attention to just these causal links, I will call *narrow* accounts. In chapters 4 and 5 I will argue that this is a fundamental mistake, that no account committed to a narrow causal individuation of mental states can do justice to our folk psychological concept of belief. But before our stance turns critical we should take a more detailed look at the sort of account of belief that the theory-theory can offer.

2. Belief and the Theory-Theory: Some Problems

Thus far I have been discussing the theory-theory as a general account of the meaning of mental terms. In the current section I want to explore the prospects of applying this account to belief ascriptions—ascriptions of the form 'S believes that p'. In setting out the theory-theory, a commonly used illustration is pain, or some specific sort of pain, like a toothache. But there are a number of important differences between mental states like having a toothache, and mental states like believing that Socrates was wise, differences which make it hard to see how the theory-theory can provide an account of belief at all. First, pain has relatively strong and direct links to both environmental stimuli and to behavior; the links between belief and stimuli or behavior are much more tenuous. Second, folk psychology specifies relatively few links between pains and other mental states; beliefs, by contrast bristle with causal links to other mental states (including other beliefs). Third, just about all the varieties of pain for which our folk vocabulary provides labels have had many instances in the actual world. By contrast, folk psychology provides standard designations for an endless variety of beliefs that no one has ever held. Finally, pain is not prima facie a relational notion; 'has a toothache' is a one-place predicate. But belief at least *appears* to be a relational notion. It is tempting to say 'John believes Socrates was wise' expresses a *relation* between John and something, though, notoriously, it is not easy to say just what the second element of the relation is. These four differences will serve as convenient foci in the discussion to follow.

To see how the first of these differences makes belief problematic for the theory-theorist, consider the sort of account that could be given of a mental state like having a pricking pain in the finger. What folk platitudes might contribute to an implicit functional definition of this notion? Well, pricking pains in the finger are typically caused when the skin on the finger is pricked with a pin or other sharp object. In turn, pricking pains typically cause the finger to be quickly withdrawn. Pricking pains often cause wincing and a variety of verbal exclamations, many of which are not printable. They may also cause brief rubbing of the site of the wound. A few more platitudes might be added, but we already have a good sampling of the folk wisdom about pricking pains in the finger. On the theory-theorist's account, the pricking pain is defined as the state which has these characteristic causes and effects. If we try to tell a parallel story for beliefs, however, problems quickly crowd in on us. For, in contrast to pain, there is generally no characteristic environmental stimulus which typically causes a belief. There is no bit of sensory stimulation which typically causes, say, the belief that the economy is in bad shape, or the belief that Mozart was a Freemason. Beliefs about one's current surroundings are arguably an exception here; the belief that one is standing before an elephant *is* typically caused by having an elephant before one's eyes. But the fact remains that the bulk of our beliefs have no typical or characteristic environmental causes.* Nor do most beliefs have typical behavioral effects. My belief that Ouagadougou is the capital of Upper Volta does not cause me to do much of anything. It does (or would) typically cause

---

*This is not, of course, to say that these beliefs do not sometimes *have* environmental causes, but only that they do not have typical or characteristic causes of the sort needed for the theory-theorist's implicit definition. Your belief that the economy is in bad shape may have been caused by the sight of a price sign at your local gas station; mine was caused by the sight of the letter detailing my laughable pay increase.

me to say 'Ouagadougou is the capital of Upper Volta' in response to 'Fifty bucks if you can name the capital of a central African nation.' But it certainly does not cause most people who share my belief to utter what I would, given the same stimulus. For most of the people who share my belief, including most of the inhabitants of Upper Volta, neither speak nor understand English.

Since beliefs generally do not have typical stimulus causes or typical behaviorial effects, the theory-theorist must look elsewhere for platitudes to incorporate in implicit functional definitions. With links to stimuli and to behavior generally unavailable, the only alternative open to the theory-theorist is to build implicit functional definitions from principles detailing the relations of beliefs to other beliefs and to mental states of other sorts. This path is strewn with obstacles, however, and in what remains of this chapter, I will survey some of them.*

The most salient and systematic of the causal relations linking beliefs with other mental states are those that fall under the headings *inference* and *practical reasoning*. Here are some examples: Typically, if a person believes that everyone aboard the morning flight to Bamako was killed in a crash, and if he comes to believe that the prime minister of Mali was on that flight, those two beliefs together will cause him to believe that the prime minister is dead. Typically, if a person wants to go to New Zealand, and if she comes to believe that she must get a visa in order to make the trip, she will acquire a desire to get a visa. Endlessly many further examples might easily be constructed. But therein lies a problem, for there is no hyperbole in the prospect of *endlessly many* further examples. There are literally infinitely many inferential paths leading both to and from every belief. Moreover a description of each of these inferences (or at least of an infinite subset of them) is arguably part of our shared fund of folk platitudes about belief. An example may help to make the point obvious. Consider the inferences that would typically be drawn from the belief that Niger is west of Mali. If a person believes this and comes to believe that if Niger is west of Mali, then Niger has more than one million inhabitants, he will typically come to believe that Niger has more than one million inhabitants. If a person believes that Niger is west of Mali and comes to believe that if Niger is west of Mali then Niger has more than two million inhabitants, he will typically come to believe that Niger has more than two million inhabitants. And so on, ad infinitum. Moreover, obviously, this is only

*At this point we part company with Lewis who, as far as I know, has not addressed the problem of providing implicit functional definitions for belief predicates. The only serious and detailed attempts to provide a causal role analysis of belief that I know of are in Armstrong 1968 and 1973. For a critique of Armstrong's analysis, see Stich 1983.

the beginning. (Suppose he believes that if Niger is west of Mali, then Niger grows 5 percent more grain, or that if Niger is west of Mali, then Mali is more politically stable, or . . .) If we are to construct our implicit functional definition of 'believes that Niger is west of Mali' from the conjunction of these commonsense platitudes about inference, then the definition will have to be *infinitely long*! Now some stout-hearted souls are not intimidated by infinitely long conjunctions, provided they can be recursively summarized.[16] But when we reckon in inductive inference as well as deductive inference, it is far from clear that the class of inferences recognized by common sense *is* recursively characterizable. Even if we assume it is, there is considerable awkwardness in the view that the meaning of workaday belief attributions can be specified only by an infinite conjunction. Thus we have some motive to hunt for an alternative account.

The problem we have been discussing derives from the fact that common sense is so rich in platitudes about belief. But there is also a sense in which common sense is not rich enough in such platitudes, and this generates another sort of problem for the strategy of analyzing belief ascriptions in terms of intramental causal links. While there are infinitely many inferences with a claim to being embedded in common sense, there are also infinitely many logically valid inferences which people neither draw nor expect others to draw. If we know that Maggie believes all Italians love pasta, and if we know she has just learned that Sven is an Italian, we expect Maggie will come to believe that Sven loves pasta. But suppose that instead of believing Sven is Italian, Maggie comes to believe some claim which is logically equivalent, though it would take a clever logician a week of hard work to prove the equivalence. Plainly, we would not, then, expect Maggie would come to believe that Sven loves pasta. All this is unproblematic. Trouble arises because the line between cases of the first sort and cases of the second sort is anything but sharp. There are enormous numbers of inferences which some people expect their fellows to draw, while others do not. Which of these are we to take as part of the body of platitudes which define belief predicates? Advocates of the theory-theory give little guidance here, and I suspect that any answer will be ad hoc and implausible.

Another problem for the intramental definition strategy emerges when we reflect on the motive for invoking the notions of *typical cause* and *typical effect* in theory-theoretic accounts. Briefly, the story goes like this. Folk psychology recognizes that the causal regularities from which it is woven do not always obtain. For a given stimulus to produce a given mental state or for one mental state to produce another, conditions have to be suitable. Some of the ways in which conditions can be suitable or unsuitable are incorporated into further folk principles. But many are not. This causes no problems so long as the causal links folk theory specifies generally obtain under familiar circumstances. Thus a pricking pain in the finger can be characterized as the state typically caused by a pin pricking the finger, etc., and this characterization will pick out the right state, despite the occasional instance of a finger pricking causing no pain or of a pricking pain in the finger caused by a blow on the head. Note, in all this, that the notion of typicality being invoked is an utterly pedestrian one. A typical effect is just an effect that arises *in a substantial majority of the relevant cases.*

When we try to transfer this notion to the case of belief, however, things get very messy, for there are just not enough actual beliefs to go around. To jaded academic ears this may sound like an odd claim, since it often seems (as a colleague once put it to me) that every belief, no matter how outrageous, has at least a few adherents. But surely this is more pessimism than the facts warrant. No one believes—no one has *ever* believed—that Buckingham Palace is filled with pickles from floor to ceiling. And a few minutes of playful thought will be enough to convince you that there are endlessly many other beliefs that no one has ever held. Once this is granted, the strategy of defining beliefs by specifying their *typical* causes and effects runs into trouble. In the case of pain, 'typical' was unpacked as 'true of a substantial majority.' But what about such predicates as 'believes that Buckingham Palace is filled with pickles'? Since no one has ever held this belief, it has never caused or been caused by anything. What then are we to make of talk about its *typical* causes and effects? In chapter 5 we will see that an analogous problem arises for the account of belief ascription I want to defend. The solution I sketch there, however, will be of no help to the theory-theorist pursuing the intramental link strategy on beliefs.

A final difficulty with the strategy we have been considering is that it entails what Field has called the "orthographic accident view."[17] There is, as we noted earlier, a very strong temptation to insist that a statement like 'Jack believes that Bamako is the capital of Mali' expresses a *relation*. Jack is said to stand in some relation to a proposition, or fact, or sentence about Bamako. 'Jack believes that Niamey is the capital of Mali' asserts that Jack stands in the same relation to a different proposition or sentence. But on the view I have been sketching, predicates like 'believes that Bamako is the capital of Mali' are treated as one place predicates, whose meanings are implicit in a theory specifying the potential causal antecedents and consequences of the state denoted by the predicate. On this view it is simply an accident of nomenclature that 'believes' occurs in both 'believes that Bamako is the capital of

Mali' and in 'believes that Niamey is the capital of Mali,' an accident of no more significance than the fact that 'It' occurs in both 'Italy' and 'It's raining.' It is also an orthographic accident that 'Mali' occurs in both belief predicates. Indeed, it seems to follow from this view that beliefs are not (or at least need not be) a natural folk psychological category at all. The states attributed by 'believes that Socrates was wise', 'believes that Frege was mistaken', and 'wants to visit New Zealand' are each characterized by a set of typical causes and effects specified by folk theory. There is nothing to indicate that the first two are states of the same kind, different from the third. To make matters worse, the orthographic accident view makes it something of a mystery how we ever succeeded in mastering the language of belief ascription. We all understand infinitely many predicates of the form 'believes that p', though on the orthographic accident view each of these is a logically atomic predicate like 'is red'.

All of this is wildly implausible.* Surely it is more promising to view belief sentences as expressing a relation of some sort. And, conveniently enough, this thought leads directly to the *mental sentence* theory of belief, which is the topic of the next chapter. But what shall we conclude about the theory-theory account of belief? Well, at a minimum it is clear that the view must confront some very substantial obstacles. Perhaps enough has already been said to convince you that the theory-theory strategy cannot produce an account which does justice to our folk notion of belief. If not, then read further. In chapters 4 and 5 an argument will be developed which applies, mutatis mutandis, against any account of belief which individuates beliefs on narrow causal lines. Since the theory-theory is committed to narrow causal individuation, that argument gives yet another reason to conclude that the theory-theory tells the wrong story about the commonsense concept of belief.

---

*Though not so implausible that it lacks eminent advocates. Quine 1960 comes very close to adopting the orthographic accident view.

Chapter 3
Beliefs as Mental Sentences

At the end of the previous chapter we reviewed some reasons for thinking that the notion of belief is best construed as a relational notion. By and large, relational accounts of belief divide into two categories, the division turning on the sort of thing that fills the second slot in the belief relation. Theories in one of the categories take belief to be a relation between a person and a proposition. These accounts differ among themselves on just what a proposition is and on the nature of the relationship between the person and the proposition that is the object of that person's belief. But there are two points on which propositional accounts agree: propositions are some sort of *abstract* entity, and propositions are not sentencelike creatures—they do not have a *syntactic* structure. Theories in the second category take belief to be a relation between a person and a *sentence*. On this view, to have a belief is to have a sentence token suitably inscribed or encoded in one's brain. In this book I will have very little to say about propositional theories of belief. This for two reasons. First, these theories have made relatively little impact on cognitive science; those who hope that contemporary cognitive science will reunite the scientific and the commonsense world views are almost always advocates of a sentential account of belief. Second, I think it is already abundantly clear that propositional theories, whatever their virtues, simply do not tell the right story about belief as it is conceived in folk psychology. The case for this point has been well stated by others.[1]

The bulk of this chapter will be devoted to answering the two obvious questions about sentential theories of belief: What, precisely, do they claim, and what reason is there to accept them? Before attending to either of these matters, however, a few remarks are in order on the divergent goals of sentential theorists on the one hand and theory-theorists like Lewis on the other.

1. Protoscience and Conceptual Analysis

In the discussion of philosophical behaviorism I noted that it brought in its wake a subtle shift in the sort of questions philosophers have asked about the mind. For Descartes or Hume the central questions were ontological: What sort of thing or stuff is a mind or mental state? How is it related to matter? These are questions about the nature of things and, apart from their generality, they are of a piece with the questions that would be asked by a natural scientist interested in the mind. For the philosophical behaviorist, by contrast, the central questions are those of conceptual analysis: How is the concept of mind (or belief, or pain) to be analyzed? What is the meaning of mental state terms? As philosophical behaviorism has lost its grip on contemporary philosophy of mind, the protoscientific questions have once again come to the fore. Thus most defenders of the mental sentence view do not take themselves to be doing conceptual analysis. Rather, they view themselves as engaged in a process which is continuous with the doing of science. They want to know what sort of thing a belief is, and not merely how our ordinary concept of belief is to be understood. Since they are attempting to build a theory about a part of the natural world, they feel free to marshal arguments and evidence from any quarter which may prove helpful. There is no need for them to restrict themselves to facts about our commonsense concept. Still folk notions are not irrelevant to the protoscientific project. If we want to know the nature of the entities denoted by a certain commonsense term or falling under a certain commonsense concept, then we had better keep a sharp eye on the way that concept is used, lest we end up describing the wrong critters. Conceptual analysis also has a more substantive role to play in the protoscientific project. For it is sometimes possible to argue that, given the contours of our commonsense concept, the entities falling under the concept must have (or are likely to have) certain features. What is more, the features need not be the ones which are, in any sense, *entailed by* or *built into* the folk notion. In effect such arguments attempt to show that, in virtue of various facts, including some about our commonsense concept, the *best hypothesis* about the entities falling under the concept is that they have certain features. I am laboring this point to forestall a possible misunderstanding of mental sentence theories. In arguing that belief is a relation between a person and a sentence token in that person's brain, mental sentence theorists are *not* claiming that this is part of our ordinary *concept* of belief. Rather, they are arguing that this is the best hypothesis *about belief*, given a range of facts including some about our commonsense concept and locutions.

2. Some Features of the Concept of Belief

Let us begin our discussion by assembling some of the facts about our ordinary notion of belief which sentential theorists have used in arguing for their view.[2]

(1) First, and most obviously, beliefs (and related states like fears, wants, hopes, etc.) are standardly named and attributed by linguistic constructions involving an embedded sentence or sentential transform. There are other ways of referring to beliefs, of course. My students sometimes refer to a belief of mine as "Stich's favorite belief." But if asked what that belief is, they would reply, "the belief that Ouagadougou is the capital of Upper Volta." Moreover, as Vendler has shown,[3] there are striking parallels between the syntactic behavior of belief sentence complements and the syntactic behavior of the complements in sentences of the form: 'S said that p' or 'S asserted that p'.

(2) As we have noted, 'believes' seems to express a two-place relation. Ordinary language provides us with the resources for distinguishing between a belief and the second element in the belief relation, which might be called *what is believed* or *the object* of the belief. The distinction emerges clearly in a passage like the following:

> John believes that war builds character. Given his early education, his belief is to be expected. Though, of course, what he believes is utter nonsense.

Ordinary language also provides us with natural ways of expressing the fact that a pair of beliefs share the same object:

> John believes that war builds character, and after his rousing lectures many of his students believe it too.

Beliefs can also share the same object with other attitudes:

> John believes that we have turned the corner on inflation, but Maggie doubts it. I wish it were true.

(3) As they are conceived and spoken of in our folk theory, both beliefs and the objects of beliefs can have semantic properties. Thus we may say either

> Maggie's belief is true.

or

> What Maggie believes is true.

However, the truth value of a belief must be the same as the truth value of the object of the belief. Thus common sense finds nothing but paradox in a claim like

> John's belief is true, though what he believes is false.

Also, the truth value of both a belief and of what is believed must match the truth value of the embedded sentence that would be used in ascribing the belief. So if Maggie believes that there are no pandas in Tibet, then Maggie's belief is true if and only if the sentence

There are no pandas in Tibet

is true.

The situation is analogous for entailment, logical equivalence, and other semantic relations. These relations can obtain both between beliefs:

Maggie's belief entails John's

and between the objects of beliefs:

What Maggie believes entails what John believes.

Here too, the semantic relations between the objects of belief must parallel the semantic relations between the embedded sentences used in ascribing the beliefs. So if Maggie believes that there are no pandas in Tibet, and John believes that there are no pandas in northern Tibet, then what Maggie believes entails what John believes if and only if

There are no pandas in Tibet

entails

There are no pandas in northern Tibet.

The various parallels we have noted can hardly be an accident. A theory about the nature of belief should give us some explanation of the fact that the semantic properties of beliefs, the objects of beliefs, and the sentences embedded in belief ascriptions all coincide.

(4) A bit of terminology will prove useful. Let us call sentences of the form

S believes that p

belief sentences, and let us call the embedded sentence, p, *the content sentence.* What we have just seen is that the semantic properties of beliefs and of the objects of beliefs parallel those of the associated content sentences. When our attention turns to the semantic properties of belief *sentences,* however, the situation is much more puzzling. For, though content sentences are embedded within belief sentences, the semantic properties of belief sentences seem to be quite independent of the semantic properties of their own content sentences. The logical perversity thus engendered has been, until recently, the main focus of philosophical interest in belief. To underscore the semantic puzzles posed by belief sentences, it is useful to compare them with superficially analogus forms like negations. Syntactically, negation functions as a sentence forming operator. Given any declarative sentence, p, we can form a new sentence by embedding p in

It is not the case that _____ .

The situation for 'believes that' is quite similar. Given any declarative sentence, p, we get a new sentence by inserting p for '_____' and an arbitrary name for ' . . . ' in

. . . believes that _____ .

But when our focus shifts to semantics, the analogy quickly breaks down. In the case of negation, the semantic properties of the compound sentence are determined by the semantic properties of the embedded sentence. 'It is not the case that p' is true if and only if p is false. With belief sentences, the truth value of the content sentence tells us nothing about the truth value of the compound. From the (rather surprising) fact that

Los Angeles is east of Reno

is true, we can conclude neither that

Quine believes that Los Angeles is east of Reno

is true, nor that it is false.

The entailment relations of belief sentences also fail to follow those of their content sentences. Thus, from the fact that p entails q, it does not follow that

S believes that p

entails

S believes that q.

If it did, our beliefs would be closed under entailment, which would make mathematics much less of a challenge, and our fellow citizens much less exasperating. (Or perhaps it would make them much *more* exasperating. It seems likely that each of us has at least one pair of contradictory beliefs. And if we believe everything entailed by our inconsistent beliefs . . . .)

The failure of belief sentences to mirror the entailments of their content sentences deserves special note when the content sentence inference is of the following form:

$$
\begin{array}{ll}
\text{Fa} & \text{(e.g., Bart is a spy)} \\
\underline{a = b} & \underline{\text{(e.g., Bart is the president of Yale)}} \\
\text{Fb} & \text{(e.g., The president of Yale is a spy.)}
\end{array}
$$

If we embed the first premise in a belief sentence, we get the following inference:

S believes that Fa   (e.g., David believes that Bart is a spy)
a = b   (e.g., Bart is the president of Yale)

S believes that Fb   (e.g., David believes that the
                           president of Yale is a spy)

And this latter inference is certainly not generally valid. However, a venerable tradition insists that there is a *sense* of 'believes that' on which the second inference is valid. This (alleged) sense is called the *relational* or *de re* sense, and referring expressions (like 'Bart' or 'the president of Yale') are said to occur *transparently* in the content sentences of *de re* belief sentences. In contrast, the sense of 'believes that' on which this last inference is not valid is labeled the *de dicto* sense, and referring expressions are said to occur *opaquely* in the content sentences of *de dicto* belief sentences. One of the less orthodox theses of this book is that the putative distinction between *de dicto* and *de re* belief sentences is a philosophers' myth, corresponding to nothing sanctioned by folk psychology. But that is a story for a later chapter. For the moment we are accumulating uncontroversial facts about our commonsense notion of belief. And a point beyond dispute is that (at least on one reading) inferences like the last one displayed are not generally valid.

(5) Another central theme of folk psychology is that mental states interact causally with one another, producing new mental states and, ultimately, behavior. These causal interactions are not random. Rather, folk theory maintains that the pattern of causal interactions often mirrors various *formal* relations among the content sentences that would be used in ascribing the states. Thus, for example, if Maggie believes that all Italians love pasta, and if she comes to believe that everyone at Sven's party is Italian, she will likely come to believe that everyone at Sven's party loves pasta. The folk generalization of which this is an instance is that a belief of the form:

All As are B

and a belief of the form:

All Bs are C

typically causes a belief of the form:

All As are C

What is important here is the natural, indeed all but inevitable, way in which our folk theory leads us to talk about the *logical form* of the objects of belief. What is believed, folk psychology seems to suggest, has some sort of logical form, and often it is in virtue of the logical forms of their objects that one belief causally interacts with another. Much the same point can be made about the causal interactions among beliefs and other "contentful" mental states. Suppose Sven wants to visit New Zealand, and suppose that he believes that if he is to visit New Zealand then he must obtain a visa. Here, folk psychology urges, we might typically expect Sven to form the desire to obtain a visa. The folk generalization in this case is (roughly) that a desire of the form:

Do A

along with a belief of the form:

In order to do A it is necessary to do B

leads to a desire of the form:

Do B.

For current purposes, details are not essential. What is important is that in capturing the generalizations of practical reasoning, it is plausible to view the objects of belief and desire as having a logical structure which determines the ways in which they interact.

A caveat should be thrown in here. The mental sentence theorist need not claim that *all* the causal interactions among contentful mental states are dependent on their form. Plainly folk psychology recognizes other sorts of causal interactions, some systematic and others not. All the mental sentence theorist need claim is that some quite central causal patterns recognized by folk theory seem to turn on the logical form of the objects of belief.

3. Sentences in the Head

I have been collecting facts about our commonsense notion of (and talk about) belief, with the aim of reconstructing an argument to the effect that the best explanation of all these facts would be the hypothesis that belief is a relation between a person and an internally inscribed sentence. The chore now is to see how that hypothesis would account for the evidence collected. Before beginning I had best address a question that may have been troubling the reader since this talk of mental sentences began, to wit: What does it *mean* to talk of having a sentence in the head?

Let me address the most skeptical group of readers first, those who suspect that talk of sentences in the head is *conceptually incoherent*.

Surely this is too strong a criticism. For consider. We might, on a close examination of the contents of the head, discover there a tiny blackboard on which English sentences are literally inscribed in chalk. Or, if fancy runs to more contemporary technology, we could discover a tiny television monitor or CRT with thousands of English sentences displayed on the screen. Since there is nothing conceptually incoherent about this fantasy and since it would surely count as discovering that there are sentences in the head, we can safely conclude that the sentence-in-the-head hypothesis is not conceptually incoherent.

It is instructive to note that even if, *mirabile dictu*, we all have CRTs covered with sentences inside our heads, this would not be nearly sufficient to establish that beliefs are sentences in our head. The sentences on the screen would, at a bare minimum, have to stand in some plausible correlation to what the owner of the head actually believes. So, for example, if the only sentences to be found in my head are the text of Gibbon's *Decline and Fall of the Roman Empire*, these sentences could hardly be the objects of my beliefs. Suppose, then, that the sentences found in my head are the right ones—that for every true sentence of the form

Stich believes that p

there is a token of p on my internal CRT. Suppose, further, that the screen is regularly updated. When an elephant comes into view, a token of 'there is an elephant in front of me' is added to the sentences on the screen, and when the elephant ambles away, the sentence disappears from the screen. This, no doubt, would make it much more plausible that these sentences could be identified as the objects of my beliefs. But something more would still be required. For suppose that the sentences on my CRT, while keeping an accurate record of what I believe, play no causal role in the dynamics of my mental and behavioral life. Surgically removing the screen has no effect on my behavior or on my stream of consciousness. Here, I think, we would be inclined to treat the sentences not as objects of belief but as some sort of epiphenomenon, a psychologically irrelevant causal product of my beliefs. The situation would be different if the sentences on my CRT played causal roles of the sort attributed to beliefs in our folk psychology. Suppose, for example, that inference is causally dependent on what appears on the screen. Imagine that there is an "inference device" which scans the screen, causing new sentences to appear on the screen depending on what it has scanned. Thus, if the inference device scanned tokens of 'All Italians love pasta', and 'Sven is an Italian', it would cause a token of 'Sven loves pasta' to appear on the screen. To test whether the token on the screen was really *causally* involved in the inference process, we might obscure the bit of the screen displaying 'Sven is Italian' and see if this breaks the causal chain, so that the inference device now does not cause 'Sven loves pasta' to be added to the display. Analogously, let us imagine that the sentences on the internal CRT play the right sort of causal role in practical reasoning, details here being left to the imagination of the reader. If all that we have imagined were true—if there are internal sentences, if they correspond to what the subject actually believes, and if they play a suitable causal role in mental processes and the production of behavior, then surely we would be on safe ground to conclude that beliefs are relations between persons and internal sentences.[4]

All of this might be enough to establish the *intelligibility* of the mental sentence view. But what about its *plausibility*? We know that there are neither blackboards nor CRTs in the head; indeed there is nothing in the head that *looks* anything like a sentence token. Here the defender of the mental sentence view must insist that appearances are deceiving. We have many familiar examples of sentences encoded in a medium which cannot be detected by direct inspection. I relieve the tedium of my daily commute by listening to books recorded on cassette tapes. These tapes are, in a quite unproblematic sense, covered with sentence tokens, though the tokens are unrecognizable without the aid of a sophisticated piece of electronic apparatus. Similarly, the mental sentence theorist does not expect to find the sentences in the brain inscribed in Roman letters. Rather, if they exist at all, they will be recorded in some neural or neurochemical code.

This leaves us with the nice question of just when some complex neurochemical state is to *count* as being an encoding of a sentence, be the sentence in English or in some other language. My guess is that there can be no satisfying, fully general answer to this question. Certainly none has been offered. Part of the answer will inevitably require that there be a coding or mapping of units in the language (words, morphemes, or whatever) onto types of neurochemical states. A particular instance (or token) of the state to which a word is mapped will then count as an encoded token of the word. The code will also have to map at least some syntactically salient relations among words or units (for example, the relation of being the next word in the sentence) onto relations among neurochemical states. This will enable us to identify a sequence of suitably related neurochemical states as an encoding of a sequence of words. If that sequence of words is a sentence, then the sequence of suitably related neurochemical states will be the encoding of that sentence. This is hardly the last word on the question of coding. Indeed, before we end this chapter we will have reason to puzzle further over just what is to count as the neural encoding of a sentence.

But for now I think enough has been said. Let us grant to the mental sentence theorist that the existence of sentences in the brain is both intelligible and not incompatible with anything we know about the brain.

4. Explaining the Facts about Belief

The contention of the mental sentence theorist, recall, is that we can best explain facts about our commonsense notion of belief by hypothesizing that belief is a relation between a person and an internally represented sentence. It is time to see how these explanations are supposed to work. To show the view in its best light, let us assume that in all of our heads there are enormous numbers of sentence tokens which are unproblematic encodings of just those English sentences which express the contents of our current beliefs. Indeed for the sake of vividness we can imagine for the nonce that we really do have a little CRT in our heads covered with sentence tokens. Further, let us assume that these sentence tokens play the causal role of beliefs as this is depicted in folk psychology. Given these favorable assumptions, what can be said about the various facts assembled earlier in this chapter?

First, it is no surprise that beliefs are standardly attributed by a construction involving an embedded sentence. On the mental sentence hypothesis, my belief that Ouagadougou is the capital of Upper Volta is a relation between me and a token of 'Ouagadougou is the capital of Upper Volta'. So the belief sentence

> Stich believes that Ouagadougou is the capital of Upper Volta

wears its logical form on its face—well, almost on its face. To say that a relation obtains between a pair of objects, we flank a relational predicate by *names* of the objects, and while 'Stich believes that Ouagadougou is the capital of Upper Volta' has my name to the left of the relational predicate 'believes that', to the right it has a sentence, not the name of a sentence. It would be more accurate to write

> Stich believes 'Ouagadougou is the capital of Upper Volta'

thereby making it clear that the second element in the relation is a sentence. It is not surprising that this is not ordinarily done, since ordinary usage is notoriously sloppy about the distinction between use and mention.*

---

*Actually,

   Stich believes 'Ouagadougou is the capital of Upper Volta'

still does not quite capture what the mental sentence theorist intends, since quotation

Once we have made the implicit quotation marks explicit, the various logical peculiarities of belief sentences have a straightforward explanation. They are all just what we would expect, given that the content sentence is mentioned, not used. Changes made within a quoted context produce the name of a *different* sentence, and there is no reason to expect that a person who had an internal inscription of the first sentence will also have an internal inscription of the second just because the two sentences have the same truth value or are logically equivalent. In particular, it is no surprise that

David believes 'Bart is a spy'

may be true, while

David believes 'the president of Yale is a spy'

is false, even though Bart is the president of Yale. This latter identity guarantees that the two content sentences will have the same truth value, but they are still very different sentences, one of which may be internally represented in David while the other is not. So, on the mental sentence view, the inference from

David believes that Bart is a spy

and

Bart is the president of Yale

to

David believes that the president of Yale is a spy

is strictly parallel to the inference from

'Bart is a spy' was written on the blackboard

and

Bart is the president of Yale

to

'The president of Yale is a spy' was written on the blackboard.

Since the latter inference is patently invalid, we should expect the former to be invalid as well.

---

mark names denote types, not tokens. What is needed is something like:

Stich believes a token of 'Ouagadougou is the capital of Upper Volta'

or perhaps even better:

($\exists$t) (t is a token of 'Ouagadougou is the capital of Upper Volta' and Stich believes t).

But let us not quibble over small points.

The mental sentence view has an equally easy time explaining the semantic facts about what is believed (i.e., about what I have been calling the *objects* of belief). Here, recall, the most striking fact was that the semantic properties of the object of a belief coincide exactly with those of the associated content sentence. But this is exactly what would be expected if the object of the belief just *is* a token of the content sentence. We noted that common sense ascribes truth and other semantic properties to beliefs as well as to the objects of belief and that these too matched the semantic properties of the appropriate content sentence. Here, I suppose, the best line for the mental sentence theorist to take is that talk of the truth, consistency, or entailments of a belief is just a shorthand for talk about the truth, consistency, or entailments of the object of that belief.

Finally we saw that many of the most useful generalizations of folk psychology require that beliefs (and other contentful mental states) be categorized according to the logical form of their objects. For this to make sense, the objects of belief must be the sort of things which *have* logical forms. And of course sentences are possessors of logical form par excellence. Glimpsing ahead a bit, we can see why mental sentence theorists are so sanguine about integrating the contentful states of folk psychology into serious scientific psychology. For if beliefs and their kin are relations to sentence tokens whose causal interactions are largely determined by their logical forms, then we have a clear research program. What we want to discover are the forms of various mental representations and the principles governing the devices or processes which manipulate representation tokens in virtue of their forms. While we may have no good leads on the neurophysiology of these token-manipulating mechanisms, we know that there is nothing in principle mysterious about physical devices which manipulate sentence tokens in virtue of their form. For this, near enough, is just what is done by an electronic digital computer.

Some of the defenders of the mental sentence account would insist that their view offers more than a research *program* in cognitive psychology. They contend that the view is "presupposed by the best—indeed the only—psychology that we've got."[5] If this is correct, it is a powerful independent argument for the mental sentence theory of belief. In chapter 9 we will take a careful look at the arguments offered in support of the claim that the best in contemporary psychology presupposes the mental sentence view.

5. The Language of Thought

All that we have said so far makes the case for the mental sentence hypothesis look remarkably good. But before we get carried away we should note that the argument we have been reconstructing rests precariously on a single implausible assumption, viz. that the sentences in our heads which are the objects of our beliefs are *English* sentences. Note that the assumption I am questioning is that the objects of belief are tokens of English sentences, not the fanciful proposal that they are written on an internal CRT. The latter conceit is offered merely as an aid to the imagination, and nothing said in the previous section depends on it. The assumption might be passingly plausible if "our heads" referred only to yours and mine, English speakers both. But interpreted less xenophobically, the assumption is hopeless. Surely we do not expect to find tokens of English sentences inside the heads of monolingual Korean speakers, not to mention the heads of prelinguistic children or the family dog. Yet folk psychology clearly ascribes beliefs to all of these.[6] So something else will have to be said about the objects of belief.

There are two proposals that have been taken seriously. The first, suggested by Harman,[7] and tentatively endorsed by Field,[8] is that the objects of belief (and other contentful mental states) are sentences in the language of the *believer*, or perhaps something a bit richer, like sentences in the believer's language paired with their phrase structure trees. On this view, my beliefs are relations to internal tokens of English sentences, and the monolingual Korean's beliefs are relations to internal tokens of Korean sentences. What to say about beasts and babies is less clear. The other view, championed by Fodor,[9] takes the objects of belief to be sentences in a species-wide mental code, *the language of thought*. On this view, the Korean who believes that dry food is good for man is related to the same sentence in universal mental code as was Aristotle, who held the same belief, though he expressed it in Greek. Since the language of thought is supposed to be species wide and innate, the beliefs of prelinguistic children pose no special problems. Fido presumably holds his beliefs in the language of canine thought. Since Fodor's view has been rather more influential, I will focus my discussion on it. But just about all the points to be made can be made mutatis mutandis if we assume instead that the objects of belief are sentences in the language spoken by the believer.

When we were pretending that all beliefs had English sentences as their objects, we had a relatively easy time explaining the facts we had collected about our commonsense notion of belief. On dropping that pretense, however, many of those explanations begin to come unglued. Consider the story we told about why beliefs should standardly be ascribed by a locution involving an embedded sentence. What could be more natural if the belief simply is a relation between the believer and an internal token of *that very embedded sentence*? But what are we to say now that we are assuming belief is a relation between the believer and a sentence in the language of thought? Why do we standardly attribute this state using a locution involving an embedded *English* sentence? And what is the relation between the English content sentence and the object of the belief which, ex hypothesis, is a sentence in the language of thought? This last question is perhaps the central one, for until we have some account of the relation between content sentences and the objects of belief, most of the other explanatory stories told in the previous section cannot be reconstructed. It is, for example, a renewed puzzle why the semantic properties of the objects of belief should coincide with the semantic properties of content sentences, a puzzle that will be solved only if the relation between mental sentences in the language of thought and content sentences in English turns out to be one which preserves semantic properties. Similarly, the story we told to explain the opacity of belief sentences rested heavily on the assumption that the relation between content sentence and object of belief was the relation of type to token. With this assumption denied, the explanation no longer hangs together.

Well, what can the mental sentence theorist say about the relation between content sentences and the objects of belief? One idea that seems natural enough derives from the observation that the content sentence is the one *we* (i.e., English speakers) would use to express the belief which we attribute to others by embedding that sentence in a belief sentence. So, for example, we would express the belief that it's raining by *saying*, 'It's raining'. French speakers would express the belief in other words, and babies (if they have such beliefs) would not express them linguistically at all. Following up on this idea, Fodor introduces a function F, "from (e.g. English) sentences onto internal formulae,"[10] that is, onto what we have been calling sentences in the language of thought. He then proposes the following "principle" to connect the object of the belief that it's raining (which, recall, will be a token of an internal formula) with the English sentence 'It's raining':

> 'It's raining' is the sentence that English speakers use when they are in the belief-making relation to a token of F(it's raining) and wish to use a sentence of English to say what it is that they believe.[11]

A bit later, he writes that

> F(it's raining) is distinguished by the fact that its tokens play a causal/functional role (not only as the object of the belief that it's raining, but also) in the production of linguistically regular utterances of 'it's raining'.[12]

This last quote could do with a brief gloss. It is only *chez nous*, among English speakers, that utterances of 'It's raining' count among their causes tokens of the mental sentence F(it's raining). In another possible language utterances of 'It's raining' might typically be caused by tokens of F(there is nothing but cabbage for dinner). There are other short-comings in Fodor's story about the function from English sentences to mental formulas which are less easy to patch.[13] But I am inclined to think that Fodor's basic idea is on the right track. What is of crucial importance for our current concerns is that if anything much like Fodor's account is accepted, then the problem of the relation between sentence types and their mental or neurochemical tokens must come to center stage once again.

6. Sentence Type and Mental Token

To see just why this issue assumes critical importance, let us trace through the sort of account a Fodor-style theory would have to give of a belief sentence like

Otto believes that it's raining.

What, precisely, does this sentence tell us about Otto? Or, to put the question more fashionably, what are the sentence's truth conditions? Well, first off, the sentence is ascribing a belief to Otto, and ex hypothesis to have a belief is to have a token of a sentence (or formula) of the language of thought properly stored in the head. A long story could be told about "properly stored"—it must be stored in such a way that it functions as a belief, interacts with other beliefs and with desires in the proper way, and so on. But this part of the account is not now in question, so let us take it for granted. What about Otto's mental sentence token itself? What does our belief ascription tell us about it? Here is where the content sentence comes in, with the story going something like this: the content sentence is 'it's raining.' Among us, English speak-ers, that content sentence is correlated with a particular internal code sentence, viz. the one whose tokens typically cause us to say 'It's raining'. So now we have specified a sentence type in internal code. And what about Otto? What is his relation to this sentence type? Well, it's simple; the sentence token he has in his head is a token of the very same internal code sentence type, though Otto, who speaks only Ger-man, would express his belief by saying 'Es regnet'. In short, Otto and the English speaker who sincerely says 'It's raining' have in their re-spective heads *tokens of the same mental sentence type*. So for a Fodor-style account of belief sentences to hang together, we must have some workable notion of what it is for two distinct people, speaking different languages, to have in their heads distinct tokens of the same sentence type.

At first blush this might seem to pose no problem. After all it seemed in section 3 that we could make plausible sense of a person having a sentence token in his head. So why not use the same account in talking of a pair of people with tokens of the same sentence? To see where the problem lies, remember the story told in section 3 about the encoding of a sentence. The idea was that the first of a pair of mappings would take sentence parts (like words) onto types of neurochemical states, and the second would take syntactic relations (like the relation of being the next word) onto relations among neurochemical states. The trouble with this, as it were, purely syntactic story about the type-token relation is that it simply will not do the work needed in a Fodor-style account of belief sentences.

A bit of science fiction will help underscore the difficulty. Let us revert to an earlier fancy and suppose that inside each person's head there is a tiny CRT covered with sentence tokens. Suppose further that these sentence tokens are functioning as the objects of belief, playing the causal role assigned to beliefs by folk psychology. Finally, let us suppose that all the sentences on all human belief screens appear to be written in the same language. Indeed to make matters really simple, suppose them all to be written in what appears to be *English*. Granting all this, the obvious mapping from English sentence types to "mental tokens" is simply the one which maps sentence types to their CRT inscriptions. With the generous assumptions we are making, it should be particularly easy to tell Fodor's tale about Otto. Let us assume that when you and I produce "linguistically regular utterances" of 'it's raining', the causally implicated mental sentence is a token of 'it's raining'. When we say 'Otto believes that it's raining', we are saying that Otto has on his CRT a token of the same type as the tokens that are causally implicated in our production of "linguistically regular utterances" of 'It's raining'—that is, that he has a CRT inscription similar in shape to the following:

It's raining.

But, I claim, this purely syntactic story simply cannot be right. Merely having an inscription of the right shape on his belief-CRT can't be all there is to Otto's believing that it's raining. Suppose, for example, that we note the following correlation: Whenever Otto is awake and alert, and it begins to *snow* around him, a token of 'it's raining' appears on his CRT. Suppose further that Otto regularly opens his umbrella when 'It's snowing' appears on his CRT but never does so when 'It's raining' appears. And, looking around at the other sentences on his CRT, we find tokens of 'Rain is white', 'It generally rains in the winter and snows in the summer', 'In the spring, the flowers need plenty of snow' etc. Finally suppose that when Otto wishes to express the belief whose object is the token of 'It's raining', what he says is 'Es schneit'. Given all of this, what are we to say Otto believes when a token of 'It's raining' appears on his CRT? Clearly the right answer is that Otto believes that it's snowing. But on the purely syntactic story about the type-token relation, he believes that it's raining! For on *that* story, to believe that it's raining simply is to have an 'It's raining' token on the belief CRT.

At this point it might be protested that, with a bit of fiddling, what I have been calling the purely syntactic story could perfectly well attribute to Otto the belief that it's snowing when a shape similar to

It's raining

appears on his CRT. We have been tacitly assuming that the mapping from English sentences to mental tokens is the same in all people, and thus if my mental token of the sentence 'It's raining' is similar in shape to the inscription just displayed, Otto's must be too. But since this leads to absurd consequences, let us give up the assumption that everyone uses the same mapping. Perhaps in Otto's encoding of the language of thought, the word 'rain' does not map onto CRT inscriptions similar in shape to

rain

but rather to CRT inscriptions similar in shape to

snow.

Making this assumption (and assuming that the rest of Otto's mapping works just like mine), we can attribute to Otto the belief that it's snowing since the inscription on his CRT which is shape-similar to

It's raining

is in fact a token of (i.e., is mapped onto) the sentence type 'It's snowing'.

All this is true enough. Unfortunately it leads us out of the frying pan and into the fire. For recall that we started out attempting to reconstruct a Fodor-style account of the truth conditions for 'Otto believes that it's raining'. On the first proposed mapping, the one that mapped 'rain' to shape-similar tokens, we got the wrong truth conditions. To remedy the problem, it was noted that we can map 'rain' to inscriptions shape-similar to

snow.

And so we can. But we can also map 'rain' to inscriptions shape-similar to

sleet

or, for that matter, to inscriptions shape-similar to

dark of night.

Mappings, after all, are just functions, and functions are cheap. So if a brain state (e.g., an inscription on a cerebral CRT) counts as a token of a sentence merely in virtue of there being *some* mapping from the sentence onto states of this type, then any brain state (and thus any CRT inscription) will count as a token of any sentence we choose, and we are left without any coherent account of the truth conditions for 'Otto believes that it's raining'.

It appears then that we are confronting the following dilemma. If we assume that the mapping from English sentence types to mental sentence tokens is a "purely syntactic" one on the lines sketched in section 3, then if the mapping is uniform from one person to the next, we get wildly incorrect truth conditions for belief sentences. However, if the mapping is not uniform from one person to the next, we get no coherent account of the truth conditions for belief sentences. The conclusion to draw is obvious enough. The purely syntactic mapping from English content sentences to mental sentence tokens must be abandoned. What is needed, in its stead, is a mapping which preserves or mirrors some more interesting properties of the sentences mapped.

One defender of the mental sentence account of beliefs who has confronted this issue directly is William Lycan, and it will be instructive to consider his view in some detail. In setting out his view, Lycan adopts Sellarsian dot quote notation, where dot quotes "are common noun forming operators that also serve to ostend the linguistic tokens that they enclose."[14] With this notation,

Jones believes that broccoli causes erysipelas

would be rendered

Jones believes some ˙Broccoli causes erysipelas˙.

"A slight variation would be to express the force of [this last sentence] as

Jones believes one of *those.* / Broccoli causes erysipelas."

Belief, then, "is construed as a dyadic relation which a person bears to a linguistic or quasi-linguistic token that falls into a certain category."[15] The object of Jones's belief that broccoli causes erysipelas is a mental sentence token, one falling within the extension of the predicate 'is a ˙Broccoli causes erysipelas˙'. This, of course, is just Fodor's view with a different notation. In Lycan's Sellarsian notation, the question pondered in the last few paragraphs—what mental state would count as a token of a given content sentence—is transformed into a question about the extension of dot quote predicates:

> How are we to determine the extension of the predicate 'is a ˙Broccoli causes erysipelas˙'? Alternatively, how are we to tell when some linguistic or quasi-linguistic token of some quite other shape *is* 'one of *those*'?[16]

Lycan notes a pair of plausible alternatives. The first, a Sellarsian idea, is to group tokens by their *inferential role*: "an item will count as a ˙Broccoli causes erysipelas˙ just in case that item plays approximately the same *inferential role* within its own surrounding conceptual framework that the sentence 'Broccoli causes erysipelas' plays in ours."[17] This idea needs a bit of interpreting, since, as quoted, it seems to be comparing the inferential role of a sentence token (a physical state or object) with the inferential role of a sentence type (an abstract object). But the Sellarsian standard need not make a detour through sentence types. Rather, I think, the proposal is best viewed as comparing foreign mental sentence *tokens* with domestic ones. A state or token in Jones's head counts as a ˙Broccoli causes erysipelas˙ if it plays an inferential role similar to that of the states or tokens that underlie normal assertions of 'Broccoli causes erysipelas' in me, or perhaps in English speakers generally. Inferential role here is simply part of the broader causal role that the tokens in question play in the cognitive dynamics of their respective heads. And it is not entirely clear just how much of this causal network Lycan or Sellars would wish to count under the rubric of inferential role. Practical reasoning, I suppose, would naturally be included. But what about the causal links tying the objects of belief to perception? For example, we would expect that a good glimpse of broccoli in front of him would generally lead to the production of a ˙There is some broccoli in front of me˙ in the appropriate place in Jones's brain. It is less natural to count this strand of the causal network as part of the "inferential role" of the sentence token. However, there is no need here to settle just what Lycan or Sellars may have intended. I raise the issue to serve as a backdrop for the introduction of some terminology of my own. On the Sellarsian view, as I have been interpreting it, what is essential in grouping mental sentence tokens together as being of the same type is some part of their causal network— the way in which the token causally interacts with other states and processes of the organism. If a principle for typing mental sentence tokens counts a pair of tokens as type identical when (and only when) the tokens have similar patterns of potential causal interaction, then, recalling the terminology of the last chapter, let us call it a *causal* account of typing. If the only relevant potential causal links that a typing scheme recognizes are those obtaining between mental tokens and other mental states, those obtaining between mental tokens and stimuli, and those obtaining between mental tokens and behavior, then let us call it a *narrow causal* account.

Causal accounts of the typing of mental tokens contrast with the purely syntactic shape-similarity account that was invoked in my tale about Otto and his tiny CRT. On a shape-similarity account, Otto has a token of the same type as the one which leads me to say 'It's raining', since we both have mental inscriptions shape-similar to

It's raining.

But Otto's inscription is not in the least *causally* similar to mine. Its causal network is much more closely akin to the one that would be exhibited by a token of 'It's snowing' on my CRT. So on a causal account of typing mental tokens, Otto's inscription, despite its shape, counts as a token of 'It's snowing'. And thus the causal account, along with commonsense intuition, ascribes to Otto the belief that it's snowing.

The second sort of classification scheme for mental tokens that Lycan describes turns not on the causal properties of the tokens, but on their *semantic properties.* "We might count a thing as a 'Broccoli causes erysipelas' just in case the thing has the same truth conditions as does our sentence 'Broccoli causes erysipelas', or if and only if the thing has the same truth conditions computed according to the same recursive procedure."[18] In a similar vein Field suggests that tokens of mental sentences may be classified together if they have the same meaning or content.[19] Just what this criterion of sameness of content comes to is less than obvious. Much of chapter 5 will be devoted to pondering the matter. For present purposes, we need only the roughest of ideas and a label. I will call any scheme for typing mental tokens which relies on their meaning or content or truth conditions a *content account.* Content accounts, like causal accounts, contrast with the shape-similarity story. On the content account, Otto's CRT inscription counts as a token of 'It's snowing' despite its shape and because of its content or truth conditions.

A more interesting question is how causal accounts and content accounts compare with each other. Do they categorize mental tokens differently, or do they inevitably come out with the same categorization? On this issue, opinions divide. According to Fodor the two sorts of classification schemes coincide, "plus or minus a bit." Indeed Fodor sees this as *"the* basic idea of modern cognitive science."[20] Any thoroughgoing functionalist in the philosophy of mind will also end up on this side of the divide. On the other side, denying that causal and content accounts converge, are Field, Lycan, Perry, McDowell, and the truth.[21]

The distinction between causal and content accounts of mental token typing makes it possible to give a quick and clean statement of three central theses of this book. First, the mental sentence theory of belief, if fleshed out with a narrow causal account of typing, just does not comport with our workaday folk psychological notion of belief—it is not an account of belief, as the term is ordinarily used. Second, the mental sentence theory, if fleshed out with a *content* account of typing, is a good first pass at saying what beliefs are, as they are conceived by folk psychology. But, third and most important, beliefs so conceived have no role to play in a mature cognitive science.

Chapter 4

Some Evidence Against Narrow Causal Accounts of Belief

In this chapter I begin my argument for the claim that accounts of belief which invoke a narrow causal standard of individuation do not characterize a notion of belief plausibly identified with our common-sense notion. My focus throughout the argument will be on the narrow causal version of the mental sentence theory sketched in the previous chapter. With appropriate adjustments of detail, however, an entirely parallel case can be constructed against theory-theory (or functionalist) accounts which are committed to the narrow causal individuation of mental states.[1] Since the case I shall present is complex, I had best begin by sketching a general overview of the argument.

My first task will be to assemble some evidence for the lack of fit between the folk notion of belief and the account of belief offered by the narrow causal version of the mental sentence theory. Basically my theme will be that a narrow causal account dictates judgments about how beliefs are to be characterized and when they count as the same or different, which do not comport with the judgments of folk psychology. There are two sides to this story. Sometimes the problem is that a narrow causal account draws its distinctions too coarsely, because it is incapable of distinguishing between mental states that folk psychology takes to be importantly different. On the other side the problem is reversed. A narrow causal account is sometimes too finicky, forcing distinctions that folk theory does not draw.

The evidence to be marshaled for these conclusions will be evidence about our commonsense intuitions. The use of such intuitions is standard practice in philosophical analysis. Still perhaps a few words are in order on what I take to be the proper use of intuitive data. Intuitions are simply spontaneous judgments. At best intuitions can tell us something about the boundaries or extension of our folk concepts. Thus for example, if we present a subject with pieces of furniture varying along several dimensions and ask for his spontaneous judgments on which ones are couches, we can learn a good deal about what sort of objects do and do not fall under his concept of couch. We might also ask a subject for his judgments about putative principles of classifications, principles of the form: an object is a couch if (and/or only if) it is F. Intuitions about the principles guiding our judgments on particular cases are notoriously unreliable, however, and I shall generally try to avoid them.[2] What is more, there is no guarantee of accuracy accompanying intuitions about individual instances either. We sometimes are poor judges about what we would say on a particular case, especially when that case is verbally described.[3] And even when we correctly report on what we would say of a particular case, there is no guarantee that this is what we *should* say, that our judgment correctly reflects the extension of our concept.* Despite their fallibility, however, intuitions are often the best and most systematic evidence available in determining the contours of a folk concept. In the absence of an argument that intuitions in some domain are particularly likely to be mistaken or misleading, it would be folly to ignore them.

I would, however, be very uncomfortable indeed to rest my case against narrow causal theories of belief on the sort of intuitive data presented in this chapter. There are two reasons for my reluctance, one general, the other local. The general reason is that the facts about intuitions are negative data, and negative data hardly ever suffice to scuttle a theory. There are endless moves, principled or ad hoc, that a theorist can make to blunt the force of prima facie negative data. Nor are these moves always symptoms of intellectual bad faith.[4] To do in a theory we need another theory, preferably one that does a better job at explaining all the evidence available, including the negative evidence that troubled the old theory. Thus my case against narrow causal theories spills over into the next chapter, where I will develop my own account of the commonsense concept of belief. The local reason for my reluctance to rest my case on intuitive data is that, when it comes to judgments about what hypothetical subjects would properly be said to believe, intuitions are notably labile. It is often possible to evoke conflicting intuitions about a given subject's beliefs simply by framing the question in a somewhat different way. I take this lability as itself a bit of evidence about the folk notion of belief. A virtue of the theory to be developed

---

*How could it happen that an intuition correctly reporting what we would say of a given case might nonetheless be mistaken about the extension of our concept? The most interesting possibility is that the concept points outside itself, so to speak, in specifying its extension, requiring information about which we are ignorant or misinformed. If we present people with pieces of furniture and ask for their intuitions on which ones count as couches, we are likely to get a good fix on the extension of their couch concept. But if we present people with gemlike stones and ask for their judgments on which are diamonds, we will get a much less accurate indication of the extension of their diamond concept.

in the following chapter is that it explains why intuitions about a given case vary with the setting in which the intuition is evoked.

The evidence to be presented in this chapter falls under three headings. In the section on *Holism* I will present some cases suggesting that our intuitions about how a belief is to be described depend in part on the other beliefs the subject has. This dependency makes for intuitive distinctions that cannot be captured by a narrow causal theory. In the section on *Reference* I will use much the same strategy, this time focusing on intuitive distinctions rooted in the reference of words or concepts. Once again the theme will be that folk psychology draws distinctions more fine grained than those available to narrow causal accounts. Finally, in the section on *Irrelevant Causal Differences*, we will look at the other side of the coin, noting how under suitable circumstances commonsense intuition can be much less demanding than a narrow causal theory, classifying together cases narrow causal accounts must take to be clearly different.

1. Holism

Before considering cases, I should elaborate a bit on what I take to be the commitments of narrow causal theories. Recall that the narrow causal version of the mental sentence theory classifies mental sentence tokens as type identical if the tokens have the same (or similar) causal interrelations with other mental states, with stimuli, and with behavior. It is essential to realize that this talk of causal interrelations must be interpreted as pertaining not only to the causal interactions between a given token and other *actual* states or stimuli but also to the interactions that *would* obtain between the token and *possible* further mental states or stimuli. An illustration may serve to make the point. Suppose, as we have been supposing intermittently, that human mental sentences are written on little cerebral CRTs, and that the sentences in the language of thought look, for all the world, like tiny English sentence tokens. Now let us reflect on what is necessary, on the narrow causal account, for an inscription on Otto's CRT to count as type identical with the inscription on my CRT which I express by saying, "All men are mortal." I will assume that the mental token on my CRT looks similar in shape to the one I have just written. Of course on the causal account, looks are irrelevant. Otto may also have a mental token which looks like the one just written, though to count as the belief that all men are mortal it must enter into the same causal interactions. But the same causal interactions with *what*? I believe that Socrates was a man, and that belief (whose object, let us suppose, is a token on my CRT similar in shape to: Socrates was a man) along with my belief that all men are mortal, once caused me to infer (i.e., add to my CRT) a token of 'Socrates was mortal'. Otto, by contrast, does not believe that Socrates was a man. Perhaps he has never heard of Socrates (and thus no inscriptions containing tokens of 'Socrates' appear on his CRT). Or he might have some quite mistaken belief about Socrates—that he was a deity, perhaps, or a dachshund. Since Otto has no token of 'Socrates was a man' on his CRT, his token of 'All men are mortal' does not interact with a token of 'Socrates was a man' to yield a token of 'Socrates was mortal'. So there is a sense in which the causal interrelations of my 'All men are mortal' token differ from the causal interrelations of Otto's. However, it is alien to the spirit of the causal account of token typing to count *this* difference in reckoning whether Otto's 'All men are mortal' token and mine are of the same type. What matters is not whether Otto's 'All men are mortal' token actually *has* causally interacted with a token of 'Socrates was a man', but rather what *would* happen if Otto were to have such a token on his CRT. To count as type identical with mine, it must be the case that were Otto to have a 'Socrates was a man' it would causally interact with his 'All men are mortal' in the expected way. The causal patterns of interest to narrow causal accounts of typing are not merely those that have obtained among actual states, but also those that would obtain among nonactual though possible states. The essential point is that, for a narrow causal theorist, the type identity of a mental state is determined by its *potential causal interactions* with other mental states, with stimuli, and with behavior. Its type identity does not depend on the other mental states the subject happens to be in at the moment in question. Thus the type identity of a mental sentence token will not depend on the other mental sentence tokens that happen to be in the subject's head at a given moment.

This said, let us turn to cases. What I want to demonstrate is that intuitive judgments about whether a subject's belief can be characterized in a given way and intuitive judgments about whether a pair of subjects have the same belief are often very sensitive not only to the potential causal interactions of the belief(s) in question but also to other beliefs that the subject(s) are assumed to have. The content we ascribe to a belief depends, more or less holistically, on the subject's entire network of related beliefs.

The cleanest case I have been able to devise to illustrate the holism in content ascription turns on the sad fate of people afflicted with progressive loss of memory as the result of the degeneration of brain tissue. Often these people are troubled by the loss of many cognitive faculties, but to make the point I am after, let me ignore these other cognitive problems and describe in a somewhat idealized way the history of Mrs. T, a real person who was employed by my family when I was a child. As a young woman, around the turn of the century, Mrs. T had an active interest in politics and was well informed on the topic. She was deeply shocked by the assassination of President William McKinley in 1901. In her sixties, when I first knew her, she would often recount the history of the assassination and spell out her analysis of the effects it had had on the politics of the day. As Mrs. T advanced into her seventies, those around her began to notice that, though her reasoning seemed as sharp as ever, her memory was fading. At first she had trouble remembering recent events: who had been elected in the Senate race she had been following; where she had left her knitting. As time went on, more and more of her memory was lost. She could not remember the difference between the Senate and the House, nor the length of the president's term of office. As her affliction got worse, she could no longer remember what the president did, nor could she recall who George Washington was. Some weeks before her death, something like the following dialogue took place:

S: Mrs. T, tell me, what happened to McKinley?
Mrs. T: Oh, McKinley was assassinated.
S: Where is he now?
Mrs. T: I don't know.
S: I mean, is he alive or dead?
Mrs. T: Who?
S: McKinley.
Mrs. T: You know, I just don't remember.
S: What is an assassination?
Mrs. T: I don't know.
S: Does an assassinated person die?
Mrs. T: I used to know all that, but I just don't remember now.
S: Do you remember what dying is?
Mrs. T: No.
S: Can you tell me whether you have died?
Mrs. T: No, I just don't remember what that is.
S: But you do remember what happened to McKinley?
Mrs. T: Oh, yes. He was assassinated.

Neurologists are far from a detailed understanding of what happens to the brains of people like Mrs. T.[5] But to make the point I am after, let us engage in a bit of speculation. Suppose that what afflicted Mrs. T was a more or less pure case of progressive loss of memory, without involving other cognitive faculties. And suppose that it was real memory *loss*, with the memories or beliefs in question simply being erased from the victim's head. The mental sentence theorist can take this erasure metaphor quite literally. Memories and beliefs, on his view, are relations to sentence tokens, and to lose a memory is to erase the token. For vividness, let us imagine, yet again, that our mental sentences are written on tiny CRTs. Then the effect of Mrs. T's disease was progressively to erase areas of her CRT screen.

Now the question I want to pose for our intuitive judgment is this: Shortly before her death, Mrs. T had lost all memory about what assassination is. She had even forgotten what death itself is. She could, however, regularly respond to the question, "What happened to McKinley?" by saying, "McKinley was assassinated." Did she, at that time, *believe* that McKinley was assassinated? For just about everyone to whom I have posed this question, the overwhelmingly clear intuitive answer is no. One simply cannot believe that McKinley was assassinated if one has no idea what an assassination is, nor any grasp of the difference between life and death.

Consider, now, what the narrow causal version of the mental sentence theory must say about this case. We assume that before her illness Mrs. T had many thousands of sentence tokens on her CRT, including many about McKinley, many about death, many about assassination, and so on. But as the screen is erased, fewer and fewer of these sentences remain. At the time of the dialogue recounted above, almost none of this remains on the screen, apart from the single token of 'McKinley was assassinated'. Still, for a causal theory, the existence of this token entails that Mrs. T does believe that McKinley was assassinated, for the token has lost none of its former causal potential. We have assumed that only Mrs. T's memory is affected, and thus, ex hypothesis, were her belief screen to be restocked as it was in her prime, the isolated 'McKinley was assassinated' token would interact with these (possible) tokens in just the right way. Since in causal potential her 'McKinley was assassinated' token is quite similar to mine, and since mine is the belief that I express by saying 'McKinley was assassinated', it follows that Mrs. T's token is of the same type as mine and that she too believes that McKinley was assassinated. Plainly, here, we have a folk psychological distinction that the narrow causal version of the mental sentence theory just does not capture. On the commonsense view, before her illness Mrs. T believed that McKinley was assassinated. After her affliction had become quite severe, she no longer believed it. But if the causal potential of her few remaining mental sentence tokens has not changed, a causal account must view them as the same beliefs they have always been. Causal accounts do not reflect the holism of belief ascription.

Intuitions reflecting the holism of belief ascription are sharpest in cases like Mrs. T's, where the subject's belief tokens are a radically reduced subset of our own. However, kindred intuitions can be evoked in cases involving subjects with a much richer set of beliefs. Consider the following case. Let us imagine that some of our descendants have developed a rich and fruitful scientific theory, along with a new set of technical concepts and terms to express them. We may suppose that all of this theory is inscribed on the CRTs of these future scientists. As an aid to the imagination, we can continue the fiction that the language in which their beliefs are inscribed is English, though of course it will not be present day English but some extension of that language enriched with new terms to represent the new scientific concepts. The narrow causal version of the mental sentence view has no problem in conceding that these future scientists have beliefs that we don't, though it would add that we cannot ascribe any content to these beliefs since our language lacks suitable content sentences. Now let us suppose that via some strange set of circumstances which can here go unspecified, one of our contemporaries, Paul by name, comes to have imprinted on his belief screen a token of one single sentence which, in the heads of our scientifically sophisticated descendants, represents some deep strand of their new doctrine; let it be the mental sentence they express by saying, "Hydrogen atoms are single-petaled superheterodyning negentropy flowers."[6] In saying that Paul's belief is a token of the same mental sentence whose tokens appear in the heads of our future scientists, I am invoking the standard of the narrow causal account. Paul's token has the same causal potential as the tokens in future heads. Of course the token in Paul's head is largely inert, for lack of further theoretical sentences to interact with. But no matter. On the causal account Paul and the future scientists share the same belief. Here again commonsense intuition surely disagrees. From the fact that Paul has this odd, isolated sentence in his head, even if, as we may suppose, it sometimes leads him to *say*, "Hydrogen atoms are single-petaled superheterodyning negentropy flowers," it does not follow that Paul and the fabled scientists share the same belief. Indeed from the perspective of folk psychology, Paul's isolated mental token hardly counts as a belief at all. On a narrow causal account of belief, these folk intuitions are simply an unexplained anomaly.

Though I have told the tale about Paul in rather fanciful terms, other, more familiar situations prompt parallel intuitions. A majority of literate Americans over the age of seven have a belief which they express by affirming "$E = mc^2$." And it is not implausible to suppose that, by the standards of the causal account, this belief is identical to the one that a sophisticated physicist expresses with the same sentence. For scientifically unsophisticated people, however, the belief underlying their affirmation of '$E = mc^2$' is a largely isolated one. In reflecting on these cases there is a substantial intuitive pull in the direction of denying that the scientist and the man in the street are expressing the same belief. When my eight-year-old son asserts that $E = mc^2$, I am strongly inclined to think that the belief underlying his assertion is radically different from the one which he will express with the same sentence if he retains his avid interest in science for a decade or two. But the changes that will make the child's belief intuitively type identical with those of the scientist need not involve significant changes in the causal potential of the underlying mental state. Rather, what is needed is the addition of a rich set of further beliefs in which his current belief will be embedded.

An interesting variant on these cases arises when we consider our intuitions about beliefs we share with people whose belief systems elsewhere diverge from our own. Consider, again, the future scientists. It is plausible to suppose that they will have mental tokens which are, by the standards of the causal account, type identical to the mental token I express by saying, 'The Hindenburg exploded because it was filled with hydrogen'. But we have also supposed that many of their beliefs about hydrogen are radically different from mine. Question: Is the belief they express by saying, 'The Hindenburg exploded because it was filled with hydrogen' the same as the one I express with the same words? I find that to most ears not previously contaminated by philosophical theory, the question has a distinct "yes and no" feel to it.[7] It is sort of the same belief but also sort of not. This ambiguous intuition is yet another anomaly for a causal account, since unless we suppose that the two beliefs differ in causal potential, that account straightforwardly entails that the two beliefs are the same.

This is a convenient point for a brief detour to caution against an all too common confusion. When I discuss cases like the ones we have been considering, philosophers often ask just what, on my view, is the content of the child's belief, or the future scientist's belief, or Mrs. T's belief. My reply, in all these cases, is that the question invokes an undefined notion, and, absent a definition, it is senseless. Let me elaborate. On the mental sentence view as I have portrayed it and also on my own view to be developed in the next chapter, no mention need be made of an entity called a *content*, which beliefs can have (or lack). There are of course content *sentences*, which are simply sentences embedded in belief sentences. On the mental sentence view, there are also *objects* of belief, which are sentences in the mental code or language of thought. Finally, we *do* something that might be described as "ascribing content" to a belief; that is, we attribute a belief to a person by using a belief sentence containing a content sentence, or we talk about a belief using related locutions also containing embedded content sentences (e.g., 'Otto's belief that snow is white'). But in all of this there is no need to suppose that there are things, contents, which beliefs have. *To ascribe content to a belief is simply to describe it in a certain way.* I do not wish to deny that some reasonable sense might be *given* to the notion of there being a thing which is a belief's content. For example, it might be urged that sentences in the language of thought express propositions, and these propositions might be stipulated to be the content of the belief which has the associated mental sentence as its object. But, and this is the essential point, any such move requires some terminological stipulation. There is no preexisting notion of a content-entity to be found in folk psychology. Talk of there being some thing which is "the content" of a belief is a theorist's term of art, often used though rarely explained. What is more, it is a term of art which finds no natural place in mental sentence theories, unless the theorist wants to pursue the proposition gambit. And most don't.

So what is to be said about cases like the future scientists' belief? Well, if the mental sentence theory is correct, then it has as its object some sentence in the language of thought. There is also presumably some sentence in the language of the scientists which they use to express this belief. But there is no sentence in *our* language that is used to express that belief. Thus we cannot ascribe content to it; we cannot attribute this belief by uttering a sentence of the form: 'S believes that p', for the unexciting reason that we have no suitable p.* If the belief has truth conditions, and there is no reason to insist that it doesn't, then these are not specifiable in contemporary English either. But does the belief have a content, and if so what is it? My answer here is that pending some terminological stipulation, the question makes no sense.

To return from the detour, what I have been arguing is that intuitions about sameness of belief and about the appropriateness of describing a belief as the belief that p do not match up with the judgments mandated by the causal version of the mental sentence theory. My diagnosis of the mismatch is that, in all these cases, our intuition seems to be taking into account not only the causal potential of the mental sentence token but also the network of further beliefs that the subject has or lacks at the time in question. Sometimes, as in the case of Mrs. T, intuition seems to give a clear answer which is just the opposite of what a causal account requires. But it is interesting to note that sometimes intuition renders a less settled judgment. It is not clearly wrong to

---

*If we know the sentence scientists use to express the belief, we can use *that* sentence as a content sentence in a belief ascription. But this is a puzzling move, since we are assuming that we do not know what the content sentence means! Still, we often do invoke the words of the subject in ascribing a belief to that subject, even though we don't understand the words. (Cf. 'Heidegger believed that nothing noths'.) The theory developed in chapter 5 will have an explanation of why this sometimes works.

describe a certain belief as the belief that p, but it is not clearly right either. These yes-and-no intuitions play a prominent role in the following section, and any account of the folk notion underlying our intuition should explain their prominence. Cases evoking conflicting intuitions count as evidence against the narrow causal account not because intuition and theory are in direct conflict, but because intuition pulls in both directions, while the causal account pulls in only one.

2. Reference

The common strand in cases considered under this heading is that they all involve some aspect of reference. My theme will be that our intuitions about the appropriate description of a belief and about the sameness or difference of beliefs are affected by the reference of the terms that a subject would use to express the belief. Since reference is generally not fixed by the pattern of potential causal interconnections among a subject's beliefs, other mental states, stimuli, and behavior, however, it often happens that the narrow causal version of the mental sentence theory dictates judgments about a belief that conflict with our intuition. For convenience, I will group the cases to be considered under three headings: Proper Names, Kind Terms, and Indexicals.

Proper Names

A traditional view about proper names holds that their denotation is determined by the beliefs the speaker would express using the name, or by the sentences he would accept in which the name occurs. During the last fifteen years a new view has come to be widely accepted, however, growing out of the work of Donnellan, Kaplan, Kripke, Putnam, and others.[8] Stripped to its barest essentials, this new "causal" account holds that a name denotes a person on a given occasion of use if there is a suitable causal chain linking the person and the use of the name. I am inclined to think that the causal story is only part of the truth about the denotation of proper names. For present purposes, however, I propose to stay as far as possible from tangled issues in the philosophy of language. The story I want to tell focuses on beliefs and what we would find it intuitively natural to say about them.

Consider the following example involving the beliefs of two subjects, Tom and Dick. Tom is a contemporary of ours, a young man with little interest in politics or history. From time to time he has heard bits of information about Dwight David Eisenhower. We can assume that most of what Tom has heard is true, though there is no need to insist that all of it is. Let us also assume that each time Tom heard something about Eisenhower, Eisenhower was referred to as 'Ike'. Tom knows that this must be a nickname of some sort, but he has no idea what the man's full name might be and doesn't very much care. Being little interested in such matters, Tom remembers only a fraction of what he has heard about Ike: that he was both a military man and a political figure; that he played golf a lot; that he is no longer alive; that he had a penchant for malapropisms; and perhaps another half dozen facts. He has no memory of when or where he heard these facts, nor from whom. The mental sentence theorist will hold that all these beliefs are stored sententially in the appropriate place in Tom's brain. For vividness, I will assume that the appropriate place is a tiny CRT, and that the sentences are stored in English.

To tell you about Dick, I must indulge in a bit of fiction, though I suspect that readers with a richer knowledge of history could produce a more realistic example. Dick, in my story, is a young man in Victorian England. Like Tom, he is bored by politics and history. Dick has heard some anecdotes about a certain Victorian public figure, Reginald Angell-James, who, for reasons that history does not record, was generally called 'Ike'. And (the plot thickens) in all the stories that Dick has heard about Angell-James, the gentleman was referred to as 'Ike'. Angell-James and Eisenhower led very different careers in different places and times. However, there were some similarities between the two men. In particular, both were involved in politics and the military, both liked to play golf, and both had a penchant for malapropisms. Moreover, by a quirk of fate, it happens that the few facts Dick remembers about Angell-James coincide with the few facts Tom remembers about Eisenhower. What is more, of course, Dick would report these facts using the very same sentences that Tom would use, since the only name Dick knows for Angell-James is 'Ike'. Indeed, we can suppose that the only mental sentences about Angell-James to be found in Dick's head are, on the narrow causal standard, exact duplicates of the sentences about Eisenhower to be found in Tom's head. That is, each of Tom's sentences about Eisenhower can be paired with one of Dick's sentences about Angell-James, and the sentences so paired are identical in point of their causal potential. (It will do no harm to suppose that the sentences on their CRTs look the same too.)

Now let me try to evoke some intuitions about these cases. Suppose that one fine day in 1880 one of Dick's friends asks him what he knows about Ike. Dick replies, "He was some kind of politician who played golf a lot." A century later, one of Tom's friends asks him an identically worded question, and Tom gives an identically worded reply. First intuition probe: Were Tom and Dick expressing the same belief? Most people on whom I have tried this case are initially inclined to say no. They buttress this view by noting that Tom's belief was about Eisenhower, while Dick's was about Angell-James. This intuition tends to be even stronger if we alter the story by adding that, in fact, Angell-James did not play golf at all, though it was widely believed that he did. On this version, Dick's belief is false, while Tom's is true. On reflection, however, some people concede that they can "sort of see" why someone might want to say that Tom and Dick held the same belief, though they insist that it is odd or misleading. (In fairness, I should report that I have found one informant—a noted psychologist—who claims his intuitions run just the other way.) When asked how they would describe what Tom and Dick believe, many people give an interesting response. Tom, they say, believes that Eisenhower was a politician who played golf a lot, whereas Dick believes that Angell-James was a politician who played golf a lot.

Plainly these intuitions pose a problem for the narrow causal version of the mental sentence view. For on that view Tom's belief and Dick's ought to count as identical, since Tom's mental sentence and Dick's have identical causal potential. On the narrow causal account there is no explanation of the strong intuitive pull toward counting Tom's belief and Dick's as different.

Three observations about this case will prove useful when it comes time to build a better theory. First, the case is quite distinct from the holism cases discussed above. The network of beliefs about Eisenhower in which Tom's belief is embedded is entirely parallel to the network of beliefs in which Dick's belief about Angell-James is embedded. Indeed, by the narrow causal standard these networks are identical.* So the intuitions in this case cannot be attributed to the effects of related beliefs. Second, there is a striking parallel between our intuitions about our subjects' beliefs and our intuitions about the denotations of the names they use to express their beliefs. Both Tom and Dick might utter 'Ike was a politician'. However, there is a strong intuitive pull toward saying that their utterances of 'Ike' *refer* to different men; when Tom uses 'Ike' he is referring to Eisenhower, while when Dick uses 'Ike' he is referring to Angell-James. Were the story retold in such a way that intuition would find their utterances of 'Ike' referred to the same man, then the intuition that they had different beliefs would dissolve. Third,

---

*In the philosophical literature there is a quaint tradition of making this point by imagining a separate planet, Twin Earth, in some far off corner of the universe, on which are to be found doppelgangers, molecule for molecule replicas of people on earth. Having frequently used such examples myself, I offer a pair of sociological observations. First, nonphilosophers often find such cases so outlandish that they have no clear intuitions about them. Second, Twin Earth examples drive psychologists up the wall, reinforcing the widespread conviction that the concerns of analytic philosophy are frivolous. To avoid these problems, I will refrain from using Twin Earth examples whenever possible.

it is at least prima facie problematic for the narrow causal account that we find it so natural to describe Tom's belief as "the belief that Eisenhower was a politician." For presumably you and I have mental sentences containing tokens of both 'Ike' and 'Eisenhower', and these tokens are causally distinct. Tom, by contrast, has only 'Ike' tokens in his beliefs about Ike. And if we were to assert, "Tom believes that Eisenhower was a politician," Tom would deny it. The theory in chapter 5 provides a framework for explaining why we nonetheless feel comfortable describing Tom's belief as we do.

Kind Terms

My second case unfolds against the background of a curious difference between American and British English. The facts, as I understand them, are as follows. In American supermarkets one can buy a number of green salad vegetables, including a rather bitter curly leafed variety called 'chicory' and a smooth leafed, tightly packed conical variety called 'endive'. What appear to be exactly the same vegetables are available at British greengrocers; the labels are reversed, however. What Americans know as 'chicory', Englishmen call 'endive', and vice versa.*

The beliefs I want to focus on are those of a pair of subjects, one American, the other English. John, the American, is a "meat and potatoes man" with no taste for vegetables or salad. He has heard mention of salad greens called 'chicory' and 'endive' though he cannot remember ever seeing or tasting either of them. Nor could he tell which was which. However, he has heard, and remembers, that chicory can be rather bitter. The action in our story takes place on a day when John is a guest for dinner at the home of friends. After the main course the hostess asks John whether he would like to try some chicory salad. Tact not being John's strong suit, he declines, saying, "No thanks, chicory is bitter." The other protagonist in my tale is Robin, an Englishman. Robin shares John's dislike of vegetables and his limited knowledge of them. Like John, Robin has heard of the existence of salad greens called 'chicory' and 'endive', but he has never seen either. Robin has heard some misinformed fellow Englishman say, "Chicory is often rather bitter," and he believed it. By now the rest of the story will be obvious. Robin, too, is invited to a dinner party (this one in England) and, on being offered "a chicory salad," declines saying, "No thanks, chicory is bitter."

*Since first writing this, a number of cosmopolitan friends have assured me that I am oversimplifying. The accounts they have given of trans-Atlantic diversity in salad terms are considerably more complex and patently inconsistent with one another. No matter. For the purposes of my example, please simply *assume* that the facts are as I have stated them.

To evoke the intuitions relevant to this case, reflect on the following two questions. First, was the belief John was expressing when he said "Chicory is bitter" the same as the belief that Robin was expressing when he uttered the same words? Second, how are John's belief and Robin's best described? Most of the people on whom I have tried this case report conflicting intuitions, with a strong pull in the direction of saying that John and Robin do not have the same belief, and a somewhat weaker pull in the direction of saying that they do. American informants are inclined to think that "John believes that chicory is bitter" would be the natural way of saying what John believes. However, American informants tend to be more cagy about Robin. "What he believes," one student told me, "is that the stuff he calls 'chicory' is bitter." Many feel it is natural to say that Robin believes *endive* is bitter, though adding a gloss to the effect that he calls endive 'chicory'. Interestingly, though, just about everyone agrees that if they had to say in Chinese what Robin believes, they would use the Chinese word for endive, not the Chinese word for chicory. After reflecting on how they would describe Robin's belief in Chinese, most people I've asked are considerably less reluctant to describe Robin's belief as "the belief that endive is bitter."

As in the proper name case, these intuitions pose problems for the narrow causal version of the mental sentence theory. As I have told the story, it would be plausible for the mental sentence theorist to suppose that John and Robin have type identical sentences in their store of beliefs about endive and chicory. More specifically, the narrow causal account would classify the mental sentence that John expresses with 'Chicory is bitter' as type identical with the mental sentence that Robin expresses with the same words. The intuitive inclination to say that these are different beliefs is left unexplained. Note also that reference seems to be implicated in our intuitions, since when uttered by John 'chicory' refers to chicory (the curly, bitter stuff), while when uttered by Robin, 'chicory' refers to endive (the smooth leafed, conical shaped one).*

Indexicals

The beliefs that a person would express with a sentence containing an indexical like 'I', 'here', or 'now' pose what is perhaps the most obvious problem for narrow causal theories. For in these cases we need no

---

*This example is inspired by those of Putnam (1975) and Burge (1979), though it avoids difficulties that trouble some of their examples. See, in particular, the discussion in Fodor (1982). In focusing directly on intuitions about sameness of belief and about how beliefs are appropriately described, I think the intricate puzzles Fodor raises can simply be sidestepped.

contrived examples to see that common sense sometimes invokes a standard of sameness of belief different from the one urged by the causal account. If two sincere and confident presidential candidates each asserts, "I will be the next president of the United States," there is a strong intuitive inclination to say that they have different beliefs. Indeed given the facts about American presidential elections, their beliefs are incompatible; they cannot both be true. But there is also a discernible tug in the other direction. If two lottery ticket holders both show up at the pay-off window each thinking that he has won the lottery, it would be natural enough to explain their behavior by saying that they have the same belief. If, as seems inevitable, the mental sentence view will include indexicals in the language of thought, then presumably each presidential candidate has a token of 'I will be the next president of the United States' in his brain. And since these tokens will be causal isomorphs of each other, the narrow causal theory cannot account for that strand in our intuition which insists that the two candidates have different beliefs. As in our two previous cases, reference seems clearly implicated, since 'I' in the mouth of one candidate has a different reference from 'I' in the mouth of the other.

Cases involving indexicals also pose some difficulty for the Fodor-style account of how content sentences are related to mental sentences.[9] Recall that for Fodor the mental sentence being ascribed to the believer is identical to the one that the speaker would ordinarily express by using the content sentence. But now consider the case proposed by Perry,[10] in which I see some unfortunate fellow attacked by a bear. Following the recommended defensive strategy, the victim rolls up like a ball and remains motionless. In explaining why he does this, it would be natural to begin by saying, "He believes that he is being attacked by a bear." But the belief that I would express by saying, "He is being attacked by a bear" can hardly be identical to the one the victim has, *by the standard of the narrow causal account*. For this belief causes me to run and seek help, not to roll up like a ball. The belief which would lead me to behave as the victim does is the one which I would express by saying, "*I* am being attacked by a bear." When I am the observer and he is the victim, however, I obviously cannot attribute the correct belief by saying, "He believes that I am being attacked by a bear."

One other curiosity is worth noting about the way in which self-referential beliefs are ordinarily described. In the case of the two presidential candidates, if one is named 'Smith' and the other is named 'Jones', it would be natural enough to describe the situation by saying, "Smith believes that Smith will be elected, while Jones believes that Jones will be elected." It is possible, though, to embellish the story in a way which makes this a much less natural description. If, for example,

Smith does not know that he is named 'Smith', and if this fact looms large in the tale, then the intuitive acceptability of 'Smith believes that Smith will be elected' declines.[11]

3. Irrelevant Causal Differences

Under the headings of Holism and Reference we have looked at cases where the discriminations drawn by common sense were finer than any that would be available on the narrow causal version of the mental sentence theory. In this section I want to look at a few cases where the situation is reversed, the narrow causal account draws distinctions which our intuition ignores.

Consider first the beliefs of people who are afflicted by some minor perceptual handicap like color blindness. The potential causal pathways leading from stimulus to belief in these people differ in a clear way from the pathways available to normal subjects. If, for example, a normal subject is shown a copy of one common color blindness test, he will see (and thus come to believe) that there is a figure 8 on the sheet. A color-blind subject will not see the figure 8 and will not come to believe that there is a figure 8 on the sheet. It follows from the narrow causal account that the belief a normal subject expresses by saying, "There is a figure 8 on this sheet" differs in type from the belief that a color-blind subject would express using the same words. But in most circumstances common sense recognizes no such distinction. If a pair of subjects, one color-blind and the other normal, are both *told* that a certain sheet of paper (which neither of them can see) has a figure 8 on it, and if both subjects trust their informant, it would be intuitively bizarre to insist that they must have formed different beliefs.

It might be thought that in the color blindness case our intuition is being guided by the fact that the difference in potential causal paths leading to the two beliefs is relatively minor. Perhaps the causal account can be saved from embarrassment in cases like this if it counts beliefs as type identical when they are *approximately* the same in their potential causal interactions. I think there is an important insight lurking in this suggestion. But as it stands it clearly will not do, since common sense will often count a pair of beliefs as the same even though their difference in causal potential is enormous. Consider, for example, what we are inclined to say about the beliefs of people who are totally blind. Suppose that I tell both a blind person and a sighted person that there is a cat in the next room, and they both believe my report. It seems intuitively natural to say that they both come to have the same belief—the belief that there is a cat in the next room. Our intuitions remain the same if we change the example by replacing the (merely) blind subject with a person like Helen Keller whose perceptual deficiencies are staggering. Under most circumstances we would find it intuitively natural to say that if Ms. Keller and a normal person are both told there is a cat in the next room, and if they both accept the report as accurate, then they both come to believe the same thing. Yet here, surely, the narrow causal theory is in trouble, since the difference between the potential causal pathways leading to Ms. Keller's belief and those leading to the normal subject's belief are vast by any measure.

I have been writing as though our intuitions about the beliefs of perceptually handicapped subjects were unequivocal and quite stable. But this oversimplifies the actual situation. Many people are distinctly uneasy with the claim that a blind subject forms the same belief we do in response to verbal reports, particularly when the visual deficiencies of the subject become salient to the situation. Suppose, for example, that I tell both a sighted subject and a congenitally blind subject that in the next room there is an auburn cat with light blue eyes and a dark brown tail. Assuming that both subjects take my report to be accurate, do they both form the same belief? Intuition wavers.

I noted earlier that intuitions about how beliefs are to be described and whether they count as the same or different are often very labile. Very similar cases may provoke quite different intuitions depending on the context in which the question about the subject's belief arises. Unlike the theory developed in chapter 5, the narrow causal account has no explanation for this phenomenon. Let me illustrate the phenomenon with a pair of examples focusing on the beliefs of a color-blind subject. People suffering from one sort of color blindness report that red and green look very similar to them, and when asked to characterize the color of objects they are looking at, they often perform very poorly. However, color-blind people learn to use other visual cues to make essential distinctions—the red traffic light is the one on the top, the green one is the one on the bottom. As a result, color blindness often goes undetected. Indeed, the very existence of color blindness was unknown until the late eighteenth century, when it was discovered by Dalton.[12] Now imagine the case of Peter, a store clerk, who suffers unknowingly from severe red-green color blindness. One day, after the Christmas sales are over, Peter and a fellow worker are asked to take down the Christmas decorations and box them, with a separate box for each color. Peter's fellow worker, Greg, notes with some concern that Peter often puts red decorations in the green box and vice versa. Finally, after watching Peter take down a bright green Christmas ball, examine it carefully, and put it into the red box, Greg says, "Peter, you can't really believe that ball is red. There must be something wrong with your eyes." Here, I think, we are inclined to agree that Greg's characterization of Peter's cognitive state is quite appropriate. It would seem more than a bit intuitively odd to explain Peter's action by saying he believed the ball was red and leaving it at that. Contrast this case with the following. Peter has just been hired as a night attendant at a chemical factory. On the first day of work he is given very simple instructions. In addition to sweeping the floors, he has only one duty. If the alarm bell rings it means that something has gone wrong with the automatic equipment and there might be an explosion. Should this happen, he is to go into the control room and throw the red lever. There are many other levers of different colors in that room, and these he is not to touch. As it happens, during his first night on the job the alarm bell sounds, and Peter rushes into the control room. Unfortunately one of the engineers has left a pile of papers on top of the red lever, completely obscuring it from view. There is, however, a large *green* lever in the center of the control panel. Peter rushes to throw this lever, with disastrous results. Why did Peter throw this lever? Here, I think, it would be entirely natural to say that he did it because he believed the lever was red.

Thus far in this section we have been attending to cases in which the possible *perceptual* causes of a belief are altered. Analogous intuitions can be evoked if we look, instead, at the patterns of *inference* that may lead to and from a given belief. An intriguing example can be built around the beliefs of subjects participating in Wason and Johnson-Laird's so-called selection task experiment.[13] In one version of the experiment subjects are shown four cards like those in figure 1. Half of each card is masked. Subjects are asked to look at the cards and to decide which masks it is essential to remove in order to know whether the following claim is true about these cards:

If there is a circle on the left, there is a circle on the right.

Since the task is so straightforward and the directions so simple, it is hard to imagine that subjects don't all end up having the same beliefs about what they are being asked to do. Yet, surprisingly, though they start with the same beliefs about the setup and the task, subjects infer very different answers. A relatively small number conclude (correctly) that the masks on (a) and (d) must be removed. Many more subjects come to believe that the masks on (a) and (c) must be removed; still others conclude that only the mask on (a) must be removed. Moreover, subjects who end up with a mistaken belief often defend their conclusion with a perverse vigor. For the narrow causal theory these subjects are something of an embarrassment. Both the subjects who get the right answer and those who get the wrong answer start with what common sense classes as the same beliefs about the problem. But since they

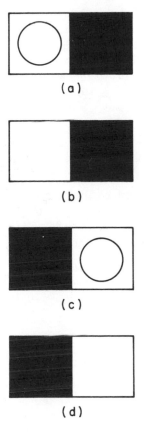

Figure 1

draw different inferences from them, the narrow causal version of the mental sentence theory must classify these initial beliefs as different in type.

Here, as in the analogous case of minimal perceptual difference, it might be objected that I am construing the narrow causal standard too strictly, since the difference between the subjects who get the right answer and those who get the wrong answer marks only a very minor difference in the causal potential of their beliefs. And as in the perceptual case, I think there is some merit in the protest. For if we consider cases in which the inferential patterns exhibited by a subject's beliefs grow increasingly different from our own, it becomes increasingly intuitively uncomfortable to describe their beliefs with the same content sentences we use in describing our own beliefs. For a particularly clear illustration of this phenomenon, let me again indulge in a bit of science fiction. Suppose, as we did earlier, that beliefs are stored on a tiny cerebral CRT and that various mental processes, including inference and practical reasoning, depend on what is written on the CRT. Let us imagine that for each of these cognitive processes there is a separate device which scans the CRT and makes appropriate modifications to the store of beliefs, the store of desires, or whatever. Now what I want to consider is a sequence of cases, each involving a subject who suffers a sudden breakdown in his inference-making device. Let us call our subjects Dave[1], Dave[2], . . . , Dave[9], and let us imagine that as we proceed down the list of Daves the breakdowns in the inference-making device get more severe. For example, we might suppose that Dave[1] simply loses his capacity to infer via transitivity of the conditional. So, though he may have tokens of both

If my wife works late, then my wife does not feed the dog.

and

If my wife does not feed the dog, then I must feed the dog.

in his belief store, he does not infer that he must feed the dog if his wife works late. Dave[2], let us suppose, shares Dave[1]'s deficiency and adds to it an incapacity to reason normally with disjunctions. Though he has a token of the sentence

Either the car keys are on my desk or the car keys are in the kitchen

on his CRT, adding

The car keys are not on my desk

does not lead him to infer

The car keys are in the kitchen.

Dave[3] adds yet another quirk, and Dave[4] still another. However, in each case it is assumed that the inferential breakdown is quite sudden and does not alter the set of sentences stored on these men's CRTs. What are we to make of the beliefs of these subjects immediately after their breakdowns? The answer, I think, is that as we proceed down the list it becomes increasingly unnatural to characterize a given belief the way we would have before the breakdown. Suppose, for example, that along with his other problems Dave[8] has lost his ability to infer by modus ponens. Though his CRT continues to display a token of

If it's raining, then I should take my umbrella

and though he continues to affirm this sentence when asked, this belief no longer leads him to infer

I should take my umbrella

when a token of

It's raining

appears on his CRT. Does he still believe that if it's raining then he should take his umbrella? My intuition here is strongly inclined to give a negative verdict.

It appears that real mental breakdowns are never quite so neatly restricted to a single cognitive capacity. But inferential peculiarities are often part of the clinical profile. One sort of schizophrenic typically infers from

Napoleon was a great leader

and

I am a great leader

to

I am Napoleon.

Does a person who has come to affirm 'I am Napoleon' as a result of this pattern of inference really believe that he is Napoleon? To my intuition, the answer is neither clearly yes nor clearly no.

The example of inferential breakdown seems to suggest that our intuitions are guided by the degree of causal similarity between a subject's belief and our own. And this is not entirely uncongenial to the narrow causal version of the mental sentence theory, though advocates of that account generally pay little attention to degrees of similarity. But there are further complications to be confronted. A number of writers have noted that it is often overwhelmingly intuitively plausible to ascribe beliefs to animals using some of the very same content sentences we would use in ascribing beliefs to quite normal people.[14] There is, for example, no intuitive awkwardness in Russell's story of the Christmas turkey rushing toward its executioner with the mistaken but inductively well-supported belief that it was about to be fed. But the turkey is a singularly stupid bird, and it is likely that despite Dave[8]'s enormous cognitive deficits, normal human inferential capacity is closer to his than to the turkey's. The narrow causal account has no explanation of why we should be more ambivalent about Dave[8] than we are about the turkey.

Before bringing this chapter to a close, I should remind you of its relatively modest aim. What I hope to have established with these examples is that there are many different cases in which the judgments of intuition are not what would be expected if we were relying on a commonsense notion of belief which could be analyzed along the lines of the mental sentence theory with tokens typed on the narrow causal standard. None of my examples suffices to show that narrow causal accounts of belief are beyond prudent patching. But collectively perhaps they are enough to convince you that the fishing might be better somewhere else.

Chapter 5
A Content Theory of Belief

At the end of chapter 3, I drew a distinction between two sorts of mental sentence theories, a distinction which turned on how they handle the problem of typing mental sentence tokens. The burden of chapter 4 was that things do not look promising for theories invoking a narrow causal account of typing. In the present chapter I will look at the other alternative, the one which types tokens according to their content. As indicated earlier I think this is the right place to look. What I propose to do is to set out in some detail a theory in the spirit of the mental sentence theory, with tokens typed by content, and to argue that this theory provides plausible explanations for all the data we have assembled about our folk psychological concept of belief. In saying that the theory I will defend is in the spirit of mental sentence theories, I intend "spirit" to be interpreted rather broadly. For there are many points, some of considerable importance, on which I part company with these theories. Indeed it will prove convenient to set out my theory by first reviewing the essential points of the content version of the mental sentence theory and then noting in detail where I differ and why.

Before setting out on this task, a word is in order on the intended scope of my analysis. Just about all of the recent philosophical discussion of belief has been wedded to the view that there are two distinct senses of the word 'believes': the *de dicto* or notional sense, and the *de re* or relational sense. On this view, belief sentences are generally ambiguous, since they may be understood as invoking either the *de dicto* or the *de re* sense of 'believes'. A great deal has been written on how these senses are to be characterized and on whether one can be defined in terms of the other. However, it is my contention that no matter how the putative senses are characterized, the ambiguity thesis is simply mistaken. *In their ordinary usage 'belief', 'believes', and related terms are not ambiguous.* And though belief sentences may sometimes be ambiguous, the ambiguity is always to be traced to some other component of the sentence. The verb 'believes' introduces no systematic ambiguity. Thus I intend the account developed below to describe the single, univocal ordinary meaning of 'believes'. If I am right in rejecting the claim that ordinary language belief sentences are systematically ambiguous, however, then the vast majority of philosophers who have written about belief in the last three decades are wrong, and some explanation is in order on just how they were led astray. In the next chapter I will take a look at the evidence and arguments that have been offered for the ambiguity thesis, and I shall argue that the data can be better explained by the theory developed below.

1. Content Mental Sentence Theories

Let me begin by sketching the essential points of mental sentence theories which type tokens according to content. Figure 2 depicts two people: A (the attributor) is uttering 'S believes that p' and thereby attributing to S the belief that p. S is the person about whom A is speaking. The aim of the theory is to explain just what A is saying about S—to analyze the meaning of his assertion.

The first point to note is that A is saying that S has (or is in) a certain sort of psychological state, viz., a belief. The mental sentence theory makes two rather different claims about states of this sort. First, to count as a belief at all, a state must play a certain sort of causal role in the mental dynamics of the subject. This causal role can be recounted in terms of characteristic causal interactions with stimuli and with other categories of mental states, which are themselves characterized by their interactions with beliefs, with each other, with stimuli, and with behavior. Thus to attribute any belief to a subject is to presuppose that the subject's psychology exhibits an overall pattern or global architecture along the lines depicted in figure 2. (A, of course, is presumed to have the same global psychological architecture, though details have been omitted from my sketch.) The second thing that mental sentence theories tell us about beliefs is that they are sentence tokens, either in the language of the subject or in a species wide language of thought. A bit more precisely, mental sentence theories claim that to have a belief is to have a sentence token inscribed in the brain in such a way that it exhibits the causal interactions appropriate to beliefs. Generally mental sentence accounts tell a parallel story about desires: to have a desire is to have a sentence token represented in the brain in such a way that it exhibits the causal interactions appropriate to desires.

In saying 'S believes that p', of course, A is not merely telling us that S has some belief or other. He is using the content sentence, 'p', to specify which belief it is. In explaining how this specification works, the content version of the mental sentence theory invokes a pair of relations to link the content sentence to S's belief. The first of these

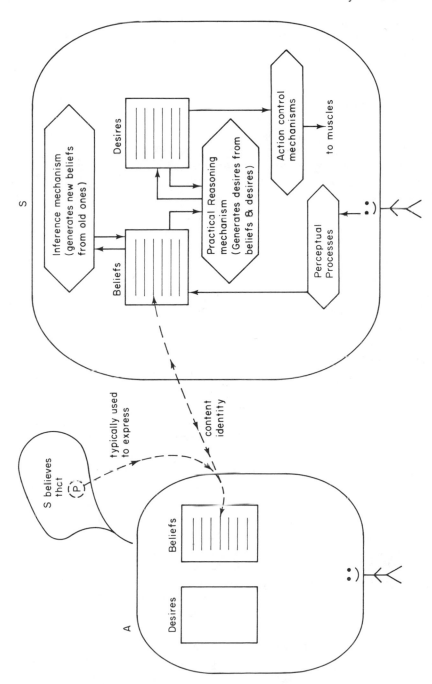

Figure 2

relations links the content sentence to an actual or possible belief state of the attributor. Though details are generally left sketchy, the core idea is that the belief in question is the one which the attributor would typically express by uttering the content sentence. Or, as Fodor has put it, it is the belief which plays "a causal/functional role in the production of linguistically regular utterances" of the content sentence.[1] The second relation is identity of content, and it serves to link the attributor's belief to the subject's. So, stripped to essentials, here is what the theory claims: When A says, 'S believes that p', he is saying that S has a mental token of a sentence stored in the way characteristic of beliefs, and this token is content-identical to the one which he (A) expresses by uttering 'p'.

2. Elaborations and Revisions

Though the theory sketched in figure 2 is a plausible first approximation, considerable tinkering will be required before we have an account which does justice to our commonsense concept of belief. In this section I will indicate where and why I think modifications are in order.

Conceptual Analysis and Protoscience

As the attentive reader will have noted, I have already smuggled in one modification of the mental sentence view as characterized in chapter 3. Mental sentence theorists generally take themselves to be doing protoscience, not conceptual analysis. Theirs is a theory about the nature of the psychological states spoken of in our folk psychology, not an attempt to analyze the concepts of folk theory. By contrast the account I shall offer aspires to be a descriptive analysis, cleaving as closely as possible to the contours of our commonsense concept. Given the broader purposes of this book, I have no choice but to aim for a descriptive conceptual analysis. If one is convinced that a term in common use denotes some real entity or class of entities, one is free to build a theory about the nature of those entities exploiting whatever evidence or argument may prove useful. But to assume that stance here would be to beg what I take to be a fundamental question. On my view it is up for grabs whether the terms of folk psychology denote anything at all. Perhaps the concepts of folk psychology, like many of those in folk medicine or folk cosmology, will turn out to be true of nothing; perhaps there are no such things as beliefs. If one takes this possibility seriously, then the inevitable strategy is to get as clear as possible on the workings of our folk concept and then assess the prospects of pressing this concept (or some elaboration of it) into service in a serious empirical theory.

Since conceptual analysis has had a bad press of late, I should say

something about how I conceive of the endeavor. There is a long philosophical tradition, stretching back to Socrates, which sought to give
an analysis by giving a definition, a set of necessary and sufficient
conditions for the application of the concept. If this exercise is to have
any point, the terms used in the definition will have to be simpler or
more perspicuous than the term or concept being defined. Thus the
project of providing necessary and sufficient conditions takes on a
reductivist cast. But things have not gone well for this reductivist project.
A plausible case could be made that in two and a half millennia of
trying, we haven't succeeded in defining *anything* of any interest.[2] So
it might be thought that it is time to give up conceptual analysis as a
lost cause. But I am inclined to think that this pessimism is warranted
only if we follow the central philosophical tradition and insist that a
conceptual analysis must give us reductivist necessary and sufficient
conditions. Outside philosophy, where the demand for reductive definition has less sway, descriptive conceptual analysis seems to be flourishing. In social anthropology it has long been common practice to
describe a set of exotic folk concepts by detailing their interrelations
with one another, with community practices and rituals, and with the
society's ecology and tradition. Such an account, when well done, can
give us deep insight into the conceptual web of exotic folks. But it does
not yield reductivist definitions of native concepts. In more recent years
a rather analogous attempt at conceptual analysis has been launched
by people working in artificial intelligence and cognitive simulation.
Their focus has been on domestic concepts rather than exotic ones.
Typically their goal has been to describe some interrelated set of commonsense concepts in sufficient detail to assemble a computer simulation
which can process information invoking these concepts in ways similar
to the ways people process them. Now on my view, philosophical
conceptual analysis, when done properly, ought to be continuous with
the project of the cognitive simulator. The philosophical analyst can
be viewed as giving a rather coarse-grained discursive characterization—
a sort of sketchy verbal flow chart—for the more detailed program that
the cognitive simulator is trying to write. This is how I would have
the project of the current chapter construed.[3]

The move away from reductivist definition as a goal in philosophical
analysis is not really all that new. Many writers in the last two decades
have embraced the view that our commonsense concepts are folk-
theoretic concepts, best analyzed by making explicit the largely tacit
structure of folk theory.[4] However, I am inclined to think that something
new and interesting is added by viewing philosophical analysis as
continuous with cognitive simulation. Although cognitive simulation
is hardly past its infancy, it has already established one important fact

beyond serious argument. Folk conceptual systems have again and again shown themselves to be unexpectedly rich, complex, subtle, and interconnected. They are so complex that it is hard to imagine them explicated in detail without exploiting the resources of computer languages and couching one's account as a complex program. If this is right, then philosophers concerned with conceptual analysis have a pair of options. They can bite the bullet and become programmers, or they can aim at informal, often imprecise description which leaves much of the detail unspecified. I think both strategies are respectable. While the informal philosophical strategy must sacrifice specificity, it can often offer greater scope and perspective. This informal strategy is the one I shall be pursuing in the pages to follow.

Mental Sentences and Complex Mental States

In practice the shift from the protoscientific stance of the mental sentence theorist to the strategy of conceptual analysis that I adopt will make surprisingly little difference in my account, save on one point. Mental sentence theorists hold that the objects of belief are sentence tokens, though they do not argue that any such view is entailed by our folk theory. Rather, they maintain, the hypothesis that beliefs are relations to internally inscribed sentence tokens is compatible with folk theory and provides a natural bridge between folk psychology and contemporary research in cognitive science.[5] I have no quarrel with any of this. But since my aim is to describe our folk concept rather than to elaborate on it, I am uncomfortable with the claim that the objects of beliefs are sentence tokens. There is ample reason to suppose that our folk theory takes beliefs to be internal *states* whose role in the psychological economy of the subject fits the pattern sketched in figure 2. Also, it seems clear that folk psychology takes beliefs to be *complex* states whose components, often labeled 'concepts', can recur in distinct beliefs, as well as in desires and in other intentional psychological states. For example, it is intuitively natural to suppose that my concept of water is a component in my belief that water is H_2O, and in my belief that (most of) the stuff in Lake Michigan is water, and in my desire for a glass of water. It is also noteworthy that there is a conspicuous correlation between the concepts we would ordinarily say are involved in a given belief and the words we would use to express the belief. As far as I can see, however, there is nothing *in our folk theory* to motivate the move from viewing beliefs as complex internal states to viewing them as sentence tokens. Nor do I see much reason to think that folk psychology is committed to a systematic language of thought. Thus I will presume, in my account, that a belief is a relation between a subject and a complex internal state of the sort depicted in figure 2.

I should emphasize though that my departure from the mental sentence theory on this point may be more apparent than real. For mental sentence theorists typically leave the notion of an internalized sentence token as little more than a *metaphor*. And it may well turn out that when the metaphor has been unpacked, it claims no more than that beliefs are relations to complex internal states whose components can occur as parts of other beliefs.

The Relation between the Content Sentence and the Attributor's Belief
In figure 2 the link between the content sentence and the attributor's belief has been labeled "expresses," and in my gloss of the sketch I followed Fodor in explaining that a content sentence expresses the attributor's belief if the belief plays a causal role in the production of "linguistically regular" utterances of the sentence. I think the basic insight here is a sound one. In saying what someone else believes, we describe his belief by relating it to one we ourselves might have. And we indicate this potential belief of our own by uttering the sentence we would use to express it. But while the central idea is sound, the details cry out for more careful elaboration. Two problems are especially conspicuous. First, there is reason to suspect that the convenient appeal to "linguistically regular" utterances is actually circular. It is clear enough why some such qualification was called for, since sometimes, as when we aim to deceive, the belief that p plays no role in the causal history of an utterance of p. The belief that p plays the intended causal role only when our assertion of p is sincere. So it looks suspiciously like 'linguistically regular utterance of p' is being used as a synonym for 'sincere assertion of p'. However, it is hard to see how this latter notion could be unpacked without invoking the idea of an utterance *caused by the belief that p*. And now we are standing on our own tail. For the whole idea was to characterize the belief that p in terms of an utterance to which it stands in a special causal relation. In explaining that special relation we find ourselves invoking the very notion it was to be used to explain.

A second problem with our explanation of the "expresses" relation echos a difficulty noted in chapter 2 in our discussion of the theory-theory. To put it starkly, there are just not enough sincere assertions to go around. Adopting an earlier example, it is probably the case that no one has ever sincerely asserted that Buckingham Palace is filled with pickles. And since there are no such sincere assertions, there is no belief which has played a causal role in the production of such assertions. But this bodes ill for belief sentences like 'S believes that Buckingham Palace is filled with pickles'. For absent sincere assertions of the content sentence, our proposed analysis cannot get off the ground.

To patch these problems, I propose to use a pair of tools: first, the idea of a typical causal pattern linking belief states to utterances, and second, a counterfactual. Let me begin by explaining my notion of a typical causal pattern. The basic thought is that there is a typical or characteristic sort of proximate causal history that underlies most of our assertions, and this pattern is the hallmark of straightforward sincere assertion. This is not of course to deny that many of our assertions have causal histories that do not fit the pattern. We sometimes assert what we do not believe, and we sometimes have the most devious of reasons for asserting what we do believe. Yet it remains true that most of our assertions are sincere and straightforward expressions of belief. Now what I am assuming and what I think commonsense psychology assumes is that there is a common causal pattern underlying most cases in which we sincerely and straightforwardly express a belief. Since sincere, straightforward assertion is the preponderant mode of speech, the presumed common causal pattern is the *typical causal pattern* underlying our assertions. No doubt the pattern, like all patterns, admits of some variation from case to case. Yet I think that we ordinarily suppose that the proximate causal histories underlying sincere, straightforward assertions are distinguished by some important common features—that they constitute a single *kind* of psychological process. It is perhaps a symptom of this tenet of folk psychology that we find the idea of constructing a generally reliable lie detector well within the bounds of conceptual possibility. Indeed I am inclined to think that the impressive success of state-of-the-art lie detector technology is some evidence that our folk theory is correct in this assumption.

Granting the notion of a typical causal pattern underlying our assertions, it might be thought that we could identify the belief that p simply as *the* belief which can play a role in a typical causal history leading to an assertion of p. But on reflection, this pretty clearly won't do, since many beliefs in addition to the belief that p may play a role in a typical causal history leading to a sincere assertion of p. Thus for example, on one occasion I may assert 'Ouagadougou is the capital of Upper Volta' because I believe it and because I believe you have just asked me what the capital of Upper Volta is. On another occasion I may make the same assertion because I believe Ouagadougou is the capital of Upper Volta and because I believe that you have just asserted that Abidjan is the capital of Upper Volta. On other occasions still other beliefs may play a role in a typical causal pattern leading to an utterance of 'Ouagadougou is the capital of Upper Volta'. However, in all these cases I think we assume the belief that p plays a special central role in typical causal histories leading to the utterance of p. If pressed to specify this central role, I would proceed as follows. First, concentrate on those sentences that Quine calls "eternal"—i.e., sentences whose truth values remain fixed despite variation in the identity of the utterer, or the time or place of utterance. Now in the class of eternal English sentences there are some which have been uttered with considerable frequency. Further, there will generally be only one belief which is part of the causal history of *each* typically caused utterance of a frequently uttered eternal sentence. It is the sort of role played by this belief that I am calling the *central* role. However, I am inclined to think that in elaborating this way of picking out the central causal role a belief can play in typical causal histories, we are going well beyond what is embedded in our commonsense psychology. I suspect folk theory gets by with the mere assumption that *there is* a special central role for the belief that p to play in typical causal histories of utterances of p, without ever detailing necessary and sufficient conditions for this role.* To characterize the role and to recognize cases of deviant causal chains linking a belief with an utterance in a nontypical way, my guess would be that folk theory relies on a few *exemplars* or *prototypical* examples to which new cases can be compared.[6]

With the notion of a central role in a typical causal history in hand, we can piece together a better account of the relation between an utterance of 'p' and the belief that p. The basic idea is this: We are to imagine that (contrary to fact) the ascriber is uttering the content sentence with a typical causal history. The belief which he aims at identifying is the one which would play the central role in the typical causal history leading to his imagined utterance of 'p'. So on my account, a rough paraphrase of what A is saying would run as follows: S is in a belief state identical in content to the one which would play the central causal role if I were now to produce an utterance of 'p' with a typical causal history.

Ambiguity and the Logical Form of Belief Sentences

In my account as it has been developed thus far, I have been following the Carnapian strategy of treating belief ascriptions as though they expressed a relation between the believer and the content sentence; though, of course, the relation I have sketched is at best a distant kin

---

*Grice (1975) notes that folk theories are likely to be "law-allusive," alluding to the existence of laws which they do not themselves specify or have need to specify. My suggestion here is of a piece with Grice's, though "theory-allusive" might be a better term, since what I am suggesting is that our folk theory alludes to the existence of some detailed theory which specifies both the nature of a typical causal pattern and the details of the special causal role. For its purposes, folk theory need not and thus does not specify the theory it alludes to.

of what Carnap had in mind.* There is reason to think we should give up this vestige of Carnapian doctrine, however. For on the Carnapian account it is a sentence *type* to which the believer is related. And if we take this tack, we are left with no explanation of the fact that the ambiguity of belief ascriptions is not nearly so great as the ambiguity of sentence types whose tokens are embedded within them. An example will serve to make the point. Suppose that you and I are walking down the street and we spot a mutual acquaintance, Charlie, pacing back and forth in front of the building across the street. Since you know that Charlie should be in his office at this hour, you ask me, "What's Charlie doing over there?" I reply, "He believes his girl friend has gone to the bank, and he is waiting for her to come out. They had a nasty quarrel this morning, and he wants to patch things up." Now the first thing to note about this example is that the sentence *type*, 'His girl friend has gone to the bank' is ambiguous. The word 'bank' may mean either a financial institution or the edge of a river, and the phrase 'his girl friend' might be used to refer to any of an indefinitely large number of women. Thus there are *many* beliefs which, under suitable circumstances, I might express by sincerely uttering a token of the content sentence. Or, to put the matter the other way around, there are many beliefs which might play the central causal role in a typical causal history leading to an utterance of (a token of) the content sentence. And according to my analysis, as we left it in the previous section, to say that Charlie believes that his girl friend has gone to the bank is to say that Charlie is in a belief state content-identical to the one I would express by earnestly uttering 'His girl friend has gone to the bank'. But, as we have just seen, there are indefinitely many such beliefs, all quite distinct. So if my analysis were correct as it stands, we should expect the belief ascription in my little tale to be comparably ambiguous. Yet of course we find no such thing. It was perfectly clear that the belief I was attributing to Charlie was a belief about *his* girl friend and the financial institution in front of which he was pacing. The ambiguity in belief ascriptions that my account leads us to expect just is not there.

In general when a belief ascription is used to attribute a belief to a person, the referring expressions in the content sentence have the denotation they would have were the content sentence alone to have been issued in the identical setting. This is true when the referring terms are pronominal expressions like 'his girl friend', and also when the referring expressions are names. Thus if I were now to tell you

---

*Actually, the account as we left it in the last section portrays belief as a three-place relation, with the relata being the believer, the content sentence, and the attributor. For Carnap's view, see chapter 2, section 1.

that former President Ford believes Nixon erased the famous gap in the Watergate tapes, I would be unambiguously ascribing to Mr. Ford a belief about his predecessor, no matter how many people there may be named 'Nixon'. Similarly a token of a *semantically* ambiguous content sentence generally renders a belief attribution in which it is embedded ambiguous only to the degree that a token of the content sentence would be semantically ambiguous if uttered alone in the same setting. Some strategy must be found to take account of these facts in the analysis of belief attributions.

One attractive solution is to borrow an idea due to Davidson.[7] In his account of indirect discourse, Davidson urges that we abandon the Carnapian strategy of analyzing sentences like

(1)   Galileo said that the earth moves

as expressing a relation between Galileo and a sentence type, viz., 'The earth moves'. Instead, Davidson proposes that we view each use of a sentence like (1) as expressing a relation (he calls it the relation of "samesaying") between Galileo and the utterance following the word 'that'. More precisely, Davidson urges that the word 'that' be construed as a demonstrative, referring to the speech act which follows.[8] The speech act is, in the nonphilosophical sense, an *act*; it is a sort of skit produced not as an assertion but as a demonstration. Its function is analogous to that of a rude gesture that might accompany my utterance of

When the teacher's back was turned, the boy whom she had just reprimanded went like that.

The analogy with a gesture is an illuminating one, since the type of gesture performed and its import are very much a function of the surrounding context. If I say,

After chewing out the recruit, the sergeant went like that.

and accompany my utterance with a sweeping motion of my open palm, the gesture I am attributing to the sergeant will vary dramatically, depending on whether the motion of my hand stops in midair or adjacent to the cheek of a man in my audience. Similarly, if I report,

The scout paused, examined the tracks carefully, and pointed like that

the information I convey may be critically dependent on the direction in which I point. The context of the act plays an analogous role in belief ascriptions. Questions of ambiguity and reference in the speech act (i.e., the skit or demonstration) following the demonstrative 'that' will be largely resolved by the setting in which the act takes place, just as they would be were the act to have been performed in earnest.

When we weave this Davidsonian idea into my account of belief ascription, the picture that emerges looks like this. In saying

Andrea believes that lead floats on mercury.

(under ordinary circumstances) I am doing two rather different things. First, I am claiming that Andrea has a belief. Second, I am performing a little skit, doing a bit of play acting. The words following the demonstrative 'that' in the sentence I utter constitute the script for the play. The two components of my belief ascription are related because the skit is designed to exhibit the typical or characteristic effect of the belief I am attributing to Andrea. A bit more precisely, I am saying that Andrea is in a belief state content-identical to one which would play the central role in the causal history leading up to my play-acting assertion, were that assertion to have been made with a typical causal history. This view of belief ascription is very much in the spirit of an account once advocated by Quine. Consider the following passage:

> In indirect quotation we project ourselves into what, from his remarks and other indications, we imagine the speaker's state of mind to have been, and then we say what, in our language, is natural and relevant for us in the state thus feigned. An indirect quotation can usually expect to rate only as better or worse, more or less faithful, and we cannot even hope for a strict standard of more and less; what is involved is evaluation, relative to special purposes, of an essentially dramatic act. Correspondingly for other propositional attitudes, for all of them can be thought of as involving something like quotation of one's own imagined verbal response to an imagined situation.
>
> Casting our real selves thus in unreal roles, we do not generally know how much reality to hold constant. Quandaries arise. But despite them we find ourselves attributing beliefs, wishes and strivings even to creatures lacking the power of speech, such is our dramatic virtuosity. We project ourselves even into what from his behavior we imagine a mouse's state of mind to have been, dramatize it as a belief, wish, or striving, verbalized as seems relevant and natural to us in the state thus feigned.[9]

Content Identity and Content Similarity

The central feature of content-style mental sentence theories as sketched in figure 2, the feature that distinguishes them from narrow causal theories, is the relation of content-identity that links the belief state of the believer with the hypothetical or counterfactually characterized belief state of the attributor. This is also the feature about which I have so far had the least to say. In this reticence I have followed the lead of the literature, which is singularly vague and uninformative about the relation of content-identity. I once thought that the way to remedy this problem was to seek a definition of the content-identity relation along familiar analytic lines. This would involve seeking a set of necessary and sufficient conditions for content identity, then testing the proposal against intuitions about cases. If the proposed definition rules that a pair of beliefs are content-identical and intuition agrees or if the definition (along with the rest of our analysis) agrees with intuition in describing a given belief as the belief that p, than we have some evidence that our definition has captured our intuitive concept. If the definition departs from the dictates of intuition, then it must be reworked. What I am describing of course is standard practice, the stock in trade of analytic philosophy. However, I am now convinced that for all its comfortable familiarity, the route I have been describing is not the way to get a handle on the intuitive notion I have been calling 'content-identity'. Not to put too fine a point on the matter, the reason is that *there are no necessary and sufficient conditions for the application of this intuitive concept*, at least not along the lines traditionally conceived.

Several lines of thought converge in leading me to this conclusion. Consider first the fact that many of the intuitions we noted in the previous chapter seemed to lie along a continuum. Recall for example the case of Mrs. T, the woman suffering from gradual, progressive loss of memory. Before the onset of her illness Mrs. T clearly believed that McKinley was assassinated. By the time of the dialogue reported in chapter 4 she clearly did not believe it. But at what point in the course of her illness did her belief stop being content-identical with mine? The question is a puzzling one and admits of no comfortable reply. What we are inclined to say is that her belief gradually became less and less content-identical with mine; it became less and less the belief that McKinley was assassinated. The same apparent impossibility of drawing a natural boundary, even a rough one, can be seen in the case of Paul, who somehow comes to accept a single sentence of a radically new theory. To see this, suppose we imagine the process repeated, with Paul coming to have internal inscriptions of the fundamental sentences of the new theory one at a time. At what point would we be prepared to say that Paul and the future scientists *first* have content-identical beliefs? Well, at no *point*. Their beliefs simply become more and more identical in content. Note the parallel here with children learning some new concept or theory. How much physics must my son know before it is appropriate to say he believes that $E = mc^2$? The more the better, of course; but there are no natural lines to draw. The case of Dave[1], . . . , Dave[9] makes the point in a different way. Where, as we proceed from Dave[1] to Dave[9] do the beliefs of these imagined subjects stop being content-identical with the beliefs *we* would express using the same sentences? The answer, surely, is that there is no such point. Their beliefs and ours simply become less and less content-identical. What these cases suggest is that the relation I have been calling 'content-identity' is actually a *similarity* relation, one which admits of a gradation of degrees.

The suggestion that content-identity (so called) is actually a similarity relation is reinforced by the context dependence of many intuitions about how beliefs are appropriately described. We saw an example of this in the previous chapter in the case of the color-blind store clerk turned night watchman. Whether or not we were prepared to say without qualification that he believed the object he was looking at was red depended on the focus of our interest. Much the same phenomenon could be illustrated with many of our other examples. Consider, to choose just one case, the child who accepts and repeats a few isolated sentences of a complex scientific theory. If we tell a story in which it is important that the child *assert* $E = mc^2$ or *deny* $E = mc^4$ it can seem quite natural to say that the child does indeed believe (or know) that $E = mc^2$. (Here is the outline of such a story: The quiz show producers are pondering what questions to set for little Alice. Their plan is to allow her to win a small sum, but to be sure that she does not win the grand prize. "For the grand prize, how about asking her what E equals in Einstein's famous equation," proposes one producer. "No," protests the other, who has interviewed Alice at length, "she knows that $E = mc^2$".) If, by contrast, we tell a story in which it is important that Alice be able to use the belief to solve some contextually important problem, our inclination is to deny that she believes $E = mc^2$. This shift in judgment, as a function of the focus of our interest in the context where the judgment is called for, is quite characteristic of similarity judgments. If we are discussing climate and terrain and I ask, "Is the USSR more similar to Canada or to Cuba?" Canada is the clear intuitive choice. But if our discussion has been about political systems and I raise the same question, the natural answer is Cuba.

Another consideration encouraging me to believe that what I have been calling 'content-identity' is actually a similarity relation is that analogous similarity relations have recently come to play a large role in the empirical study of the mental representation of concepts and the use of concepts in categorization. The work I have in mind has developed in reaction to the traditional view that concepts are represented by definitions—lists of properties or features which are individually necessary and jointly sufficient for the application of a concept. The theories that have been proposed in opposition to this tradition are still very much in flux.[10] Typically they claim that a concept (the concept of a bird, say, or of a robin) is represented by a set of features few if any of which are necessary. In deciding whether a given object falls under a concept, the theories claim that a subject performs a similarity match, determining the extent to which the features in his representation of the object coincide with the features in his representation of the concept. A variation on this theme suggests that concepts are stored not as a set of features but, rather, as one or more stored *prototypes* or *exemplars*. On this version, we determine the applicability of a concept to an object by matching the features in our representation of the object with those in our prototypical representation(s). The effect of context may shift our focus from one prototype to another or affect the weight that is given, in the similarity measure, to one sort of feature or another. These latter complications are only beginning to be studied, however.

It turns out that feature matching or prototype similarity theories explain an impressive range of data that are problematic for the traditional view that concepts are represented by mental definitions. Here are a few striking illustrations. First, people find it a fairly natural task to rate various objects or subcategories falling under a concept with respect to how typical or representative of the concept each is.[11] For example, people rate robins and sparrows as more typical birds than eagles, and eagles as more typical than chickens. Moreover, the typicality rankings obtained correlate with a surprising range of further phenomena. They predict both the speed and the accuracy with which subjects will respond when asked to determine whether an item or a subcategory falls under a category. People are faster to judge that a robin is a bird than to judge that a chicken is a bird. Typicality rankings also predict which concepts will be learned first by children and which subcategories will be mentioned first when subjects are asked to list items falling under a category.[12] Perhaps most suggestive to philosophers is the finding that all of the above mentioned typicality-correlated phenomena also correlate with what has been called the "family resemblance measure." This latter measure is determined by asking subjects to list features characteristic of members of various subcategories of a given category. For example, if the category is furniture, subjects are asked to list features of a table, a chair, a rug, a vase, etc. The more mentioned features a subcategory has in common with other subcategories, the higher is its family resemblance measure.[13]

Now none of the results I have been describing bear directly on the analysis of belief ascription. The reason I find them relevant is that they suggest that context-dependent judgments of similarity may play quite a fundamental role in the mental mechanism underlying our intuitions on how things are to be categorized or described.* And, as we have already seen, there are ample hints suggesting that this is afoot in the case of our judgments about the appropriateness of belief ascriptions. So let me mold these various hints into an explicit hypothesis. What I am proposing is that in figure 2 we replace the content-identity relation with a notion of context-dependent similarity. If this is right, then we will have the following rough paraphrase of what we are saying when we say 'S believes that p':

> p.
> S is in a belief state similar to the one which would play the typical causal role if my utterance of that had had a typical causal history.

The 'that', of course, is a demonstrative, referring to the play-acting utterance of 'p' that preceded. I offer this account as an hypothesis to be tested against our intuitions. But before seeing how well it does, some elaboration is needed on just how the notion of similarity is supposed to work.

Basically I conceive of the similarity measure as a feature-matching measure along the lines sketched above and characterized in greater detail by Tversky.[14] Unlike Tversky's account of similarity, however, the one needed in my account will have to discriminate among features in a context-dependent way, sometimes giving heavier weight to features of one sort, sometimes to another. I have no detailed proposal to make on how this sort of context sensitivity is best built into a feature-matching similarity tester. It is one of those (many and important) problems of detail that I will foist off on the cognitive simulator. Without actually building a model or writing a program, we have no choice but to sketch the forest while ignoring the trees.

Still, even at this relatively coarse-grained level of description, something must be said on how beliefs are represented—what the features are in virtue of which similarity among beliefs is to be assessed. I think that the features which are most salient in our mental characterization of beliefs can be grouped under three headings. The first and in a sense the most central is *functional* or *causal-pattern* similarity. A pair of belief

---

*An important caveat: Though I think the prototype-cum-similarity-match theory is an important advance in the study of concepts and categorization, I am inclined to think it is much too *simple* a story. Rather than a prototype or a cluster of features, I suspect our concepts are represented in structures more akin to Minsky's frames (Minsky 1975, Winograd 1981). Though I adopt the prototype theory as a metaphor for my view, the account I am developing is comfortably compatible with a more complex framelike picture of conceptual representation.

states count as similar along this dimension if they have similar patterns of potential causal interaction with (actual or possible) stimuli, with other (actual or possible) mental states, and with (actual or possible) behavior. A strong causal-pattern similarity is the single standard for sameness of belief proposed by the narrow causal version of the mental sentence theory. In addition to the global causal-pattern similarity stressed by causal accounts, however, there are various dimensions along which a pair of belief states (or other mental states) can be *partially* causal-pattern similar. For example, a pair of belief states may interact similarly with other beliefs in inference but may not have terribly similar links with stimuli. These beliefs would count as highly similar when the context primes for inferential connections but as rather dissimilar when the context focuses interest on the connections between belief and perception. Causal-pattern similarity is the basic sort of similarity since it is presumed to some degree by the other features used to gauge similarity of belief. What we do, in effect, is to locate a pair of belief states which are (or are assumed to be) passingly similar in causal pattern, then, when relevant, attend to other features in our representation of belief.

The second sort of feature which we use to assess similarity of beliefs underlies what might be labeled *ideological similarity*. The ideological similarity of a pair of beliefs is a measure of the extent to which the beliefs are embedded in similar networks of belief. In effect, ideological similarity measures the similarity of the doxastic neighborhood in which a given pair of belief states find themselves. As in the case of causal-pattern similarity, partial ideological similarity is often much more important than global ideological similarity. Since belief states are compound entities, ideological similarity can be assessed separately for the several concepts that compose a belief. And context can determine which concepts are salient in the situation at hand. For example, under some circumstances, if Boris and Marie both say, 'Abstract art is bourgeois', we may count them as having similar beliefs if their other beliefs invoking the bourgeois-concept are similar, even though they have notably different beliefs invoking their abstract-art concept. But if the difference in their conception of abstract art looms large in the context, our judgment will be reversed, and they will not count has having similar beliefs.

The third sort of feature used in assessing belief state similarity leads to what I will call *reference similarity*. The core notion of reference similarity is straightforward enough. A pair of beliefs count as reference similar if the terms the subjects use to express the beliefs are identical in reference. Complications come quickly, however, since there is considerable dispute over just how the reference of a term is determined for a given speaker. The dominant view a decade or two ago was that reference is determined by the set of statements involving the term that the speaker takes to be true. If this were the whole story, then reference similarity would reduce to ideological similarity. But recent work has made it pretty clear that other factors are involved in determining the reference of a term. One prime candidate is the causal history of the use of the term, a causal chain stretching back through the user's concept, through the concept of the person from whom he acquired the term, and so on to the person or stuff denoted.[15] A second candidate, persuasively defended by Burge, is the use of the term in the speaker's linguistic community.[16] Neither the causal nor the linguistic community story is free from problems, and neither is a paradigm of clarity.[17] It would be out of place in this book to spend substantial time improving matters (though I would do it anyhow, if I could). Since there are different and potentially competing factors contributing to our judgment about the reference of a term, my theory would predict that context may single out one or another of these for special emphasis in the assessment of belief state similarity. And in fact I think that cases illustrating this sort of context sensitivity can be constructed.[18] It might be thought that since reference similarity is defined by appeal to the expression of a belief in language, this component of belief state similarity would play no role in our judgments about the beliefs of animals or prelinguistic children. By and large I think this is true. However, the causal history strand in the determination of reference has an analogue in the case of beastly concepts, since a dog's concept, if not its use of a term, may have a causal history linking it to some specific object or stuff. And, as we shall see below, these quasi-reference-fixing causal links will sometimes influence our intuitions about how a dog's belief is to be described.

On the theory I am proposing, the three sorts of features sketched above are the principal determinants of belief similarity and thus the principal determinants of our intuitions on sameness of belief and on the appropriateness of a content sentence in characterizing a belief. However, I make no claim about the exhaustiveness of these three sorts of features. It is no doubt the case that other sorts of features can play a role in our characterization of a belief state. And given a suitable context, one or another of these further features may play a dominant role in determining our intuition about the appropriateness of a description of the belief in question. For example, in a fascinating paper John Haugeland argues that computer simulations, current ones at least, do not really understand a text about which they can answer questions, because they lack an existential sense of themselves, a concern about who they are "as some sort of enduring whole."[19] I think that Haugeland succeeds in at least tempting our intuitions to agree that the computer does not really believe or understand. His strategy is to note an undeniable difference between the computer's "cognitive state" and our own, then to focus on contexts involving embarrassment, guilt, and threats to one's self-image where the difference is of central importance.

Before we turn to other matters, I want to consider two closely connected objections to the idea of embedding a notion of similarity in the analysis of belief ascription. The first objection protests that introducing similarity seriously distorts the picture of our intuitive notion, since similarity is a matter of degree, while believing that p is not something which admits of degrees. There is an initial plausibility to this charge. But on a closer look, I think its plausibility can be traced to a misleading grammatical quirk. Certain properties or attributes are expressed in English by adjectives admitting of comparative endings. 'Tall', 'fat', 'bald', and 'blue' are examples, and the properties they express are the ones we think of as admitting of degrees. Where a comparative form is not readily available, there is a tendency to think that the notion does not admit of degrees. But the example of such concepts as *cup*, *couch*, or *eggbeater* should convince us that this tendency is to be resisted. In each of these cases it is easy to imagine constructing a sequence of objects whose early members clearly fall under the concept and whose later members become increasingly less cuplike, couchlike, or eggbeaterlike. As we saw in the case of Mrs. T, analogous sequences can be constructed with clear examples of the belief that p at one end and increasingly less belief-that-p-like cases further along. In none of these cases can a natural boundary be drawn separating the instances which fall under the concept from those which do not. Despite appearances, then, both the *couch* concept and the *belief that p* concept do admit of degrees.

The second objection protests that the use of similarity in our analysis entails that belief ascriptions are always rather vague. But, the objection continues, this is simply not true. Many belief ascriptions, particularly *de dicto* belief ascriptions, say something exceptionally precise about the believer, so precise, in fact, that even the subtlest change in the content sentence may turn a true belief ascription into a false one.[20] My reply here is that the critic is simply mistaken in thinking that importing a notion of similarity entails that belief ascriptions are always vague. Perhaps the best way to make the point is to look at the use of similarity in another setting. If you and I are wandering through the National Gallery and I comment casually that the Valázquez portrait of Pope Innocent is very similar to Rembrandt's Portrait of a Polish Nobleman, my remark would no doubt be intended as a rather vague one which would remain true even were the Rembrandt notably different from the way it is. Take away the Polish Nobleman's earrings, for example, and the two paintings still count as similar by the contextually indicated standards. But now suppose that we are in the laboratory of the National Gallery watching an expert examine the Rembrandt and an excellent forgery. Looking up from her microscope she says, "It's remarkable. They are very similar." Note that here a vastly different standard is contextually indicated. The expert would not have said what she did if the forger had forgotten to paint in the earrings! The point I want to extract from these two cases is that while the sentence *type* 'A is similar to B' may be quite vague, individual tokens uttered in context can be very recise indeed. It is the context which makes clear the standard and aspects of similarity that are appropriate. Now it is my contention that the alleged precision of so-called *de dicto* belief ascriptions is simply a consequent of focusing on a certain sort of context. What is needed is a case involving a compatriot, someone whose beliefs and language are very similar to our own. We then make it a matter of special interest exactly what the believer would be prepared to say or assent to, making sure that slight differences in words make a big difference in that context. In this setting a minor change in the content sentence can radically change our intuition about the propriety of a belief ascription. But when the believer is less like us—a child, perhaps, or a person from an exotic culture—or when the exact words he would utter or accept are of small importance, minor differences in the content sentence are of less moment.

3. Testing the Theory Against the Facts

In this section and the two that follow I want to indicate how the theory I have been sketching handles the facts of intuition. Since my theory is billed as a descriptive conceptual analysis, these facts constitute the principal data which the theory must explain. I will divide my effort into several parts. In the current section I will go through the cases described in the previous chapter, showing how the intuitions these cases evoke are explained by the theory. In the following two sections I will look at two particularly vexing cases, the apparently absurd beliefs of exotic folk and the beliefs of animals, and I will argue that in these cases too the theory does a plausible job of explaining our intuitions.

I begin with those cases discussed toward the end of chapter 4, under the heading Irrelevant Causal Differences. The point that was being made in that section was that sometimes belief states exhibiting substantial differences in their potential causal patterns will nonetheless be ascribed with the same content sentence and intuited to be the same belief. My strategy for generating the cases was to start with a normal or near normal subject and make progressively larger changes in the potential causal patterns leading to or from his belief states. In the first sequence of cases, the changes were perceptual, leaving the inferential parts of the causal network unchanged; the second sequence worked just the other way around. What my theory predicts in these cases is as follows. First, if we keep the context fixed, then as the difference between the causal pattern of a subject's belief and the causal pattern of our own gets greater, our willingness to ascribe both beliefs with the same content sentence should diminish. This is particularly clear in the Dave^1, . . . , Dave^9 cases. As inference gets progressively less normal we get progressively less willing to use the content sentences we would have used before the subject's inferential breakdown. The theory also predicts that in cases where it is not of great contextual importance, significant differences in causal pattern will be ignored. This explains why we are generally willing to characterize the beliefs of color-blind or totally blind people with the same content sentences we use to characterize the beliefs of normal subjects. Finally the theory predicts that in contexts which prime for one or another feature of belief, differences in that feature will be of particular importance in our assessment of similarity and thus in our intuitions about the appropriateness of a content sentence. This, I would urge, is what is going on in the case of Peter, the store clerk turned night watchman. In the store clerk half of our tale, the emphasis is on his anomalous visual perception, and it sounds natural to say that he does not really believe that the ball is red. In the night watchman half of the story, the emphasis is on practical reasoning. How could he have behaved so stupidly, given that he believed that the red lever was the one which would avoid an explosion and that he wanted to avoid an explosion? Here, since the belief state in question has *inferential* interactions which are much the same as the ones that would be exhibited by our own belief that the lever is red, we are prepared to use the same content sentence for both.

I turn next to the four cases recounted in the section on Holism. There the strategy was to vary the surrounding beliefs, the doxastic neighborhood, in which a belief is embedded, thus altering its ideological similarity to our beliefs or to the beliefs of some other person to whom the subject was being compared. The theory predicts that, keeping the context constant, ideological similarity should be positively correlated with sameness-of-belief intuitions and with intuitive willingness to describe the subject's belief and our own with the same content sentence. The case of Mrs. T fits the prediction perfectly; as she loses more and more of her memory, we become increasingly reluctant to say that her doxastically isolated belief counts as the belief that McKinley was assassinated. Though none of the cases in the Holism section attempted to manipulate context, this is easily done in the case of Mrs. T. Let us imagine that at about the time of the dialogue reported in that section, Mrs. T was the subject in a somewhat gruesome Milgram-style experiment. She is led into a room where she can see someone she cares for, say Mr. T, sitting in a booth wired to a chair. She is told that Mr. T is receiving painful electric shocks, and Mr. T goes along by screaming convincingly. We then tell Mrs. T that she can stop the shocks by pushing one of two buttons. If McKinley was assassinated, she must push the red button to stop the shocks; if McKinley was not assassinated, she must push the green button. On hearing this Mrs. T rushes to the red button. Why? Here, I think, it is all but impossible to resist the inclination to say that she pushes the red button because she believes that McKinley was assassinated. This of course is just what would be predicted by my theory, since the context emphasizes the importance of the (ex hypothesis normal) inferential connections of Mrs. T's belief and deemphasizes the importance of her belief's doxastic isolation.

The case of Paul, who mysteriously comes to have a doxastically isolated belief, is comfortably explained by my theory, as is the case of the child who accepts 'E = mc^2' though largely innocent of physics. In both instances, there is little ideological similarity between the subject's belief and the belief of those we are comparing him to—the future scientists in Paul's case; ourselves in the case of the child. So we count Paul's belief as different from the scientists', and the child's belief as different from ours. There is one peculiarity in the future scientist case that merits special attention. We noted that in talking about the future scientists' beliefs it seems natural to use, as a content sentence, the sentence they would use in expressing their belief, even though that content sentence would be quite incomprehensible to us. Why should this be? The explanation I would offer turns on the counterfactual locution built into our analysis of belief ascription. As I have told the story, what we assert when we say 'S believes that p' is, roughly, that S is in a state similar to the one which would have caused me to utter 'p' just now, *had I uttered it with a typical causal history*. But just how are we to make sense of the italicized counterfactual clause? What possible world do we imagine when we imagine ourselves asserting the scientists' sentence in earnest? The one that comes first to mind, I think, is the world in which we have learned and come to believe their theory. And of course in *that* world the scientists' belief state would be ideologically similar to mine.

The final case in the Holism section concerned the future scientists' belief that the Hindenburg exploded because it was filled with hydrogen.

Is it properly so characterized? Does it count as the same belief as the one we would express with the same words? Here the theory predicts intermediate intuitions, and these, I think, are just what we have. The theory also predicts that by emphasizing or deemphasizing the importance of the ideological gap we should be able to urge our intuitions in one direction or another. Cases illustrating this prediction are relatively easy to construct, though I will not pause to elaborate one here.

Let us now consider the set of cases collected under the heading Reference. The first of these concerned beliefs whose expression invoked the proper name 'Ike'. In the mouth of Tom, a contemporary American, 'Ike' referred to Dwight Eisenhower, while in the mouth of Dick, a Victorian Englishman, 'Ike' referred to Reginald Angell-James. This difference in reference can, I think, readily be explained by the causal account of the reference of proper names. The causal history of Tom's Ike-concept traces back to Eisenhower, while the causal history of Dick's Ike-concept traces back to Angell-James. Apart from this difference, the two beliefs were portrayed to be very similar indeed. The theory predicts that when the reference of the names is of particular salience, as it is in this case, our intuitions will count the beliefs as different despite their similarities in other respects. And this, it appears, is just what most people are inclined to say. We also noted that it would be entirely natural under most circumstances to say that Tom believes *Eisenhower* was a politician, while Dick believes *Angell-James* was a politician. This choice of content sentences has a ready explanation on the theory I am defending, since Tom's belief is very similar (referentially and in other respects) to the one I would express by saying 'Eisenhower was a politician', and Dick's is very similar to the one I would express by saying 'Angell-James was a politician'. There are differences between my belief and Tom's, however. Tom would neither say nor assent to the sentence 'Eisenhower was a politician', since he has never heard the name 'Eisenhower'. And if this difference between the causal ties linking belief and behavior were of contextual importance, as it might be, for example, in a story recounting Tom's failure to give the right answer on an exam or a quiz show, we would find it much odder to characterize Tom's belief with this content sentence. Again this is just what my account would lead us to expect.

The second reference case turned on the difference between the American and British uses of 'chicory' and 'endive'. It is not clear to me whether the difference in reference in this case is due to a difference in causal history (à la Putnam and Kripke) or to a difference in accepted patterns of usage in the linguistic communities (à la Burge). But no matter. My theory predicts that in contexts where reference is of some importance, we will take the Englishman's belief to be different from the American's, though they both express their belief by saying, 'Chicory is bitter'. And, as we saw, this prediction is correct. The theory also explains why, in many circumstances, we would describe the Englishman's belief as the belief that *endive* is bitter. Though when the context focuses attention on the exact words the Englishman would use or accept (think of the quiz show again) the theory correctly predicts that this content sentence will seem intuitively inappropriate.

The reference cases we have looked at thus far illustrate the way in which reference similarity and causal-pattern similarity can pull in opposite directions, with context determining which will make the greater contribution to our intuitive judgments. It might be wondered whether, as the theory leads us to expect, there are analogous cases which pit components of reference similarity against *ideological* similarity. I think that with a bit of imagination such cases are readily constructed. Here is one. It involves the dastardly deeds of one Boris A. Nogoodnik, an agent of the KGB. In the course of his dirty work, Boris decides he must do in a minor American spy named Grimes. He devises a plot which will not only get rid of Grimes, but will also put the blame for the crime on a certain troublesome, distantly related Russian émigré named Boris B. Nogoodnik. To pull it off, KGB man Boris plans to leave a trail of incriminating clues, all pointing to émigré Boris. On the day of the crime there is a slight slip-up however. Grimes recognizes his attacker as his KGB contact Boris Nogoodnik. What is worse, Grimes does not die immediately from his wounds. He is still alive, though just barely, when FBI agent Edgar finds him. Grimes whispers "Boris Nogoodnik did it," and then promptly expires. Now Grimes, let us suppose, has never heard of Boris B. Nogoodnik, the émigré. He was referring to Boris A. whom he had recognized as his attacker. FBI man Edgar, for his part, has never heard of either Nogoodnik. But he quickly picks up the trail of clues, all pointing to poor Boris B. From the clues he comes to believe that the killer lives on Front Street, frequents the *Mauve Gloves Lounge*, drives a Fiat, smokes French cigarettes, etc. And, of course, Edgar believes that the killer's name is 'Boris Nogoodnik'. All of this is true of Boris B. In short order Edgar arranges a stakeout at the townhouse on Front Street. Question: Does Edgar believe that Boris A. Nogoodnik killed Grimes or that Boris B. Nogoodnik killed Grimes? The clear intuitive answer is that Edgar believes Boris B. did it, despite the fact that the causal history of Edgar's utterances of 'Boris Nogoodnik' trace through the expiring Grimes to Boris A., not to Boris B. What has happened, I would contend, is that ideological similarity has overwhelmed similarity of causal history in determining our intuition. It is interesting to note, however, that although we have a case of ideological similarity winning out over a *component* of reference similarity, it is not a case of ideological similarity winning out over reference similarity *simpliciter*. For in this case it seems most natural to say that when Edgar asserts, "Boris Nogoodnik killed Grimes," he is *referring* to Boris B. The case poses no problem for my account of belief ascription, though it does raise serious questions about the general adequacy of a causal theory of proper names.

Let us turn, finally, to those reference cases involving indexicals. Part of the story, but only part, is quite straightforward. We noted that if two political candidates both say, 'I will be the next president of the United States,' we have conflicting intuitions on whether the two men have the same belief. My theory explains this on lines analogous to those used in the *Ike* case. The candidates' beliefs are similar in causal pattern but different in reference, thus the intuitive conflict. What my theory, as so far developed, cannot explain is the fact that we ascribe both of these beliefs by saying, 'Jones (or Smith) believes that *he* will be the next president'. Similar problems arise with our saying, in the case of the man attacked by the bear, 'He believes that *he* is being attacked by a bear? Let us focus on the latter case. Presumably what we mean here is that the victim has a belief which he might express by saying, 'I am being attacked by a bear'. This sentence is *reference* similar to the content sentence I used in ascribing the belief (viz., 'He is being attacked by a bear'); so all is well there. But the belief I would express using the content sentence in earnest is radically dissimilar in causal pattern from the belief we wish to ascribe. The belief I would express using the content sentence leads me to run for help, while the belief I am attributing to the victim leads him to roll up like a ball. What is more, this case cannot be treated as one in which partial similarity and partial dissimilarity lead to potentially conflicting intuitions. It would simply be wrongheaded for me to say the victim believes that *I* am being attacked by a bear, in virtue of the causal-pattern similarity between his belief and the one which I would express using this content sentence. He believes no such thing.

I think the lesson to be learned from this case is that an additional wrinkle must be added to our analysis of belief ascription. When belief ascriptions use indexical expressions like 'he' (or 'himself'), 'her' (or 'herself'), 'you' (or 'yourself'), 'then', 'there', and some others, referring to the believer, the moment of belief, or the believer's location, there seems to be a linguistic convention mandating *normal* reference similarity and what might be called *transposed-causal-pattern similarity*. By this I mean simply that the belief which is causal-pattern similar to the believer's is not the one I would express using the content sentence in the belief ascription but, rather, the one I would express using the content sentence with the indexical pronoun replaced by one referring to myself, the current time, or my present location (generally 'I', 'now', or 'here'). So, for example, if I say the victim of the bear attack believed that he would die then and there, I am claiming that he is in a belief state which he would express using terms similar in reference to the terms I used (presumably he would say, 'I will die here and now' if he speaks English) though it is similar in causal pattern to a belief that I would express using a transposed content sentence (viz., 'I will die here and now'). An added indication that these cases involving indexicals are rather special ones is the fact that, to all appearances, ideological similarity drops out of the picture almost entirely in these cases. The bear attack victim's concept of himself, or, more accurately, the set of beliefs he has about himself that he would express using a self-referential pronoun, need not have much resemblance to either the set of beliefs I would express about him using 'he' or to the set of beliefs I would express about myself using 'I'.

4. Absurd Beliefs

From time to time we hear reports of people who assert, with apparent sincerity, some claim which strikes us as so patently false, so hopelessly beyond belief, so absurd, that it boggles the mind how anyone could possibly believe it. The beliefs that these people are expressing are what I will call *absurd beliefs*. A rich source of examples of such beliefs can be found in the anthropological literature describing belief systems of so-called primitive peoples. As a paradigm case, consider a belief which, according to Evans-Prichard is widely shared by the Nuer people: the belief that a sacrificial cucumber used in certain rituals is an ox![21] Other examples can be found closer to home among the avowed beliefs of people who accept political, religious, metaphysical, or "scientific" doctrines wildly different from our own.

In general the cases that concern us will be found among the beliefs of people who are, in one or more domains, very ideologically dissimilar from us. But it is important to realize that not all beliefs embedded in doxastically exotic surroundings will strike us as absurd. We saw two rather different examples of this in our discussion of the imagined future scientists who espouse a theory quite unlike anything known to us. Some of their beliefs, like the belief that the Hindenburg burned because it was filled with hydrogen, are neither absurd nor even unfamiliar. Though when context focuses attention on the links between this belief and the perplexing newfangled theory, our intuitions on whether the scientists' belief is the same as ours may waiver. Other beliefs held by our imagined scientists, the ones they express in unfamiliar theoretical vocabulary, will not strike us as absurd, though we may find them incomprehensible. In these cases, as we saw, there is some intuitive appeal to the strategy of borrowing the scientists' own sentence to use as a content sentence in reporting their belief. In contrast with these cases, absurd beliefs are ascribed using perfectly familiar vocabulary. But the content sentence is one whose falsehood, we think, should be unmistakably obvious to anyone.

There is a certain relativity in my characterization of absurd belief, since what one person takes to be screamingly false, another may take to be debatable, or even true. Consider, for example, the situation of the average freshman philosophy student when first told of Bishop Berkeley's curious belief that chairs and tables are made up of ideas. To the freshman, Berkeley's doctrine seems not merely false, but patently so. Indeed the reaction of many freshmen on first hearing of Berkeley's belief is to insist (or at least suspect) that "Berkeley must have been some kind of nut." This is an intriguing response, and it is one which I think a theory of belief ascription should try to explain. Moreover, it is not all that different from the reaction of rather more sophisticated people on first hearing reports about the Nuer belief. In this case people are unlikely to suspect madness, since the belief is purportedly shared by an entire culture. But many are tempted to conclude that if reports about the Nuer belief are correct, then the tribe must, as a group, exhibit a prerational mentality. Their minds must work very differently from ours. Oddly, though, these suspicions of madness or prerationality often decline when we learn more about the system of beliefs in which the prima facie belief is embedded. After a good introductory philosophy course which sets out Berkeley's system, his arguments, and the intellectual background of his thought, most students no longer suspect that Berkeley was mad. Indeed some come to believe he was right. Analogously, on reading a careful anthropological account of the Nuer, some people find themselves significantly less inclined to suspect that the Nuer mind is vastly different from our own. Rather, they come to see the Nuer rituals and beliefs, including the one about the cucumber and the ox, as a sensible systematic attempt to deal with the natural and social environment the Nuer confront.[22] What I have been reporting about reactions and change of reactions, in the face of absurd belief, is no doubt familiar enough. But it raises a perplexing question for a theory about our commonsense notion of belief. What is there about our folk notion that leads us to react as we do?

The explanation I would offer starts with the counterfactual embedded in the analysis of belief ascription. If you tell me S believes that p, I am to imagine that you have asserted 'p' in earnest, since you are claiming that S's belief state is similar to the one that would be centrally responsible for your utterance, had the utterance had a typical causal history. But how am I to imagine you asserting 'p' in earnest if 'p' is absurd? In what possible world might you (or I, for that matter) seriously say that a cucumber is an ox? How is the freshman to imagine a possible world in which his instructor earnestly asserts that a chair is made of ideas? In all likelihood, what will come first to mind is a world in which the speaker has taken leave of his senses—"gone bonkers" as one of my students put it. For the content sentences in question are not merely false, they are patently incompatible with many further beliefs which we hold and which we know are shared by the person making the belief ascription. So a possible world in which he succeeds in inserting such a belief into his store of beliefs must be one in which his cognitive mechanisms are no longer functioning properly; the mental subsystem responsible for filtering out blatant contradictions must be out of order. Now the explanation I would offer for the initial reaction to reports (and avowals) of absurd belief, the reaction which insists that the believer is prerational or mad, is simply this: In attempting to imagine a possible world in which the speaker might make his assertion in earnest, the world that comes most readily to mind is one in which the speaker's mind no longer filters out obvious contradictions as our mind does. In short, the most easily imagined world in which the speaker asserts the content sentence in earnest is a world in which he is no longer functioning rationally.

Some of the time, however, some of us can conjure a more flattering possibility. The problem with absurd beliefs is that they so obviously contradict so many other beliefs. But if we can imagine replacing these other beliefs with a new set, a set which is more or less consistent and not glaringly incompatible with the belief being ascribed, we can then imagine the speaker sincerely asserting the content sentence without suspecting him of any deep cognitive failing. If we can also imagine how such an alternate set of beliefs might be acquired and/or maintained in the believer's ecological setting, we will have imagined a possible world in which a speaker with a mind quite as rational as our own might sincerely utter a sentence which, on first hearing, strikes us as absurd. We now have an explanation for the fact that as we learn more about a person's system of beliefs, his practices, his traditions, and his environment, we sometimes find that what had seemed an absurd belief no longer strikes us as indicative of prerationality or madness. Rather than imagining the speaker's mind to be defective in function, we succeed in the more challenging task of imagining a radically different doxastic network.[23]

Unfortunately however, the story about absurd beliefs does not stop here. For there is a sense in which either of the two possible worlds we might conjure in evaluating the report of an absurd belief is uncongenial to the whole business of describing beliefs by appeal to content sentences. Consider first the case in which we imagine that the speaker has lost the capacity to detect and eliminate contradictions. What we are imagining is a person with serious inferential shortcomings, fully on a par with some of the more serious cases in our sequence from Dave[1] to Dave[9]. Given the marked causal-pattern dissimilarity, we are reluctant to characterize this person's nonabsurd beliefs with the content sentences we would use were he not inferentially impaired. When a person is *that* different from us, we are inclined to think that there is just *no saying* what he believes. But this global reluctance to ascribe content to the belief states of an inferentially peculiar person comes full circle and undermines our willingness to ascribe the absurd belief to him. So there is a sort of tension built into these cases. On the one hand we are inclined to say that a suitably mad person might perfectly well come to believe that a cucumber is an ox or some other patently absurd claim. On the other hand we are inclined to say that if a person's inferential capacities are that far gone, then no content sentences in our language will adequately characterize his belief states. There is a whiff of contradiction here. It seems that when the processes underlying our intuitive judgments are confronted with cases like this one, they urge two intuitions which are simply incompatible. What is more, this is not, as far as I can see, an inconsistency that can be written off by appeal to different contexts of judgment. But perhaps it is not all that surprising that our folk psychology gets into trouble in these cases. For folk psychology presumably evolved as an aid to our workaday dealings with one another. The fact that it renders contradictory judgments about exotic cases does not diminish the practical utility of folk psychology, since *real* cases like this are few and far between.[24] The moral, I suppose, is that where nature doesn't itch, folk theory doesn't scratch.

It would be a mistake, however, to conclude that cases like the ones we have been considering are of interest only as devices for probing the contours of our folk concepts. The clinical literature is full of reports of people who say absurd things and whose reasoning capacities are clearly impaired, though the problems are never quite so clear-cut as the ones we have been imagining.[25] In reading these cases one becomes acutely sensitive to the fact that the descriptive apparatus provided by common sense just is not up to characterizing the patient's cognitive states. When a man insists, apparently in all sincerity, that he is Jesus Christ and that he is a heap of dung,[26] there is no comfortable characterization of the content of his beliefs.

Let us consider now the second possibility that we might imagine in evaluating the report of an absurd belief, viz., the possibility that the speaker's doxastic network is radically different from our own. The situation here is parallel to the case of inferential breakdown. In order to accommodate the absurd belief without contradiction, we must imagine a doxastic network so different from our own that we undermine our willingness to use familiar content sentences to characterize any of the speaker's beliefs in the doxastically exotic domain. Once again a contradiction looms. Having projected ourselves into an exotic belief network, we are inclined to say both that the subject believes a cucumber is an ox and that English content sentences are not up to characterizing his beliefs at all. This difficulty plagues anthropology much as the problem of inferential failure plagues clinical psychology. One way in which anthropologists have attempted to deal with the problem is to invoke native terminology in their descriptions of native beliefs, in effect labeling the native beliefs as they are labeled by the natives themselves. This will work, of course, only when supplemented by an elaborate gloss explaining how these beliefs, characterized by native content sentences, relate to one another, how they integrate with native practices, and how they enable the natives to deal with their environment as they understand it. When native belief systems and "forms of life" differ radically from our own, there is no shorter way to characterize their cognitive world. The descriptive apparatus of folk psychology is not designed to deal with the beliefs of exotic folk.

I think these reflections on the inadequacy of folk locutions in characterizing exotic inferential patterns and exotic doxastic networks throw considerable light on a pair of arguments that have been widely discussed. In *Word and Object*[27] Quine argues against the "doctrine of 'prelogical mentality'." The thrust of his argument is that if a person makes absurd assertions we should suspect our translation or interpretation of his words, rather than impute to him an absurd belief. "The maxim of translation underlying all this," Quine writes, "is that assertions startlingly false on the face of them are likely to turn on hidden differences in language."[28] This is certainly good advice for the translator or the literary critic. But what course would Quine have us follow if diligent effort can do no better, if any interpretation we can come up with either imputes absurd beliefs or is hopelessly ad hoc? Surely we do not want to insist, a priori, that everyone's inferential patterns must approximate some decent standard of rationality, since we can perfectly well imagine that our own inferential patterns might alter radically as the result of injury or illness. I think the right thing to say here (and, reading between the lines, I suspect Quine would agree) is that in these cases we should simply give up on translation. Translation is inextricably linked with saying what a person believes when he asserts the sentence being translated. And when a person's inferential patterns are substantially different from our own, we have no content sentence which will comfortably characterize his belief.

In a similar argument, focusing on the case of a radically exotic doxastic network, Davidson has challenged the coherence of the very notion of an alternative conceptual scheme.[29] If we can translate the native's claims and thus specify the content of his beliefs, then, Davidson urges, we are not dealing with the case of a *radically* different conceptual scheme. But if we cannot translate or assign content, then why should we assume we are dealing with a conceptual scheme at all? Why should we think that the untranslatable utterances of these exotic humans constitute speech behavior? Davidson's conclusion is that we should not, that if we cannot translate their language and assign content to their beliefs, then we have no grounds for thinking that these creatures *have* belief. But as other writers have noted, there is a plausible line of argument which leads to exactly the opposite conclusion.[30] We can readily imagine ourselves gradually turning into such doxastically exotic creatures by altering the elements of our doxastic network one belief at a time. Or, to change the image, we can imagine a sequence of people each ideologically similar to his immediate neighbors, with ourselves at one end and the unfathomable native at the other. What is more, in assuming the native to be ideologically exotic we need not assume that the global architecture of his cognitive apparatus has departed from the pattern in figure 2. He can still have belief-like states and desire-like states, even though we have no content sentences to characterize them. Further, these belief-like states may serve the native in good stead, enabling him to deal with his world quite successfully. Indeed, he may do a rather better job than we do. After all, if our race survives, our own scientifically sophisticated descendants may well have doxastic networks as different from ours as are those of our imagined natives. Surely, it is urged, it would be perverse parochialism to deny that these folk have an alternative conceptual scheme and quite a snazzy one at that.

In response to this looming antinomy, I would offer three observations. First, it is misleading to assume, as we have been throughout this section, that extreme ideological dissimilarity will always undermine content ascription. In an appropriate context, causal-pattern similarity may sustain the use of a quite ordinary English content sentence despite quite radical ideological dissimilarity. Second, in those contexts where ideological differences are both important and too great to warrant comfortable use of content sentences drawn from our own language, we are not forced into silence about the native's doxastic world. We can opt for an anthropological description, using their labels for their beliefs and detailing how their beliefs fit into their own form of life.

Finally, to the extent that Davidson's argument and the argument to the opposite conclusion constitute at antinomy, its source should by now be apparent. Our folk psychology evolved and earns its keep in settings where exotic folk were few and far between. When pushed to accommodate such cases, the judgments it renders are often neither clear nor consistent.

5. Animal Beliefs

There are many ways in which animals, particularly higher animals, are (or are thought to be) rather like people. They have needs and desires. They perceive the world around them and draw inferences from what they perceive. (Master is reaching for the leash, so we must be going for a walk. I smell food so it must be time to eat.) They form plans, albeit primitive ones, exploiting their beliefs to satisfy their desires. In short, it is plausible to assume that higher animals have a psychology whose global organization fits the pattern of figure 2. But there are also many ways in which animals are (or are thought to be) quite different from people. They are causal-pattern dissimilar, since neither their perception nor their inferential capacities work quite they way ours do. And they are ideologically dissimilar, since their doxastic network differs markedly from our own. Since they have no language, reference similarity is out of the question, though the causal history component of reference similarity may have an analogue in the causal history of animal concepts. These similarities and dissimilarities lead us to expect that we will have conflicting intuitions about the appropriateness of using everyday English content sentences to characterize the cognitive states of animals. In a context where nothing more than a rough causal-pattern and ideological similarity is called for, intuition will find such characterizations of beastly belief quite unexceptional. Suppose, for example, that Fido is in hot pursuit of a squirrel that darts down an alleyway and disappears from view. A moment later we see Fido craning his neck and barking excitedly at the foot of an oak tree near the end of the alley. To explain Fido's behavior, it would be perfectly natural to say he believes that the squirrel is up in the oak tree. But suppose now that some skeptic challenges our claim by focusing attention on the differences separating Fido's belief from ours. "Does Fido really believe it is a squirrel up in the oak tree? Are there not indefinitely many logically possible creatures which are not squirrels but which Fido would treat indistinguishably from the way he treats real squirrels? Indeed, does he believe, or even care, that the thing up the tree is an *animal*? Would it not be quite the same to Fido if he had been chasing some bit of squirrel-shaped and squirrel-smelling machinery, like the mechanical rabbits used at dog-racing tracks? The concept of animal is tied to the distinction between living and nonliving, as well as to the distinction between animals and plants. But Fido has little grasp of these distinctions. How can you say that he believes it is a squirrel if he doesn't even know that squirrels are animals?'' Confronted with this challenge, which focuses attention on the ideological gap that separates us from Fido, intuition begins to waiver. It no longer sounds quite right to say that Fido believes there is a *squirrel* up the oak tree.

The ideological gap between animals and ourselves is not the only factor capable of undermining our confidence in ascriptions of content to animal beliefs. As we saw earlier, the use of a term in a subject's linguistic community serves an important role in nailing down the reference of a term and thus in determining the content sentences we find appropriate in characterizing beliefs which are expressed using the term. It was the influence of community usage that inclined us to say that John, the American, believes that chicory is bitter, while Robin, the Englishman, believes that endive is bitter.[31] And it is in some measure a consequent of community usage that you would characterize one of my beliefs as the belief that wallabies are marsupials, even though I cannot distinguish wallabies from other vaguely kangaroo-shaped creatures. But, of course, Fido does not express his belief verbally and is not a member of a linguistic community. So the fact that he does not distinguish squirrels from other (actual or possible) squirrel-like things generates puzzles about how his belief is to be characterized. If he treats squirrels and various kindred species indistinguishably, shall we say when he is chasing one of these non-squirrels, that he (mistakenly) believes it is a squirrel? Or should we say that he correctly believes it is a furrel, where 'furrel' is a new term denoting the heterogeneous collection of animals and artifacts that Fido treats indistinguishably from ordinary squirrels? Folk psychology, it would seem, provides no comfortable reply. And of course similar qualms might be directed at Fido's concept of a tree. If there is a range of tree-shaped artifacts which Fido cannot distinguish from real trees and if in fact the squirrel has run up one of these man-made ersatz, then does Fido mistakenly believe that the squirrel is up a tree? Or, rather, does he correctly believe that the squirrel has run up the tree-or-canine-deceiving-tree-shaped-artifact? Conundrums like this abound when the context makes it important to say just exactly what it is that an animal believes.[32]

Most of the writers who have addressed the question of animal belief have focused either on contexts where only rough-and-ready similarity is appropriate or on contexts which stress more fine-grained similarity.

Those who focus on contexts of the first sort insist that the attribution of beliefs to animals is unproblematic.[33] Those who focus on the second sort of context dwell on the impossibility of characterizing the content of an animal's belief and go on to urge that in the absence of finely discriminated content sentences, we should not apply the notion of belief to animals at all.[34] In one of my own papers I gave examples of both contexts, noted the conflict of intuitions, and concluded that the issue of whether animals have beliefs is moot.[35] But I would now argue that none of these three positions gets the matter quite right. If the question being asked is whether claims of the form

S believes that p

are ever true, when S is an animal, and 'p' is replaced by some quite ordinary English sentence, then the answer is clearly yes. But there are other conversational contexts in which the very same sentence, referring to the same animal and time, would be false. The apparent paradox here dissolves once we recognize that belief ascriptions are similarity claims, and similarity claims are context dependent.

6. Some Conclusions

The work of part I is not yet finished, since I still owe the reader an account of why I reject the putative distinction between *de dicto* and *de re* belief sentences. However, I think this would be an appropriate place to draw together some of the conclusions that follow from what has been said thus far. On the positive side we have an account of our commonsense concept of belief which appears to do quite a good job at capturing the data of intuition. As advertised, our account is in the spirit of the mental sentence theory, with mental sentences typed by content, though the relation of "content-identity" is ultimately replaced by a context-sensitive multidimensional similarity measure. On the negative side we have an argument against those accounts of the notion of belief which individuate beliefs along narrow causal lines. There are three reasons for rejecting accounts of belief which invoke a narrow causal standard. The first is the holism of belief ascription and individuation. Our intuitions about whether a belief-like state counts as the belief that p and our intuitions about whether a pair of beliefs count as identical in type are sensitive to the doxastic neighborhood—the network of further beliefs—in which the state resides. By altering the surrounding beliefs we can change a paradigm case of the belief that p into a state which common sense would not count as the belief that p at all. However, since these changes are quite independent of the state's causal potential, the narrow causal standard records no change.

The second reason for rejecting narrow causal accounts of belief individuation is the link between the ascription and individuation of belief on the one hand and reference on the other. The reference of a term is often determined in part by its distant causal ancestry and by the use of the term in the speaker's community. But neither of these factors need be reflected in the narrow causal profile of the belief state which would be expressed using the term. Thus it is possible to have a pair of belief state tokens which count as type identical by the narrow causal standard though intuition judges them to be quite different. The final reason for rejecting narrow causal theories is the context sensitivity of commonsense belief ascription and individuation. In one context intuition may judge that a given belief token is appropriately describable as the belief that p, while in another context intuition may find that label inappropriate. Judgments about whether a pair of belief tokens count as type identical are similarly context sensitive. If the narrow causal standard requires that a pair of belief tokens must have *identical* narrow causal profiles to be type identical, then it cannot begin to explain the context sensitivity of our judgments. If a narrow causal theory requires only *similarity* of narrow causal profiles then it has more room for maneuver, since similarity is a context-sensitive notion. But even so, the narrow causal account will be unable to explain the effect of those contexts which prime for ideological similarity or for elements of reference similarity.

Granting that the narrow causal version of the mental sentence theory does not fully capture our folk psychological notion of belief, it is worth pondering just how badly it misses the mark. Fodor, as we have seen, anticipated some slippage between the narrow causal standard of individuation and the content-based scheme of "aboriginal, uncorrupted, pretheoretical intuition."[36] However, on his view, the two classification schemes will coincide "plus or minus a bit."[37] The issue assumes considerable importance if, as Fodor maintains, the close (if imperfect) correspondence between narrow causal (or "formal") taxonomy and content-based taxonomy "is perhaps *the* basic idea of modern cognitive theory."[38] As will emerge in part II, there is reason to doubt that cognitive science need be much concerned about the size of the gap between these two taxonomic schemes. But if Fodor is right on this point, then cognitive science is in deep trouble. For it is quite clear that by any reasonable measure the divide between folk taxonomy and narrow causal taxonomy is *enormous.*

The best way to appreciate the difference between the two is to ask how far we could get in ascribing content to a belief-like state if our knowledge about the state is restricted to a complete specification of its narrow causal profile. It is my contention that if this is all we know, then we can hardly begin to judge whether a given content sentence correctly characterizes the belief. Writing on a different theme, Fodor himself began to make this point very nicely. In his delightfully irreverent paper, "Tom Swift and His Procedural Grandmother,"[39] Fodor asks what we know about the semantic properties of a computer machine language (ML) sentence when we know the program specifying how that ML sentence interacts with other ML sentences. Does a knowledge of the potential causal connections among ML sentences enable us to determine their truth conditions, or the reference of their terms, or how they are to be interpreted? Fodor's answer is that it does not. To make the point, he asks that we

> Imagine two programs, one of which is a simulation of the Six Day War (so the referring expressions designate, e.g. tank divisions, jet planes, Egyptian soldiers, Moshe Dayan, etc., and the relational terms express bombing, surrounding, commanding, capturing, etc.), and the other of which simulates a chess game (so the referring expressions designate knights, bishops, pawns, etc., and the relational terms express threatening, checking, controlling, taking, etc.). It is a possible (though, of course, unlikely) accident that these programs should be *indistinguishable when compiled*; viz., that the ML counterparts of these programs should be identical, so that the internal career of a machine running one program would be identical, step by step, to that of a machine running the other.[40]

Fodor is quite right of course. The formal computational properties of ML sentences do not tell us whether they are about a chess game or the Six Day War. So if this is all we know about these sentences we can hardly begin to assess their semantic interpretation or their content. But now there is a clear analogy between ML sentences and belief states or mental sentence tokens. If all we know is the "program"— the potential causal interactions among belief states and other mental states—then we are in no position to assign content to the belief state. We cannot tell whether it is a belief about a chess game or about the Six Day War. Here it might be protested with some justice that the analogy is not a perfect one. For in the case of the computer we are assuming that we know only interstate causal links, while in the case of mental sentences we would have a complete narrow causal profile which includes potential causal links to stimuli and behavior. To make the analogy more exact, we should have to imagine our computer connected to sensory transducers and a robot, and we would have to know the potential causal links between transducer inputs and ML sentences, on one side, and between ML sentences and robot behavior on the other. Would this additional information enable us to determine the semantic properties of ML sentences? Or, putting the question the other way around, does the information about causal links from stimuli to mental states, and from mental states to behavior, which is included in a narrow causal profile enable us to assign content to belief states or sentences in a mental code? In certain cases the answer is clearly no. Information about stimuli and behavior will not tell us that Tom believes Eisenhower was a politician, while Dick believes that Angell-James was a politician.[41] Nor will it tell us that John's belief is about chicory while Robin's is about endive.[42] Moreover, I think a plausible case could be made for a much more massive underdetermination of content by narrow causal profile. The key here is to imagine a community of people who from birth onward are embedded in devices which systematically alter the input to their natural sensory apparatus. Thus, for example, we might imagine that just after birth children in this society have tiny TV systems attached to their eyes and that the images projected into their eyes by these systems systematically alter the true color of objects in the environment. Facing a ripe tomato, children in this society would be subjected to, say, a green spherical stimulus. If we fill in the details in the right way it will be clear that the belief they acquire from this green stimulus is that the object before them is red. From this small beginning, aficionados of philosophical science fiction will see how we could construct a much more elaborate case which would in effect duplicate the old chestnut example of the brain in the vat. The difference is that what we end up with is not a bodyless brain in a vat but a full, normal body whose sensory apparatus is provided with synthetic input and whose bodily movements are monitored to provide appropriate synthetic feedback. The conclusion to be drawn from this rather outlandish case is that a full narrow causal profile will not enable us to characterize the content of the subject's belief states nor to determine the semantic properties of sentences in his mental code. To assign content we must know something about the history of his concepts, the linguistic practices prevailing in his community, and the way in which his mental states are causally related to actual objects in his environment. In short, we must know how the subject is embedded in the world.

One brief final point must be added. In arguing against accounts of belief which invoke a narrow causal standard, my thesis has been that these accounts do not capture our folk psychological notion of belief. I have not argued, nor do I believe, that psychological states which are individuated along narrow causal lines should be eliminated from cognitive science. Indeed in part II, I will argue that the narrow causal standard or something very close to it ought to be (and often is) respected in serious cognitive science. But if this is right, then since the folk notion of belief is at odds with the narrow causal standard, it has no place in a mature cognitive science.

Chapter 6

De Dicto and *De Re*: The Myth of Ambiguity

The account of belief ascription developed in the previous chapter purports to handle all ordinary invocations of belief sentences, that is, sentences of the form

S believes that p.

But a venerable tradition in philosophy holds that belief sentences are *ambiguous*, that they generally admit of two quite distinct readings. If this is correct it bodes ill for my analysis, since my account leaves no place for any such systematic ambiguity. Individual belief sentences may of course be ambiguous on my view, but only if the ambiguity can be traced to some element other than the 'believes that' construction. Absent ambiguity elsewhere in the sentence, my account holds that belief sentences are *univocal*. What I propose to argue in this chapter is that the putative ambiguity of belief sentences poses no threat to my theory for the very simple reason that this ambiguity is a myth.[1] I offer this conclusion with some trepidation, for if I am right then just about all the philosophers who have written about belief sentences in the last quarter century are wrong. And since this topic has become something of a showcase for the skills of analytic philosophers, I am taking a stand in opposition to the view of almost all the philosophers whose work I most admire. Nonetheless the story I have to tell seems to me to be both simple and persuasive. That story divides into three parts. In the first I will assemble examples of the sort of evidence typically offered by those who advocate the ambiguity thesis and will explain why they think this evidence supports their conclusion. As we shall see, the defenders of the ambiguity thesis are not of a single mind on just what sort of ambiguity will best account for the data. Some opt for a straightforward lexical ambiguity, while others argue for something more akin to syntactic ambiguity. The second part of my story drops the belief theme temporarily to take a look at the role of indefinite descriptions in ordinary discourse. Here my claim will be that this topic has been widely misunderstood, though recent work by

Chastain, G. Wilson, and others has set the matter right. The last part of my story goes back to the evidence on which the case for ambiguity rests. What I shall argue is that all of this evidence can be explained at least as well and in many instances better by the theory developed in chapter 5, supplemented with Chastain's and Wilson's insights about indefinite descriptions.

1. The Argument for Ambiguity

Though the ambiguity doctrine has its roots in antiquity, modern discussion of the topic was spurred by Quine's seminal paper, "Quantifiers and Propositional Attitudes."[2] In that paper Quine urges that there are two senses of 'believes' and of related locutions. One of these senses, the one Quine labels *notional*, can be thought of as expressing a two-place relation between a person and a proposition or a person and a sentence. The other sense, which Quine calls *relational*, expresses a three-place relation that may obtain among a person, an attribute (or open sentence), and an object. Other writers have used the traditional labels *de dicto* and *de re* to mark these putative senses. Why should we think that 'believes' is ambiguous in this way? It is no easy matter to extract an argument to this conclusion from Quine's paper, and it might be thought that he simply assumes the ambiguity is there. But despite appearances I think there is an implicit argument to be found. Quine's strategy is to recount a number of cases and to note what we are inclined to say about these cases. The tacit argument is that our reactions can best be made sense of if we postulate two senses of 'believe'. Whether or not this interpretation is true to Quine's intentions, it does yield an argument of some plausibility. So let me run through some of Quine's cases, supplementing them with some examples of my own.

Consider first the case of Ralph. Like most of us, Ralph is convinced that espionage is widespread. Though, again like us, Ralph has no reason to suspect the loyalty of any particular person. To describe Ralph's cognitive state, we might say

(1)   Ralph believes that spies exist.

Or we might instead say

(2)   Ralph believes that someone is a spy.

(This last sounds a bit strained to many an ear, mine included. Perhaps

(3)   Ralph believes that someone or other is a spy

captures the situation a bit better.) But there is also a quite different cognitive state that might be captured by (2). For suppose that Ralph has a suspect whom he has been watching for many a month and whom he is about to report to the FBI. In this case too, we might use (2) to describe Ralph's doxastic situation. But (1) or (3), though still true enough, would not capture the fact that Ralph has a suspect. If we revert to the case in which Ralph has no suspect, then (2) is true on one reading but false on another. So if would appear that (2) is ambiguous. On Quine's view the ambiguity is to be traced to the two senses of 'believe'. The reading of (2) on which it is true even when Ralph has no suspect invokes the notional sense, and might be rendered

(4)   Ralph believes^n someone is a spy

or, even more perspicuously

(5)   Ralph believes^n ($\exists$x) (x is a spy).

The reading of (2) on which it is false if Ralph has no suspect would be rendered

(6)   ($\exists$x) (Ralph believes^r z(z is a spy) of x).

('z(z is a spy)' is Quine's notation for the attribute of being a spy.) Alternatively, we might trade propositions and attributes for sentences and open sentences, rendering the two senses of (2) as

(7)   Ralph believes^n '($\exists$x) (x is a spy)'

and

(8)   ($\exists$x) (Ralph believes^r '——— is a spy', x)

respectively.*

Now it might be protested that so far we have only the most meager justification for claiming an ambiguity in 'believes', since it is very difficult indeed to hear (2) in the sense of (1) or (3). I think this protest is well taken. There are other examples in which the putative ambiguity stands out much more clearly, however. Consider for example the case of Peter Smyth who made his mark some years ago by inventing a new industrial process. Peter now lives in comfortable retirement on the income produced by a factory he owns, which manufactures widgets using his secret process. One day it comes to Peter's attention that a foreign manufacturer is using the very same process. Convinced that

---

*Quine is careful to note that the likes of (7) and (8) must be relativized to the language to which the quoted material is construed as belonging. But this is a complication we can ignore for the present. I should also note that I have made sundry minor modifications in Quine's notation.

the foreigners could not have rediscovered the process on their own, Peter concludes that he has been the victim of industrial espionage perpetrated by one of his employees. In this case we might quite naturally recount Peter's doxastic state with

(9)   Peter believes that someone who works in the factory has stolen the secret process.

Intent on discovering the culprit's identity, Peter gets a job in his own factory under the assumed name Harry Foot. Since he is an absentee owner, none of the plant's employees recognize him. The foreman of the plant is an honest fellow by the name of David Jones. Some months after Foot (i.e., Smyth) comes to work at the factory, Jones too discovers that the secret process is being used by foreign competition, and he too suspects industrial espionage. Moreover, Jones has a suspect. He has noted the curious behavior of the new man Foot and becomes increasingly convinced that Foot is the spy. Now suppose that one evening, after confiding his suspicions to his wife, Jones decides to return to the plant in hopes of catching the culprit red-handed. If, later that evening, a friend inquires about Jones's absence, it would be natural enough for his wife to report

(10)   David believes that someone who works in the factory has stolen the secret process.

She might go on to explain that David has returned to the plant in the hope of catching him. Here, I think, we have clear case of the ambiguity Quine has in mind. On the intended reading of (10) there is a clear implication that David has a suspect; it makes sense to ask *who* it is David thinks to have stolen the process. But this is not the reading intended for (9). If someone were to ask who is the object of Peter's suspicion, he would indicate that he had misconstrued the intended meaning of (9). Of course (10) might also have been used to report David's cognitive state after learning the secret was out but before noting Foot's supicious behavior. At that time, however, (10) in the sense intended by his wife would have been false. For Quine the ambiguity illustrated in this example traces to the ambiguity of 'believes'. It is the notional sense of 'believes' that is being invoked in (9) and the relational sense that is being invoked in (10). To disambiguate the two Quine would render them

(11)   Peter believes^n '$(\exists x)$ (x works in the factory & x has stolen the secret process)'

and

(12) $(\exists x)$ (x works in the factory & David believes^r '——— has stolen the secret process', x)

respectively.*

Thus far we have been focusing on cases in which the content sentence contains an existential quantifier. If the ambiguity Quine postulates is really there, however, it ought to show itself in cases where names or definite descriptions are the grammatical subjects of the content sentence. Some useful examples can be constructed by expanding a bit on our tale of industrial espionage. Suppose that on the night David Jones returned to the plant, Foot (i.e., Smyth) has used his passkey to get into the office and is about to open the office safe. Just as Foot gets the safe open Jones bursts in on him and wrestles him to the floor. Asked to explain Jones's action, we might well say

(13) Jones believed that Foot was burgling the safe.

And Jones himself would agree with this characterization of his belief. Now let us bring our melodrama to a close. Suppose that Jones calls the police and Foot explains that he is not a burglar at all, but the owner of the factory. Both Jones and the police are incredulous, so Foot calls his old friend the mayor, who comes down to the factory and identifies him. On their return to the station house, we might well imagine one of the officers using (14) in recounting the adventures of the evening to his amused colleagues:

(14) Jones believed that the owner of the factory was a burglar.

Similarly, we can imagine the mayor using (15) while regaling the city fathers with an account of the evening's doings:

(15) Jones believed that Peter Smyth was a burglar.

It seems clear that both (14) and (15) can be understood as saying something true. However, it is also clear that at the moment the police arrived Jones would vigorously deny that either (14) or (15) characterized his cognitive state while wrestling Foot to the floor. Given this obviously sincere denial, there is a strong inclination to think that both (16) and (17) can be understood as saying something true:

(16) Jones did not believe that the owner of the factory was a burglar

---

*Alternatively, (10) might be rendered

    (12a) $(\exists x)$ (David believes^r '——— works in the factory and ——— has stolen the secret process', x).

See Loar (1972) for some insightful observations on how the distinction between (12) and (12a) may be exploited within a basically Quinean framework.

(17)   Jones did not believe that Peter Smyth was a burglar.

But now we are confronting a paradox, since (16) appears to be the negation of (14) and (17) appears to be the negation of (15). How can a sentence and its negation both say something true? To resolve the anomaly, Quine would invoke the doctrine of ambiguity. Indeed (14)–(17) do each say something true, but there is no contradiction since the first pair must be understood as invoking the relational sense of 'believe' while the second pair are using the notional sense. Rendered into a more perspicuous notation, (14)–(17) become

(14a)   Jones believed^r ('——— is a burglar', the owner of the factory)

(15a)   Jones believed^r ('——— is a burglar', Peter Smyth)

(16a)   Jones did not believe^n 'the owner of the factory is a burglar'

(17a)   Jones did not believe^n 'Peter Smyth is a burglar'

The apparent contradiction has been avoided.

While Quine's lexical ambiguity thesis does a plausible job at handling the cases we have looked at so far, it buys its success at a price. On Quine's view 'believe^n' and 'believe^r' are distinct primitives giving no hint of their relation to each other. What is more, there is a threat of indefinitely many additional primitives to come. 'Believe^r' is a three-place predicate taking as arguments the believer, an open sentence, and the person or object the belief is about. But, of course, some beliefs are about more than one object. Thus consider Quine's example:

(18)   Tom believes that Cicero denounced Cataline.

In order to render the relational reading of (18) we would need something like

Tom believes^{r4} ('——— denounced ———', Cicero, Cataline)

invoking a four-place predicate 'believes^{r4}'. Still another distinct belief predicate will be required to handle the relational reading of

Sam believes that Leslie, Terry, and Maria are involved in a menage à trois.

And so on. There are various technical tricks one might explore to avoid this proliferation of relational belief predicates.[3] But at a minimum, the Quinean strategy leaves us with a pair of primitives whose orthographic similarity reflects no theoretical relation. Confronted with this awkward consequence of the lexical ambiguity thesis, a number of writers have sought to construct an analysis of one belief predicate in terms of the other. The game, of course, can be played in two different ways: we might take the notional reading as primitive and seek to define the relational reading in terms of it, or we might try to run our analysis just the other way round.[4] Whichever route is chosen, however, the resulting theory must give some account of the anomalies that motivate Quine's theory. It must explain why (2) can be read as either true or false in the case where Ralph has no suspect; it must explain the difference between (9) and (10); and it must give some account of how (14) and (15) can be compatible with (16) and (17). In general those who seek to analyze the notional and relational readings of belief sentences in terms of a single primitive share Quine's conviction that sentences like (2), (9), (10), and (14)–(17) are ambiguous. But rather than tracing the sentential ambiguity to a lexical ambiguity in 'believes', they view the ambiguity on the model of a syntactic ambiguity or an ambiguity of scope. On this view sentences containing 'believes' are generally analyzable into the chosen primitive notation in more than one way. And it is this multiplicity of possible analyses that accounts for the anomalies and ambiguities noted by Quine. To get a feel for how these analyses work, let us take a look at a simple example.

To minimize complications we can continue to view the notional reading of a belief sentence as expressing a relation between the believer and a sentence. The relational reading may then be construed as asserting that the believer stands in the belief relation to some sentence which is only incompletely specified. Pursuing this thought, the notional reading of (2) would be rendered, as before, along the lines of (7). The relational reading, by contrast, would be something like

(19)   ($\exists$t) (t is a name or definite description & Ralph believes^n a sentence consisting of t followed by 'is a spy')

Or we might adopt Quine's handy corner quote device[5] and replace (19) with

(20)   ($\exists$t) (t is a name or definite description & Ralph believes^n ⌜t is a spy⌝.)

Sticking with corner quotes, we could represent the notional and relational readings of (14) as follows:

(21)   Jones believes^n 'the owner of the factory is a burglar'

(22)   ($\exists$t) (t is a name or definite description & t denotes the owner of the factory & Jones believes^n ⌜t is a burglar⌝.

In our story a few pages back, (21) is false, while (22) is true. (The candidates for t include 'Harry Foot' and 'the man standing near the safe' among others.) The reading of (16) on which it is true in our tale is the notional reading, rendered as in (16a). Plainly there is no incompatibility between (16a) and (22).

The version of the analytic strategy I have been sketching is something of a hybrid. It is very close to the view urged by Armstrong and it resembles Sellars's account in spirit if not in detail. Kaplan's sophisticated theory starts with an account similar to this one. But, he argues, in cases like (22) it is not sufficient that t merely denote the owner of the factory; the name or definite description must also be a vivid one and be suitably causally related to its denotation. For our purposes the essential point in all these accounts is that they portray belief sentences as systematically ambiguous. This is a thesis they share with Quine, and it is the thesis I propose to deny. Before getting to that, however, we will have to take a brief look at the theory of indefinite descriptions.

2. Indefinite Descriptions

By an indefinite description I mean an expression like 'a man' or 'an aardvark' consisting of an indefinite article followed by a noun. Since Russell, the received wisdom about indefinite articles has been that they are actually natural language quantifiers. On this view the sentence

An aardvark escaped from the zoo

has the following logical form:

($\exists$x) (Aardvark (x) & Escaped from the zoo (x))

And the sentence

An aardvark bit a man

would be rendered

($\exists$x) ($\exists$y) (Aardvark(x) & Man(y) & Bit(x,y)).

Now doubtless this familiar story is correct for some uses of indefinite descriptions. But both Chastain and Wilson have argued convincingly that indefinite descriptions also have a quite different use.[6] Rather than acting as quantifiers, they serve a *referential* function. Here is how Chastain makes the point:

> Sentences containing indefinite descriptions are ambiguous. Sometimes 'A mosquito is in here' and its stylistic variant 'There is a mosquito in here' must be taken as asserting merely that the place is not wholly mosquito-less, but sometimes they involve an intended reference to one particular mosquito. Their disambiguation depends on how the speaker intends the context containing them to be related to other contexts.
>
> For example, suppose that I am reading the morning newspaper

and I come across the following story:

> D7: #Houston, Texas, March 10 (UPI)–Dr. Michael DeBakey stated at a press conference today that an artificial heart could be developed within five years. The famed Baylor University heart surgeon said that such a development would make heart transplants unnecessary.#

I then report this fact to you by saying:

> D8: #A doctor in Texas claims that artificial hearts will be developed within five years.#

Is 'a doctor' in that token of D8 a singular term? Is it possible to trace a referential connection between that expression and a particular person, such that what I said is true if and only if *that* person claimed that artificial hearts will be developed within five years? Or am I merely asserting that the class of Texas doctors claiming that artificial hearts will be developed within five years is non-empty, as the existential quantification reading of D8 would have it? In that case what I said would be true even if the news report about DeBakey were wholly erroneous and DeBakey had never made any such claim but some other doctor in Texas had, say in a private conversation, unknown to the reporter who wrote the story. Which reading is the correct one in this case? Imagine how the conversation might continue: you ask 'Who said that?' and I answer 'Dr. Michael DeBakey.' Or perhaps: you say 'I can't quite believe that' and I say 'Well, it was DeBakey who said it and he ought to know. He's a famous surgeon.' Or perhaps: you say 'What's his name?' and I say, 'Michael DeBakey.' Such continuations would be unintelligible on the existential quantification reading, for they presuppose that one and only one person is being said to have claimed that artificial hearts will be developed within five years; they presuppose that there is a unique referent of 'a doctor' whose name can be requested by asking 'Who?' or 'What's his name?' and who can be identified by saying 'Michael DeBakey'.[7]

As I see it, this single extended example is sufficient to establish the ambiguity of indefinite descriptions. For readers less ready to be convinced, Chastain's paper and Wilson's contain numerous further examples along with some acute criticism of those who deny that indefinite descriptions admit of a referential reading. For present purposes I will take Chastain's claim to be established. What makes Chastain's ambiguity important to our current concerns is Chastain's brief observation that sentences like 'There is a mosquito in here' are often simply stylistic variants for 'A mosquito is in here'. It follows that the ambiguity of indefinite descriptions is mirrored by a parallel ambiguity in expressions of the form 'There is a ϕ'. And indeed the passage quoted above would be equally convincing if D8 had begun 'There is a doctor in Texas who claims . . .' rather than 'A doctor in Texas claims . . .'. What is more, a completely parallel ambiguity can be found in many other constructions that are commonly taken to be natural language equivalents of the existential quantifier. Here is Chastain again:

> Sometimes the existential quantification
>
> ($\exists$x) (x has been eating my porridge)
>
> is a correct paraphrase of
>
> D44: #Someone has been eating my porridge.#
>
> and sometimes it is not, as we can see by considering
>
> D45: #Someone has been eating my porridge. She says her name is "Goldilocks." Here she is. What are we going to do with her?[8]

The moral of this digression is a simple one. English expressions that have been taken to be natural language equivalents of the existential quantifier are commonly ambiguous. Sometimes they are indeed functioning as quantifiers, but sometimes they serve as singular terms referring to particular persons or objects.

3. Belief Sentences without Systematic Ambiguity

What I want to argue in this section is that the alleged systematic ambiguity of belief sentences is a myth. Quine treated 'believes' itself as lexically ambiguous and used this putative lexical ambiguity to explain our intuitions about sentences like (2), (9), and (14)–(17). Those who seek to get by with a single primitive sense of 'believes' agree with Quine in treating each of these sentences as ambiguous but trace the ambiguity to alternative possible analyses. By contrast, I maintain that belief sentences are *not* systematically ambiguous and that the examples considered in the first section of this chapter fall into two quite distinct categories. Some of the sentences considered are genuinely ambiguous, but the ambiguity can be traced to an ambiguity in the content sentence. Others are not ambiguous at all; the anomalies involving these sentences can be traced to the context sensitivity that the embedded notion of similarity imparts to the notion of belief.

Let me start with the cases of genuine ambiguity. In this category I include (2), (9), (10), and in general any belief sentence whose content sentence begins with 'someone', 'there is a', 'there are', and other expressions that can sometimes function as natural language equivalents of the existential quantifier. What Chastain and Wilson have shown is that these content sentences are themselves ambiguous. Thus we should expect that belief sentences containing them will also be ambiguous, much as 'Alice believes that flying planes can be dangerous' is ambiguous in virtue of the ambiguity of 'flying planes can be dangerous'. On my account,

> (10)   David believes that someone who works in the factory has stolen the secret process

might be roughly rendered

> (23)   Someone who works in the factory has stolen the secret process.
>
> David believes that.

Or, a bit more expansively, we might paraphrase (10) as

> (24)   Someone who works in the factory has stolen the secret process.
>
> David is in a belief state similar to the one which I would express by saying that.

As explained in the previous chapter, the word 'that' in (23) and (24) is a demonstrative, and when tokens of (10) are uttered, the demonstrative refers to the speech act whose text is given by the content sentence. Since the content sentence is ambiguous, the speech act may also be ambiguous, though of course in many cases the surrounding context will disambiguate. To explain the ambiguity of (10), there is no need to postulate that 'believes' is lexically ambiguous or that belief sentences admit of systematically different analyses. The ambiguity noted by Chastain suffices to explain the facts.

Let me now turn to cases like (14)–(17) and more generally to belief sentences whose content sentence contains a name or definite description. On Quine's view and on the view of writers like Kaplan, all of these sentences are ambiguous. The primary evidence for this putative ambiguity is the existence of cases in which intuition dictates that both a belief sentence and what appears to be its direct negation are appropriate characterizations of a subject's doxastic state. So, for example, both

> (14)   Jones believed that the owner of the factory was a burglar

and

> (16)   Jones did not believe that the owner of the factory was a burglar

strike us as fitting characterizations of Jones's state of mind while wrestling Foot to the floor. But I would argue that we need not postulate an *ambiguity* to explain these intuitions, since the notion of similarity embedded in our folk concept of belief already suffices to explain them. On my analysis, when we (or the policeman back at the station house) say (14) we are saying something roughly equivalent to

(25)   The owner of the factory is a burglar.

Jones was in a belief state similar to the one which I would ordinarily express by saying that.

Is this true? Well, in many respects Jones's belief was very similar to the one the policeman would express with that sentence. Jones's belief was presumably compounded of his concept of a certain man and his concept of a burglar, and Jones's token of the burglar-concept is in all respects as similar as one could wish to the policeman's token of this concept. Jones's concept of the man on the other hand is more problematic. It is similar in reference, since the man Jones tackled is the owner of the factory. But there are marked functional or causal-pattern differences, most notably the fact that Jones would not express his concept using the words 'the owner of the factory' and thus would not express his belief by saying 'the owner of the factory is a burglar'. Is this similarity similarity enough? The answer, surely, is that it depends on the context of the utterance. When our attention is focused on the fact that Jones would vigorously deny 'the owner of the factory is a burglar', (14) strikes us as an inappropriate description of Jones's cognitive state. But when, as in the station house later in the evening, what Jones would say is of less moment than the reference of his concept, (14) seems to be perfectly appropriate.

We saw an analogous phenomenon when considering the case of Tom and Dick, each of whom had beliefs about men they knew only as 'Ike'. In settings where the difference between their beliefs was important or where the exact words they would utter or accept was unimportant, it seems quite natural to say that Tom believes Eisenhower was a politician, while Dick believes that Angell-James was a politician. However, when the context makes it important to know just what Tom or Dick would say (think of the quiz show, again, or the examination) these characterizations of their beliefs are intuitively unacceptable. If Tom cannot answer the quiz show question, we are inclined to say it is because he does not believe that Eisenhower was a politician. What I am urging is that our intuitions in these cases are not to be explained by appeal to ambiguity but rather by appeal to the context-sensitive vagueness of similarity judgments. The fact that (14) and (16) can *both* seem true given the right setting is analogous to the fact that

(26)   Cuba is similar to the USSR

seems true if we are discussing political systems, while

(27)   Cuba is not similar to the USSR

strikes us as true if we are discussing climate. The analogy is illuminating also in the case where context remains unspecified. If we are asked out of context whether (26) is true, we might well reply that there is a sense in which it is true, but also a sense in which it is false. Similarly, if we are asked to render a judgment about (14) out of context, we are likely to reply that there is a sense in which it is true and a sense in which it is false. But in the case of (26) I trust no one would be tempted to take our conflicting intuitions as evidence for *ambiguity*. The inference to ambiguity in the case of (14) is, I contend, equally unwarranted.*

What shall we conclude about the thesis that belief sentences are systematically ambiguous? It might be thought that our current situation is a standoff, since we can explain our intuitions in various ways, some of which presume systematic ambiguity and some of which do not. However, there are two additional considerations which, on my view, tip the balance strongly in favor of the account I have been urging. First, my account is more parsimonious. The apparatus I would invoke to explain our intuitions is motivated by considerations quite independent of the anomalies assembled earlier in this chapter. The hypothesis of systematic ambiguity, by contrast, is put forward specifically to explain these cases. Second, and more important, none of the accounts invoking the systematic ambiguity hypothesis count as serious competitors with the theory I have been developing, since all of those accounts take the concept (or concepts) of belief as *primitive*. In my theory, however, the explanation of our intuitions about puzzling cases is integrated into a systematic analysis of our folk concept of belief. In the absence of an analysis for the primitive (or primitives) invoked by those who would postulate a systematic ambiguity, the choice between the two theories is no contest.

---

*Hornsby (1977) attempts to handle some of the cases involving names and definite descriptions by arguing that both names and definite descriptions admit of a systematic ambiguity analogous to the one Chastain notes for indefinite descriptions. Though I find her argument less convincing than Chastain's, if it turns out that she is right we will have another strategy for explaining our intuitions about these cases without the hypothesis that belief sentences are systematically ambiguous.

PART II

Cognitive Science and the Concept of Belief

Chapter 7

The Strong Representational Theory of the Mind

In part I my central aim was descriptive. I tried to give an accurate portrait of the way the folk psychological language of belief is ordinarily used and to sketch the network of more or less tacit assumptions that underlies this usage. In this chapter I will start out in a new direction. The question I shall pose is whether the folk psychological notion of belief is likely to find a comfortable place in cognitive science. As will come as no surprise, my answer will be negative. It would be satisfying, I suppose, to begin with a definition of *cognitive science*, but I have no such definition to propose. I intend the term to encompass much of the contemporary work on memory, language processing, reasoning, problem solving, decision making, and higher perceptual processing. Fortunately this very rough characterization is all we shall need; the argument can proceed without any more precise specification of what counts as cognitive science.

A more pressing matter is to get clear on just how the folk concept of belief might be invoked in a cognitive theory. What would it be like to have a cognitive theory which made serious use of the language and concepts of folk psychology? In this chapter I will explore one sort of answer to this question. The answer claims that cognitive theories fit (or ought to fit) a certain model or paradigm which I will call the *Strong Representational Theory of the Mind* (abbreviated *Strong RTM*). The first chore that faces us is to explain just what the Strong RTM claims about the explanatory strategy of cognitive theories. This is the project undertaken in section 1. In the remainder of the chapter I will marshal some arguments for thinking that the idea of building a cognitive theory along the lines recommended by the Strong RTM is a bad idea. My brief against the Strong RTM will not be completed in this chapter, however. Additional arguments will be developed in both chapters 8 and 9.

The 'Strong' in 'Strong RTM' carries the obvious suggestion that there is another version of the RTM which is not so strong, and so there is. But this version, the *Weak RTM*, will not make its appearance until chapter 9. The Weak RTM offers a significantly different view of what it would be like for cognitive science to make serious use of the concepts of folk psychology. Though, as I shall argue, the Weak RTM is no more attractive a model for the cognitive theorist than the Strong RTM. A third model or account of the explanatory strategy of cognitive science will appear on the scene in chapter 8, this one to be called the *Syntactic Theory of the Mind*. Unlike the two versions of the RTM, the Syntactic Theory does not portray cognitive theories as invoking anything much like the intentional notions of folk psychology. This is the account I propose to defend.

1. Cognitive Generalizations Couched in Terms of Content

Of the several writers who have advocated the Strong RTM, none has been more eloquent or explicit than Jerry Fodor.* So let me begin my discussion of the view of assembling a few quotes from Fodor's work. (Since we will have occasion to recall these quotes substantially further on in the text, I shall number them for easy reference.)

1.

We were driven to functionalism . . . by the suspicion that there are empirical generalizations about mental states that can't be formulated in the vocabulary of neurological or physical theories. . . . But now if we think about what these generalizations are like, what is striking is that all of the candidates—literally *all* of them— are generalizations that apply to propositional attitudes in virtue of the content of the propositional attitudes. We don't need the clever examples from linguistics or psychology to make this point; commonsense psychological etiologies will do. So consider: seeing that a is F is a normal cause of believing that a is F; . . . statements that P are normally caused by beliefs that P; . . . and so on and on. The point of such examples is not, of course, that any of them are likely to figure in a serious cognitive psychology. It's rather that our attempts at a serious cognitive psychology are founded in the hope that *this kind* of generalization can be systematized and made rigorous. . . . And: YOU CAN'T SAVE THESE GENERALIZATIONS WITHOUT APPEALING TO THE NOTION OF THE CONTENT OF A MENTAL STATE, since, as previously re-

---

*Note that 'consistent' is not among the adjectives I have used to characterize Fodor's advocacy, and for good reason, since Fodor can be (and has been) read as an advocate of both the Strong and the Weak RTM. Thus in the current chapter Fodor is a principal spokesman for the Strong RTM, whereas in the following chapter he emerges as a critic of the view. The roots of Fodor's apparent ambivalence are explored in chapter 9.

marked, these generalizations are precisely such as apply to mental states in virtue of their contents.[1]

2.

The paradigm situation—the grist for the cognitivist's mill—is the one where propositional attitudes interact causally and do so *in virtue of* their content.

. . . If there are true, contingent counterfactuals which relate mental state *tokens* in virtue of their contents, that is presumably because there are true, contingent generalizations which relate mental state *types* in virtue of their contents.[2]

3.

There have been three strands to this discussion. . . : the idea that mental states are functionally defined; the idea that in order to specify the generalizations that mentalistic etiologies instantiate, we need to advert to the contents of mental states; and the idea that mental states are relations to mental representations, the latter being viewed as, inter alia, semantically interpreted objects.[3]

Two ideas in these passages will assume considerable importance in the discussion to follow. The first is that "serious cognitive psychology" is founded on the hope that the empirical generalizations of common-sense psychology can be systematized and made rigorous. The second is that the generalizations of commonsense psychology, and thus also the generalizations of cognitive science, will "advert to the contents of mental states." This last idea is the essential one in what I have been calling the Strong RTM. The claim that cognitive science seeks (or ought to seek) "generalizations which relate mental state types in virtue of their contents" is what makes the Strong RTM *strong*.

Though it is only hinted at in the quotes and will not loom large in our discussion until chapter 9, I should say something about what it is that makes the Strong RTM *representational*. The basic idea is that mental states—both those postulated by folk psychology and those postulated by cognitive science—are to be viewed as relations to some sort of representational entities. Sentences in a mental code or language of thought are the obvious candidates to serve as mental representations, but the Strong RTM need not insist that the representations be sentences. Other sorts of representations might do as well, so long as they are the sort of things which can be thought of as having content or being semantically interpreted. If the representational entities are sentences, then mental states (both those of common sense and those postulated by cognitive science) are to be taken as relations between an organism and a token of a sentence. Later chapters will clarify and elaborate on all this. But for the moment I want to focus on the claim that cognitive science seeks generalizations which specify causal relations among mental states in terms of their contents.

In view of my diatribe in chapter 4,[4] the reader will not be surprised to learn that I am a bit uncomfortable with Fodor's talk of generalizations which "advert to the contents" of mental states and mental states which interact causally "in virtue of their content." For this all sounds rather too much as though contents are things—a sort of entity—over which cognitive theories may quantify. But I think appearances are deceptive here. Fodor neither explains nor seriously uses the idea of contents *as entities*, and I think that his talk of generalizations which relate states "in virtue of their content" is best understood as shorthand for generalizations which relate states *in virtue of the content sentences we use to characterize them.* To see just what this amounts to, let us think about commonsense psychological generalizations and about how a cognitive scientist pursuing the Strong RTM paradigm might hope to systematize them and make them rigorous.

In seeking a theory which builds on the insights of common sense, a plausible place to begin is with some low-level generalizations suggested by folk wisdom. The following two generalizations are of just such a sort:

(1)   For all subjects S, if
       S desires to leave the building he is in, if the building is on fire

and

       S comes to believe that the building is on fire

then

       S will acquire a desire to leave the building he is in.

(2)   For all subjects S, if
       S believes that if a conservative is elected president, then science funding will be cut

and

       S comes to believe that a conservative is elected president

then

       S will come to believe that science funding will be cut.

With a supply of such banal generalizations at hand or taken for granted, the cognitive scientist may set out to uncover some more surprising generalizations. For example, in an elegant series of experiments Ross and his colleagues have shown that something like the following quite striking generalization holds, an instance of the phenomenon of "belief perseverance."[5]

(3)   For any subject S, if
S believes that he has done exceptionally well on a test to
see whether he is good at distinguishing real from bogus
suicide notes

and if as a result

S believes that he is better than average at distinguishing real
from bogus suicide notes

and if subsequently

S ceases to believe that he has done exceptionally well on a
test to see whether he is good at distinguishing real from
bogus suicide notes

then (it is probable that)

S will continue to believe that he is better than average at
distinguishing real from bogus suicide notes.

The principal interest of these low-level generalizations is as instances
of higher level generalizations. What is important is not how the belief
that the building is on fire interacts with the desire to leave the building
if it is on fire but rather how beliefs of this general form interact with
desires of this general form. Higher level generalizations detailing these
interactions will make up the bulk of the cognitivist's theory. But just
how are higher level generalizations which "advert to content" to be
stated? Perhaps the most natural thought is to try to generalize on (1)
as follows:

(1')   For all S, P and Q, if
S desires P if Q

and

S comes to believe that Q

then

S will come to desire P.

There are serious problems with generalizing (1) in this way, however.
For consider just what it is that the variables 'P' and 'Q' are supposed
to range over. If the answer is *sentences*, then (1') is literally incoherent,
since, in instantiating, variables must be replaced by the *names* of objects
over which the variables range. And this would yield instances like

If Tom desires 'I leave the building I am in' if 'the building is on
fire' and Tom comes to believe that 'the building is on fire', then
Tom will come to desire 'I leave the building I am in'.

which is gibberish. One way out of the difficulty would be to say that the variables 'P' and 'Q' range over *propositions* and to accept the view that sentences (at least in belief and desire contexts) name propositions. But if our fledgling cognitive science takes this route it also takes on all sorts of unwelcome obligations, like making sense of propositions, explaining how these abstract entities relate to psychological states, and elaborating a semantic theory that sustains the claim that sentences in belief and desire contexts name propositions. Fortunately, there are better options available. What we want to capture in generalizing (1) is the fact that a desire attributable by a content sentence with a certain structure and a belief attributable by a content sentence with a certain structure yield a desire attributable by a content sentence with a structure determined by the structure of the previous two. Our generalization details regularities among beliefs and desires specified in terms of *the structure of content sentences used to ascribe them*. So what we want as the generalization of (1) is something like

> (1″) For all subjects S, and all declarative sentences P and Q in our language, if
>
> S has a desire which can be attributed by a sentence of the form
>
> 'S desires p if q'
>
> where 'p' is replaced by P and 'q' is replaced by Q,
>
> and if
>
> S comes to have a belief which can be attributed by a sentence of the form
>
> 'S believes that q'
>
> where 'q' is replaced by Q,
>
> then
>
> S will come to have a desire which can be attributed by a sentence of the form
>
> 'S desires p'
>
> where 'p' is replaced by P.

Now obviously I don't propose that anyone must actually state his generalizations in this fussy and cumbersome way. (1') has obvious advantages as a perspicuous shorthand. But the point I want to make, and I think it is of considerable importance, is that the cognitive scientist who takes seriously the idea of discovering generalizations relating mental states "in virtue of their contents" must capture those generalizations by quantifying over the content sentences that could be used to attribute the psychological states in question.

Thus far we have been concerned with the form generalizations would take in a theory which adhered to the Strong RTM model. Let us now consider what would be necessary to test or to apply a theory consisting of generalizations similar in structure to (1″). Suppose, for example, that we want to generalize (3) and apply the generalization to a new case. How would the story go? Consider first the generalization, which, following the pattern of (1″), would look something like the following:

(3″)   For all subjects S, and for all declarative sentences P and Q in our language, if

S has a belief which can be attributed by a sentence of the form

'S believes that p'

and if this belief causes S to have a belief which can be attributed by a sentence of the form

'S believes that q'

and if, subsequently, S ceases to have a belief which can be attributed by a sentence of the form

'S believes that p'

then (it is probable that) S will continue to have a belief which is attributable by a sentence of the form

'S believes that q'

where 'p' is replaced by P and 'q' is replaced by Q throughout.

Now let us apply this generalization to a new case. A subject, S, has been asked to take a test labeled "Sexual Orientation Profile," and after completing the test the experimenter scores it and tells the subject, "This is very interesting. Your test indicates that you have latent homosexual tendencies." Some time later, the experimenter says to the subject, "Before you leave, I want you to understand that the test did not actually indicate that you have latent homosexual tendencies. In fact my telling you that was all part of the experiment. You see, on this sheet of paper, which I have had since you came in, it lists your name and student ID number, and specifies that you are one of the subjects who is to be told that he has latent homosexual tendencies." Finally, some days later, the subject is asked, on an allegedly anonymous questionnaire, whether or not he has latent homosexual tendencies. What prediction, if any, does (3″) enable us to make in this case?*

---

*It is perhaps worth mentioning in passing that it was concern over cases like this one that motivated Ross's work on belief perseverance. It is not uncommon in experimental

It is clear that taken alone (3″) does not enable us to predict anything about the case at hand, since (3″) only tells us about the dynamics of beliefs—how one belief does (or in this case does not) affect the other beliefs a subject holds. To apply (3″) we must know something about the way the particular experimental manipulations affect the beliefs the subject has, and we must also know something about how his beliefs are likely to manifest themselves in behavior. Without information of this sort, (3″) is quite useless. But, of course, if S is a typical experimental subject, we are prepared to make a broad range of assumptions about how his environment will affect his beliefs and about how his beliefs will be reflected in behavior. For the case at hand it is safe to assume that if a suitably professional looking experimenter says to S, "Your test indicates that you have latent homosexual tendencies," S will (or is likely to) come to believe that his test indicates that he has latent homosexual tendencies. Moreover, given the setting, that belief is likely to cause S to believe that he in fact has latent homosexual tendencies. Also, when the experimenter says, "The test did not actually indicate you have latent homosexual tendencies," and shows the subject a sheet with his name on the list headed "These subjects are to be told they have latent homosexual tendencies," this is likely to cause S to believe that the tests did not indicate he has latent homosexual tendencies. Finally, we may assume that if S believes that he has latent homosexual tendencies, and if he is given an allegedly anonymous questionnaire asking, "Do you have latent homosexual tendencies?" he will check the box marked "yes." Given all of these assumptions, (3″) enables us to predict that S will form and retain a belief that he has latent homosexual tendencies and that he will check the "yes" box on the questionnaire.* It is true that the assumptions required to get a prediction from (3″) are, in the typical case, banal and unproblematic. But it is important to see that they are not plausibly viewed as instances of generalizations which the cognitive theorist might explicitly add to his theory alongside principles like (1″). For unlike (1″) and (3″), the assumptions do not apply to all normal people. A monolingual Korean speaker, or an illiterate, or a person who had no idea what 'homosexual

social psychology to dupe a subject into having a potentially harmful belief and then explain the deception at the end of the experiment. What troubled Ross was the possibility that the subject would retain the belief he had been duped into holding, even though he no longer believed the evidence on which the belief was based.

*I am obviously oversimplifying more than a little. Most of the assumptions I have specified would have to be hedged fairly substantially. Ross's work does not enable us to predict that any given subject will check the "yes" box on the questionnaire but only that a randomly selected group of subjects who have undergone this experience are more likely to check the "yes" box than a randomly selected group who have not.

tendencies' meant, or a person from a culture in which psychologists were not authority figures and psychological testing was unknown, would not form or express beliefs as we assume the typical under-graduate subject does. None of this is offered by way of criticism. My purpose is rather to make it clear that in testing or using a cognitive theory whose generalizations "advert to content," we must surround the theory with a rich set of ad hoc assumptions about the causal interactions among particular experiences, beliefs, and behavior for the subjects at hand. The point will be of some importance in the following chapter, where we ask how content-based cognitive theories might be improved upon.

2. Some Reasons to Be Suspicious about the Strong RTM

The remainder of this chapter will be devoted to setting out reasons why the model for cognitive science proposed by the Strong RTM should be rejected. What I shall try to show is that if we insist on couching our cognitive generalizations in terms of content we will miss significant and powerful generalizations, and we will struggle with an endemic and often crippling vagueness. None of the arguments to follow establishes that a serious cognitive science could not *possibly* be constructed along the lines advocated by the Strong RTM. I have no idea how one might argue for a conclusion that sweeping. Rather, I hope to convince you that the cognitive scientist must pay a very heavy price for adhering to the Strong RTM. In the following chapter we will see that there is an alternative to the Strong RTM which has all of its virtues and none of its limitations.

Before setting out my case in detail, it may be helpful to note some of the prima facie reasons to be suspicious about the scientific utility of generalizations couched in terms of content. As it happens, I think all of these reasons for suspicion are justified. First, as I was at pains to show in chapter 5, there is an appeal to *similarity* embedded in commonsense ascriptions of content. As a result, predicates of the form 'believes that p' are both *vague* and *context sensitive*, rather like such predicates as 'looks like Abraham Lincoln'. Thus while there will be cases to which 'believes that p' clearly applies, there will also be many cases in which, out of context, there is simply no saying whether the predicate applies or not. So if the generalizations of a cognitive theory are cast in terms of such predicates, it will often be unclear whether or not the generalizations apply to a given subject.

There is a second respect in which 'believes that p' rather resembles predicates like 'looks like Abraham Lincoln'. In both cases comparison is being made to a standard or exemplar. In the case of belief *we ourselves* are the standard. To believe that p is to be in a belief state similar to the one underlying our own sincere assertion of 'p'. There is, thus, a sort of *observer relativity* built into our folk notion, and a cognitive theory written in the folk language of belief would inherit this observer relativity. There are two drawbacks to this. First and most obvious is the fact that different observers may differ substantially from one another, and when this happens they may be led to describe the subject's beliefs differently. Or, what is perhaps easier to illustrate, there may be cases in which one observer simply has no content sentence available to him which he can comfortably use to characterize the subject's belief. This last observation suggests another, and I think more serious, difficulty. Since the folk language of belief characterizes a subject's cognitive state by comparing it to our own, subjects who differ fairly radically from us will simply fall outside the reach of folk description altogether. Thus if our cognitive theory relies essentially on the content ascriptive vocabulary of folk psychology, these subjects will be beyond its purview. Yet some of these subjects may have minds which work very much as ours do. If there are important generalizations which cover both us and such exotic folk, a cognitive science in the Strong RTM mold is bound to miss them. And if there are generalizations unique to one or another category of such subjects, they will be difficult or impossible to state in the way required by the Strong RTM.

Another prima facie reason to be suspicious of the scientific utility of generalizations adverting to content turns on the role of ideological and reference similarity in individuating beliefs. Often both of these factors impose a more fine-grained individuative scheme than would be required if we were using notions individuated on narrow causal lines. The distinctions imposed are of unquestionable utility if we are concerned with the semantic properties of beliefs and the sentences that express them. But if our concern is to predict and explain behavior, there is reason to suspect that these distinctions will simply get in the way. They will force us to attach different labels to psychological states which are quite identical to one another in point of causal potential. Thus they will make it harder to capture generalizations salient to the explanation of behavior. Rather than struggle with these fine-grained distinctions which contribute nothing in the explanation of behavior, a cognitive theorist might well be tempted simply to amputate them and build a theory with the more austere concept that remains. Indeed I shall argue in chapter 9 that this is just what is commonly done in the actual practice of cognitive theorists. But, of course, a theorist who abandons the ideological and reference components of content in stating generalizations is no longer working within the explanatory paradigm proposed by the Strong RTM.

3. Problems Posed by Ideological Similarity

It is time to start substantiating the suspicions I raised about the difficulties awaiting a cognitive theorist who takes the folk notion of belief seriously. In this section I will concentrate on problems created by the fact that our folk notion attends to the doxastic surroundings of a belief in deciding whether or not a given content sentence can be used to characterize the belief. My strategy will be quite straightforward. In three separate examples, I will consider sequences of cases in which the doxastic surroundings of the subject's belief grow increasingly unlike the doxastic surroundings of the belief we might ourselves express using the same sentence. What I expect to show in all three cases is that as the ideological similarity between the subject and ourselves diminishes, it becomes quite unclear whether or not the subject's belief can be characterized by the content sentence we would use to characterize the belief which a less ideologically exotic subject expresses with the same sentence. This vagueness in the language of folk psychology makes it quite unclear whether or not the generalizations of a cognitive theory couched in terms of content can be applied to subjects whose beliefs differ significantly from our own. The vagueness is gradually resolved as we continue along the sequence, considering cases that are increasingly ideologically exotic. For it gradually becomes clear that these cases *cannot* be characterized using the content sentence we would use with more familiar subjects. Nor is any other content sentence available to us. Thus these belief states are beyond the reach of a cognitive theory which cleaves to the Strong RTM. Still, in many of these cases there are or may well be generalizations to capture which are quite parallel to the generalizations expressible in folk psychological terms. The theorist who elects to use the language of content puts these generalizations beyond reach. However, a taxonomy of mental states which typed them along narrow causal lines could count the belief of both the mildly and the extremely exotic subject as type identical to the belief of the subject whose ideological network is quite similar to ours. Thus it could capture the generalizations that the more finely grained folk psychological individuation scheme misses.

To begin our examination of cases, let us consider variations on the theme of the experimental subject who has been duped into believing that he has latent homosexual tendencies. When dealing with typical undergraduate subjects, who speak fluent English and have a passable knowledge of matters sexual, it is a fair enough assumption that if an apparently sincere and authoritative psychologist says, "Your test results indicate that you have latent homosexual tendencies," subjects are likely to come to believe that their test results indicate they have latent homosexual tendencies. If doubt should arise about the proper characterization of the belief the subject forms, we could dispel it by asking some questions about sex and homosexuality. What we expect, in the unproblematic case, is that the subject will share with us a substantial number of central beliefs about sex and homosexuality and thus will answer these questions very much as we would.

But suppose that for a given subject S¹ these expectations are not fulfilled. S¹, it turns out, describes sexual acts between certain people of opposite sex as "homosexual acts." Our first thought might be that S¹ simply did not know the definition of 'homosexual act'. But on inquiring further it turns out that matters are not so simple. Asked to define 'homosexual act' S¹ says, "A homosexual act is a sexual act performed by people of the same sex." When we ask him to explain why he classifies sexual relations between John and Mary as "homosexual" he tells us that they *are* "of the same sex." We point out to him that John is a prima facie normal man, endowed in the usual way, and Mary is a prima facie normal woman, also endowed in the usual way. But our subject is quite unmoved by these facts. He insists that

> What sex a person is, is not a function of anatomy. Maleness and femaleness are basic, irreducible properties of people. These properties are often correlated with anatomical differences, but sometimes they are not. You can't even tell for sure by examining their chromosomes. It is no easy matter to determine what sex a person is. You have to know quite a lot about their personalities, their goals and aspirations, the way they interact with other people, etc. It is often quite a subtle thing. I know John and Mary quite well, and I am convinced that, despite their anatomy, they are both female. Of course, homosexual acts never result in pregnancy, so no children will result from their sexual relations.

Finally S¹ expresses some surprise that we need to be told that anatomy is only an imperfect indicator of sex; he takes it to be common knowledge. What I am attempting to describe, of course, is a person who has a *theory* about sexuality, a set of interrelated beliefs some of which are quite different from, and incompatible with, our own.

Now what shall we say about the belief S¹ acquires when he is told about his test results in the belief perseverance experiment? To simplify matters let us suppose that S¹ is a trusting fellow who is generally much impressed by the evidence of psychological tests. On being told about his test results he forms a belief which *he* would express by saying, "I have latent homosexual tendencies." But what are *we* to say about this belief? Does he believe that he has latent homosexual tendencies? I am inclined to think that, when the question is raised without some specific context in mind, there is simply no saying.* The doxastic surround of S¹'s belief—his theory of sexuality—is sufficiently different from the doxastic surround of the belief we might express with the same sentence, that it is just not clear whether or not his belief counts as the belief that he has latent homosexual tendencies. Nor is there any other content sentence available in our language which folk intuition would find clearly appropriate in this case. What makes this vagueness important for the Strong RTM cognitive theorist is that it infects any attempt to apply his generalizations. Consider (3″). To apply it to the case of S¹, there must be some sentence Q in our language such that S¹'s belief is attributable by a sentence of the form

    S¹ believes that q

where 'q' is replaced by Q. The obvious candidate for Q is "He has latent homosexual tendencies." And to the extent that it is indeterminate whether or not this content sentence characterizes S¹'s belief, it is also indeterminate whether or not (3″) can be used in predicting or explaining S¹'s behavior or his cognitive state.

In sketching S¹'s theory of sexuality I attempted to construct a view which was not wildly different from our own. Consider, now, what happens when the difference between a subject's doxastic network and our own becomes quite radical. Suppose that we are dealing with a subject S² who first attracted our attention by claiming that sexual relations between Mary and Sara would not count as "homosexual," nor would sexual relations between Sara and Jane, or between Mary and Bill. But sex between Bill and Jane would count as "homosexual." On further questioning it turns out that S², like S¹, says "the sex of a person is a basic and irreducible property." Unlike S¹, however, S² holds that there are far more than two such properties and denies that

---

*A word about context. As we saw in chapters 4 and 5, the vagueness of belief ascriptions is often markedly reduced by the context in which the attribution is made. But the vagueness-resolving capacity of context is of little use to the cognitive theorist. This for two reasons. First, the various pragmatic factors that help to reduce vagueness are generally irrelevant to the business of scientific explanation. The cognitive scientist seeks to explain or predict a subject's behavior independent of any consideration of what the scientist's own previous conversational interests have been. To put the point in another way, the scientist's attributions of psychological states to subjects are, or ought to be, largely independent of context. Second, to the extent that the theorist's descriptions of the psychological states of subjects are not context independent, his theory itself is methodologically suspect. For in this case the question of whether or not a given theoretical generalization applies to a given subject may be answered both *yes* and *no*, depending on the setting in which the *theorist* asks the question. Terms with the acute context sensitivity of folk psychological content ascriptions make poor tools for the building of scientific theories.

they have any known correlation with anatomical characteristics. Further, S^2 denies that there is any connection between the sex of the persons involved and the possibility of having children. Instead he offers a complex hypothesis about the relation between "sexes" of the partners and the "sex" of the offspring, if any. If this is not enough by way of ideological oddity, the reader is invited to exercise his own imagination, elaborating on S^2's theory of "sex" until intuition dictates that the content sentence, "He has latent homosexual tendencies" is a hopeless nonstarter in characterizing the belief S^2 acquires in the belief perseverance experiment. When the subject's doxastic network has been made quite radically different from our own in this domain, there simply is no sentence in our language that will serve as a content sentence in characterizing the subject's belief. The ideological divide between us is so great that, apart from specific contexts, there is just no saying what he believes—no way of using a that-p clause to characterize his belief. But since the availability of an appropriate content sentence is a prerequisite for the application of (3"), the generalization cannot be applied at all. Subjects who are as doxastically exotic as this one are simply beyond the purview of a Strong RTM cognitive theory whose generalizations advert to content.

It might be thought that this is all to the good, that cognitive theory ought not to apply to such doxastically unfamiliar subjects.[6] But I would argue that that is a mistake, since it may well be that despite his doxastic oddity, S^2's underlying psychology is quite parallel to our own. It might well be that the doxastic state which S^2 expresses by saying "I have latent homosexual tendencies" behaves just as other beliefs do in the belief perseverance experiment. Shown what ought to be convincing evidence that the report of his test result was fake, S^2 continues to hold the belief that he expresses with this sentence. Indeed in this case, this is surely just what we would expect. It would be surprising indeed if the difference in ideological surround had any effect on the regularity uncovered by Ross and his coworkers. But if this turns out to be the case, cognitive scientists who couch their generalizations in the folk psychological language of content will be unable to capture this generalization in their theories.

The source of the difficulty in this case is easy enough to diagnose. Folk psychology takes ideological similarity to be important in determining what content sentence can be used in characterizing a belief. And the theorist who accepts the Strong RTM generalizes across content sentences. An obvious way out of this difficulty is for the theorist to identify belief states in some other way when generalizing across them. If a belief can be characterized in terms of its narrow causal potential or some aspect of its narrow causal potential, then the theorist can capture Ross's generalization and ignore differences in ideological similarity which affect the content sentence folk psychology assigns to the belief. In the following chapter, we will see what a cognitive theory might look like when cut free of the constraints of ideological similarity. As will come as no surprise, it might look like the mental sentence theory, with tokens typed along narrow causal lines.

For a second example, consider again the case of Mrs. T.[7] In my somewhat idealized rendition of her case history, I assumed that as her memory decayed, her other cognitive functions—inference, practical reasoning, speech processing, etc.—remained near normal. I do not know how realistic an assumption this is, since the real Mrs. T was subjected to no systematic psychological or neurological testing. Though it was certainly the impression of all those who know her well that her reasoning powers remained very much intact long after her loss of memory had reached catastrophic proportions. Now what I want to focus on is the question of whether we were correct in thinking that Mrs. T's reasoning capacities remained largely intact. It surely seems that this question ought not to be answerable a priori; it should be an open question to be settled by test and observation of Mrs. T's inferential capacities at various points in the development of her illness. But, I shall argue, for the cognitive scientist who accepts the Strong RTM it is not an open question. It cannot be the case that generalizations describing her reasoning capacities before the onset of her illness continue to characterize her doxastic dynamics as her illness grows worse, *if these generalizations apply in virtue of content*. To see the point, let us focus on the generalization about inference suggested by (2) above. Generalizing along the lines of (1″) and (3″) we get

(2″)   For all subjects S and all sentences in our language, P and Q, if

S has a belief that can be attributed by a sentence of the form

'S believes that p'

and if

S comes to have a belief that can be attributed by a sentence of the form

'S believes that if p then q'

then (it is probable that)

S will come to have a belief that can be attributed by a sentence of the form

'S believes that q'

where 'p' is replaced by P and 'q' is replaced by Q throughout.

It is clear enough that this generalization captured a regularity in Mrs. T's inferential pattern when she was in good health. But let us consider her situation as her loss of memory became serious. At some point her understanding of what an assassination is began to decay. She was still aware that an assassination was something bad and frightening. But she was not at all sure just what it was. At this point and indeed throughout her long decline, Mrs. T said "McKinley was assassinated" whenever she was asked "What happened to McKinley?" Did she, however, *believe* that McKinley was assassinated? The answer, surely, is that there is no answer. We have entered the penumbra of vagueness where, apart from a special conversational context, there is just no saying whether the content sentence is applicable. From here on, the argument parallels the one developed for the previous example. Suppose we tell Mrs. T, "If McKinley was assassinated, then he is buried in Ohio." Does (2″) enable us to predict what she will infer from the belief which our utterance causes her to form? Well, in order to predict her inference on the basis of (2″) we must know whether she has a belief which can be attributed by 'Mrs. T believes that McKinley was assassinated'. And to the extent that it is indeterminate whether she has such a belief, it is indeterminate whether or not (2″) can be applied.

As Mrs. T's condition gets worse and she loses more and more of her memory about assassination and other matters, it gradually becomes clear that, by the standards of folk psychology, her belief cannot be described as the belief that McKinley was assassinated. Nor can any other sentence in our language serve as a content sentence in describing her belief. At this point it is clear that (2″) does not apply. Yet, as in the belief perseverance case, there may well be a significant generalization here. For it may turn out that, even as she is on the brink of death, if we tell Mrs. T, "If McKinley was assassinated, then he is buried in Ohio," she would reply "Well then, he is buried in Ohio." It would be tempting to conclude from this, and a pattern of similar responses, that while her long-term memory was largely destroyed, her inferential abilities remain intact—the generalizations governing inference which applied before her illness continue to apply. But this is not a move open to cognitive theorists who adopt the Strong RTM. Their generalizations, both (2″) and others, do not apply when the doxastic surroundings of Mrs. T's beliefs become radically different from the doxastic surroundings of our own beliefs. If there is a generalization to be captured here, it is beyond the reach of a cognitive science whose generalizations advert to content. For such a theory, it is not an open question whether or not Mrs. T's inferential capacity has remained intact. Once again, in order to so much as state a prima facie plausible generalization, the cognitive theorist must find a way of classifying doxastic states which ignores ideological similarity. And, once again, some version of a mental sentence account of cognitive states looks to be a promising alternative, provided that tokens of mental sentences are typed along narrow causal lines.

For my final example I want to consider a case in which generalizations of practical reasoning like (1″) are artificially limited when couched in terms of content. The subject of my example, this time, is my daughter, age six and some months at this writing. She is a cheerful, Montessori-educated child who occasionally startles strangers overhearing her as she works out fairly complex arithmetic problems. I suspect that she sometimes works out such problems *viva voce* and in public just to achieve this effect. In any event it is perfectly clear that at present my daughter has a reasonably sophisticated grasp of numerical concepts. If asked to look at a Star of David and determine how many points there are on the star, she would quickly reply, "Six." There can be little doubt that in so saying she is expressing the belief that the star has six points.

Now let us consider an earlier stage in her cognitive development. At age four, if memory serves, my daughter was able to count to ten quite accurately, though once she got beyond ten accuracy declined rapidly. (For reasons that I do not begin to understand, fifteen seemed a particularly hard number; for several months she could count to twenty quite well, always leaving out fifteen.) At this age she could also count objects with some accuracy, though once she got beyond six or seven, accuracy declined. Arithmetic skills were very primitive. She could answer, "How much is 1 + 1?" and "How much is 2 + 2?" quite promptly. But 2 + 3 was much more difficult. To work out the answer she would count out two fingers, then three fingers, then count up the total. This particular digital calculator was useless when the sum was greater than 10, however, and she found it hard (though not impossible) to use this system when the sum was greater than 5. Such sums as 6 + 6, or even 6 + 3, were quite beyond her grasp. The question is how we are to characterize the numerical beliefs of a child whose understanding of numbers is this limited. Suppose, at this stage, we show my daughter a Star of David and ask her to count the points. She says, "There are six points." Does the belief that she is expressing count as the belief that the star has six points? To my ear, out of context, this is another of those conundrums that has no clear answer. The folk language of belief is too vague to decide the matter. But if this is right, then it is also doubtful whether generalizations like (1″) apply to the child. Suppose that on a certain occasion my daughter's teacher seats the children in the class in a circle and shows them a Star of

David. She says, "How many points are on this star? If you think the answer is six, then stand up." What does (1″) enable us to predict about this case? Clearly, if my daughter believes that there are six points and desires to stand up if there are six points, then (1″) entails that she will acquire a desire to stand up. But since the vagueness of the folk language of belief leaves it undetermined whether she has this belief, it is also undetermined whether or not (1″) applies.

As in the previous two cases, we can turn a case of vagueness into one of clear inapplicability by enlarging the ideological divide between ourselves and the subject. So let us consider a still earlier time, at about age three, when my daughter could just about count up to five. At that age she sometimes tried to get past five, but the results were, at best, mixed. Also, even the simplest sums, like $1 + 1$ or $1 + 2$, were quite beyond her grasp. Under these circumstances it seems clear that the content sentences we use in characterizing our own numerical beliefs are inappropriate in characterizing the child's. But now let us imagine another episode of the class seated in a circle and shown a Star of David. The teacher asks the children to count the points, and an older child whispers to my daughter, "There are six." The teacher then instructs the children to stand up if they think there are six points, and my daughter stands up. It is tempting to think that in explaining this behavior we would invoke a generalization which would also be applicable a few years later when she has unquestioned mastery of elementary arithmetic concepts. But of course for the theorist who adopts the Strong RTM, no such generalization is available. (1″) is not applicable to a child whose ideological distance from us is this large. As in the two previous cases, what is needed to capture the generalization is a taxonomy of mental states that is oblivious to ideological similarity.

My aim in this section has been to illustrate some of the obstacles that confront the cognitive theorist who builds his theory along the lines urged by the Strong RTM. I should note that the examples were chosen with malice aforethought. The first case was indicative of the difficulties in applying a content-based theory to ideologically exotic folks, be they undergraduates with bizarre views about sex or primitive tribes with radically unfamiliar notions about the universe. The second case was typical of problems to be expected in applying a content-based theory to a whole range of people of interest to the clinical psychologist, people who are senile, or brain damaged, or victims of a stroke, among others. The third case illustrated the difficulties to be confronted in dealing with the cognitive states of children. What I would conclude from these cases is that the price for adopting the Strong RTM in cognitive science is alarmingly high. If we follow that path we shall have to do without a cognitive developmental psychology, without a cognitive clinical psychology, and without a cognitive comparative psychology. When the price gets *that* high, it is time to see what else is on the market.

4. Problems Posed by Reference Similarity

Similarity in reference, like ideological similarity, plays a major role in determining what content sentence can be used in characterizing a belief. In this section I will illustrate some of the problems that this creates for a cognitive theory whose generalizations follow the Strong RTM pattern. In essence, the story is parallel to the one we told in the previous section. The involvement of reference similarity produces intermediate cases in which it is simply not clear whether a given content sentence can be used to characterize a belief. And in these cases the applicability of laws generalizing across content sentences is uncertain. In more extreme cases radical dissimilarity in the factors underlying reference can make it quite impossible, apart from special conversational contexts, to find a content sentence appropriate for a belief. In these cases, as in the cases of radical ideological dissimilarity, the subject is beyond the reach of a content-based cognitive theory. Here too there are plausible generalizations to explore, however, generalizations which cannot be stated in the language of folk psychology.

For a change of pace, let me begin with a case of radical dissimilarity. What we need is an example of a subject who uses a term with so peculiar a history that we are at a loss to say what the term might refer to. Here is a bit of fiction that seems to fit the bill. Suppose that our subject, a Mr. Binh, is a recent immigrant to the United States whose mastery of English is rather shaky. A bright and attentive man, Binh is anxious to learn as much as possible about his adopted country. On his first day off the plane, he overhears a conversation about a Mr. Jefferson, whose exploits are of obvious interest to the people on whom he is eavesdropping. Unknown to Binh, the people whose conversation he overhears are avid TV fans, and they are discussing the most recent travails of the fictional black dry-cleaning magnate whose apparent popularity is a sorry commentary on the state of the popular arts in America. Binh takes it all in. The next day Binh begins citizenship classes and he hears that Jefferson was a statesman, an inventor, and a major figure in the early history of America. Binh remembers, though he does not suspect that his teacher may be referring to a different Jefferson. On the third day Binh hears some discussion of a Mr. Feferman, a brilliant logician. However, with his ear not yet well attuned to spoken English, Binh hears 'Feferman' as 'Jefferson'. Finally, on the fourth day, Binh meets an old friend and has a long chat about what he has learned of his new country. "I am," he says, "very anxious to learn more about this fascinating fellow Jefferson, the black patriot and statesman who made significant contributions to logic while building a dry cleaning empire." Now, when Binh says "Jefferson was a black patriot who built a dry cleaning empire," just what content sentence shall we use to characterize his belief? The best alternative, I suppose, is the very sentence Binh himself uses. But this is the best of a bad lot. The reference of "Jefferson" as Binh uses it is so muddled that, apart from special contexts, no content sentence is likely to seem very appropriate. As a result, the belief that Binh expresses using this sentence is outside the reach of generalizations like (1")–(3"). Yet surely we expect that Binh's belief will behave in a manner quite parallel to beliefs with ungarbled reference. If, for example, Binh is taking a quiz whose instructions read, "If Jefferson was a patriot, then circle the letter A below," we would expect him to circle the letter A. And part of the explanation for this behavior would be a generalization something like (1"). But to reformulate (1") so that it applies despite the referential oddity of Binh's belief, we need a taxonomy of cognitive states which, unlike our folk taxonomy, ignores reference similarity.

Morton has also noted the mischief that garbled reference does to our ordinary ways of recounting what others believe. His illustration is a useful supplement to mine.

> Someone learns first that there was a man born in Corsica in 1769 who went on to various exploits; as he learns more about the man he just thinks 'he did that' without identifying him particularly as the man crowned in 1804 or the victor of Austerlitz or whatever. Then if the story gets mixed up—say he assimilates Louis and Napoleon Bonaparte and comes to believe that the victor of Austerlitz is the king of Holland in 1806 and the father of Napoleon III, then there may be no fact to the matter about who his beliefs refer to. What does he believe then? Not just that Napoleon became king of Holland in 1806, but that he was, where he is a creature of his private mythology, linked with both Napoleon and Louis Bonaparte. There is not, at any rate there need not be, any way of capturing his belief by saying that he believes that p, where p is some real proposition, seducible into English.[8]

For an illustration of the sort of vagueness referential similarity can introduce, I borrow, with a few changes, an example due to Burge.[9] Burge asks that we imagine a society quite like our own in all respects save one. In the imagined society the word 'arthritis' is applied not only to inflammations of the joints but also to various other ailments including inflammations of the long bones and surrounding tissue. This usage of 'arthritis' is well known to physicians, lexicographers, and other knowledgeable people in this society. However, many common folk in this society, as in our own, have only a rather hazy idea of the extension of 'arthritis'. One such less-than-learned fellow, call him Bob, will be the protagonist in our tale. Bob has long suffered from painful inflammation of the joints, and his physician has told him, "You have arthritis." On a certain morning, Bob awakes with pains in the calves of his legs, and says to himself, "Drat, the arthritis is in my calves." Now, as it happens, Bob is quite right; his diagnosis will later be confirmed by his physician. But it is also true that the sentence Bob uses to express his belief is one that could not be true if spoken by someone in our own society, since it is, so to speak, analytically false. The question to be posed here is how Bob's belief is to be described. Does Bob believe that he has arthritis in his calves? On Burge's view, the answer is no; others have conflicting intuitions.[10] I think the best answer is that there is no answer. The case is one of those many vague ones which folk psychology leaves unresolved. A particularly useful feature of this example is the fact that it admits of gradual modification to accommodate varying intuitions. If, like Burge, you think it is clear that Bob's belief cannot be characterized as the belief that he has arthritis in his calves, then imagine an intermediate case in which linguistic practice is not quite so far from our own—say one where 'arthritis' is used just as we use it, save for the fact that inflammations in the neck joints do not fall in its extension. If, on the other hand your intuitions dictate that Bob's belief *can* be characterized as the belief that he has arthritis in his calves, then imagine a more extreme case—say one in which 'arthritis' applies to only a few joint inflammations but also applies to a large variety of other maladies from corns to carbuncles. For the Strong RTM cognitive scientist, the problem resulting from vagueness traceable to reference similarity is much the same as the problem traceable to ideological similarity. The application of putative laws which generalize over content sentences is, in these cases, left indeterminate. To remove the indeterminacy, the cognitive scientist must adopt a taxonomy which is not sensitive to sociolinguistic setting or to the causal history of the terms the subject uses.

5. Problems Posed by Causal-Pattern Similarity

In the account of content ascription developed in chapter 5, similarity in causal pattern was the third dimension along which belief states were evaluated to determine the appropriateness of a content sentence. As in the case of ideological and reference similarity, increasingly exotic causal patterns produce cases of vagueness which gradually evolve into cases where the descriptive resources of folk psychology are taxed beyond their limit.[11] However, the problems posed for the Strong RTM by increased causal-pattern dissimilarity are not quite parallel to those posed by ideological and reference dissimilarity. In the latter two cases our central worry was that, despite the differences that separate us from the subjects, there may be generalizations about cognitive processes that apply to us all, generalizations that cannot be captured in the language of folk psychology. In the case of the subject who is markedly causal-pattern dissimilar from us we do not expect to find causal generalizations applicable to both his cognitive states and our own. What we might expect to find, though, are generalizations that apply to the subject and to others of his ilk—different psychological laws for organisms of different sorts. Perhaps the most appealing place to hunt for such differences is among children. Much of the work of Piaget and his colleagues points toward the conclusion that as children develop, the pattern of causal interactions among their cognitive states changes in a systematic way. If this proves to be correct, then we will need a sequence of different models or theories to characterize the cognitive functioning of children at various stages of development. If the differences that divide us from the young child turn out to be quite radical ones, however, then developmental cognitive scientists who seek to write theories in the fashion prescribed by the Strong RTM will find themselves constrained by the limitations of folk description. There just is no comfortable folk characterization of belief states whose patterns of interaction with one another and with other cognitive states differ radically from the pattern manifested by our beliefs. The problem will be compounded, of course, by the ideological gap separating children and normal adults. And if there is no content sentence theorists can use to describe the cognitive state of the young child, then they will be unable to formulate nomic regularities about children of that age which generalize across content sentences. Much the same argument applies, mutatis mutandis, to victims of strokes, injuries, retardation, and the like.

The upshot of all this is to buttress the conclusion urged in our discussion of problems posed by ideological similarity. If we insist on constructing cognitive theories whose generalizations advert to content, then we may well have to do without comprehensive theories of cognitive development and cognitive abnormality. If, by contrast, we adopt a taxonomy of cognitive states which individuates them along narrow causal lines and which takes no account of similarities or differences between the subjects and ourselves, we will avoid the obstacles that have been surveyed in the last three sections. The price for adopting the Strong RTM is that many cognitive generalizations will be beyond our grasp and many of those which we can state will be plagued by the vagueness inherent in the language of content.

Chapter 8

The Syntactic Theory of the Mind

One way in which cognitive science might make serious use of the language and concepts of folk psychology would be to build theories on the pattern commended by the Strong RTM. But the burden of the last chapter was that this option is a very costly one. Throughout that chapter I intimated that there is a better alternative, one which offers the explanatory benefits of the Strong RTM without its deficits. The alternative is what I shall call the *Syntactic Theory of the Mind*, or *STM* for short. This chapter will be occupied with explaining the STM and defending my contention that it provides a better paradigm for cognitive theorizing than does the Strong RTM. Like the Strong RTM, the STM is not itself a cognitive theory; both are, rather, views about what cognitive theories are or ought to be. Unlike the Strong RTM, however, the STM is not sanguine about the use of folk psychological notions in cognitive science. It does not advocate cognitive theories whose generalizations appeal to the notion of content.

1. The STM Vision of Cognitive Theories

The basic idea of the STM is that the cognitive states whose interaction is (in part) responsible for behavior can be systematically mapped to abstract syntactic objects in such a way that causal interactions among cognitive states, as well as causal links with stimuli and behavioral events, can be described in terms of the syntactic properties and relations of the abstract objects to which the cognitive states are mapped. More briefly, the idea is that causal relations among cognitive states mirror formal relations among syntactic objects. If this is right, then it will be natural to view cognitive state tokens as tokens of abstract syntactic objects.

All this needs to be said much more carefully, and to do so I shall have to say quite a lot about states. So I had best begin by saying just how I would have this talk construed. As I conceive of them, states are the instantiation of a *property* by an *object* during a *time interval*.

So construed, states are *particulars*, with a more or less definite location in space and time. On the view I am adopting, states admit of what might be called an *essential* classification into types. A pair of states are of the same *essential type* if and only if they are instantiations of the same property. It will sometimes be convenient to use the word 'state' to denote the property which all states of the same essential type have in common. On this way of talking, when I say of a certain organism that it is *in state P*, I will mean that the organism instantiates property P at the time in question. Similarly, to say that a pair of organisms are *in the same state* is to say that they instantiate the same essential property at the times in question. When ambiguity threatens, it will be useful to use 'state token' to refer to particulars and 'state type' to refer to properties.[1]

Although each state token has only one essential type, states, like other particulars, can be grouped into nonessential types in an endless variety of ways. A type of state token is simply a category of particulars, and we have specified such a type when we have set out the conditions for membership in the category. Similarly, state types, both essential and nonessential, can themselves be grouped into types or categories. To specify a category of state types we need but specify the property a type must have to count as a member of the category. One last complication is that a type or category of state types imposes derivative or indirect categorization on state tokens; if ϕ is a property whose possession by a state type is necessary and sufficient for the state type to be of category C, then we might think of all tokens of state types in C as tokens, also, of ϕ. *Being a token of ϕ*, then, is a property a state token has in virtue of being of a type which itself has a certain property. (Note that an analogous sort of derivative or indirect categorization is standard fare when we are talking about linguistic types and tokens. The word (type) 'linguistic' falls into the category of adjectives, and thus the token of 'linguistic' that occurs in the previous sentence in this volume may also be thought of as a token of an adjective.) This completes my brief excursion into ontology; let us return, now, to the STM.

The theorist's job in setting out an STM cognitive theory can be viewed as having three parts. First, he must specify a class of syntactic objects (types, of course, not tokens) and do so in a way which assigns a formal or syntactic structure to each of these objects. Since there will commonly be infinitely many objects in the class, this is best done with a grammar or a set of formation rules detailing the ways in which complex syntactic objects may be built out of a finite set of primitives.

Second, the theorist hypothesizes that for each organism covered by the theory, there exists a set of state types whose tokens are causally implicated in the production of behavior. He also hypothesizes that there is a mapping from these state types to syntactic objects in the specified class. Several observations about these hypotheses are in order. First, the theorist need say very little about the essential nature of the state tokens which are causally implicated in the production of behavior. Presumably they are physical states of the brain, and thus the properties which constitute their essential types are neurological properties, though an STM theorist who wishes to be coy or cautious need not even commit himself on this point. (Since it will simplify my exposition considerably, I will henceforth suppose that the states causally implicated in the production of behavior are neurological.) Second, in asserting the existence of the mapping, the order of the quantifiers is of some importance. The theorist is not claiming that the mapping is the same for each subject, but only that for each subject there is a mapping. So in different subjects, quite different neurological state types may be mapped to a given syntactic object. These first two points, of course, are in the spirit of functionalism, which stresses the possibility of multiple realizations of mental states. A third point is that the theorist need not restrict himself to claiming a single mapping from neurological states to his chosen class of formal objects. Rather, he may assert that there are several categories of neurological states and that states in each category are mapped to the formal objects. For example, if the theory takes its lead from folk psychology, it may postulate two distinct classes of states underlying behavior, belief-like states and desire-like states, with state types of *both* classes mapped to a single class of formal objects. So a given belief-like state type and a given desire-like state type may both be mapped to the same formal object. Finally, the mapping from both the belief-like category and the desire-like category is supposed to cover all of the possible state types in that category, and it will generally be assumed that an infinite number of distinct state types are possible in each category.

The third part of a cognitive theory built on the STM pattern is a specification of the theory's generalizations. The core idea of the STM— the idea that makes it *syntactic*—is that generalizations detailing causal relations among the hypothesized neurological states are to be specified indirectly via the formal relations among the syntactic objects to which the neurological state types are mapped. Similarly, generalizations specifying causal relations between stimuli and neurological states will identify the neurological states not by adverting to their essential neurological types but, rather, by adverting to the syntactic objects to which the neurological types are mapped. Ditto for generalizations specifying causal relations between neurological states and behavior.

At this point the reader may well be experiencing a certain sense of déjà vu, since if the syntactic objects chosen by the theorist are *sentences*, then the neurological states postulated by an STM-style theory are of a piece with *narrow causally individuated mental sentences*, as this notion was explained in chapter 3. Since hypothesized neurological state types are mapped to sentence types, the tokens of these neurological states might plausibly be taken to be tokens (in the derivative sense) of the sentence types to which their neurological type is matched. Since there may be different categories of hypothetical neurological states, a subject may have more than one token of a given sentence type among his mental states. He may, for example, have one token of a sentence type which is a belief-like state and another which is a desire-like state; or he may have a desire-like state which is a token of a conditional sentence and a belief-like state which is a token of the antecedent of the conditional.

It is not, strictly speaking, required for an STM theorist to view hypothesized neurological state tokens as mental sentence tokens, though talking of them in this way is often an all but unavoidable shorthand. If we wish to view tokens of the states postulated by an STM-style theory as sentence tokens, then we must say something more about the individuation or typing of these sentence tokens. Since the motivation for viewing hypothetical neurological state tokens as sentence tokens is to describe causal relations by adverting to syntactic ones, we must ask just *which* syntactic relations must be mirrored for the neurological state tokens to count as sentence tokens. There are, I think, three rather different answers that might be given. One idea is to insist that if a neurological state token is to count as a token of a sentence it must satisfy *all* the generalizations specified by the theory. This strategy has a notable disadvantage, since even small changes in the theory's generalizations entail a modification in the account of what it is to be a token of a mental sentence type. A second idea, which avoids this difficulty, is to specify a set of *essential* generalizations which a neurological state must satisfy if its tokens are to count as tokens of a given sentence type. Further generalizations may be added and modified as necessary, without altering the account of typing. But this approach, too, has its shortcomings. It is hard to see what motivation there can be for distinguishing a special set of generalizations as the essential ones, hard to see how the divide between essential and non-essential generalizations could be anything but arbitrary. A third idea is to evade the issue by insisting only that to count as a token of a sentence type, a neurological state must satisfy some substantial number of the cluster of generalizations included in a theory, without specifying any particular generalizations that must be satisfied, nor exactly how many must be satisfied. This avoids the problem that beset the first strategy, since it allows for modification in the set of generalizations, without changing our story on what it is for a state token to count as a sentence token. It also avoids the arbitrariness of the second strategy. But it does so at the cost of introducing an element of vagueness into the account of token typing. Theorists who actually develop theories along the lines urged by the STM tend to be little concerned with the issue, though I suspect that if pressed, they would opt for the third strategy as the one which best captures their intentions.*

We should note that on any of the three strategies for typing mental tokens, there is a sort of holism involved. It is only against the background of a systematic mapping of state types to sentence types that any given state token counts as a token of a particular sentence type. Or to put the point in another way, no one neurological state can count as a token of a sentence type unless many neurological states count as tokens of many different sentence types. But this holism, it should be stressed, is quite distinct from the holism imposed on the folk psychological notion of belief by the embedded appeal to ideological similarity. For the status of a state as a token of a sentence does not depend on what other cognitive states a subject currently happens to be in. It depends only on the causal interactions that the state would exhibit with stimuli, with behavior, and with other states.

Having said this much about the general pattern of STM theories, let me now focus in on a particular example. Since my aim is to compare STM theories with theories built on the Strong RTM pattern, the example I will elaborate is chosen with an eye to facilitating that comparison by mimicking content-based theories as closely as possible. But, I hasten to add, ease of comparison is bought at the price of psychological plausibility and sophistication. Nothing in the STM requires cognitive theories to mimic content-based theories, and if I am right in my contention that contemporary computational theories in psychology are STM theories, then obviously STM theories are often far from simple. The example I want to consider here takes as its abstract objects a class of sentences or, better, *well-formed formulas* (wffs) with the simple underlying syntax of first-order quantification theory. It will sometimes be convenient to talk of this class of sentences as a *language*. But it is important not to be misled by this terminology. The language is no more than an infinite class of complex syntactic objects. *It has no semantics.* To specify the language, we begin by detailing its basic vo-

*Déjà vu experiences sometimes come in pairs. The reader with a background in the philosophy of science will have noted that the last paragraph echoes the debate over the conditions under which theoretical entities postulated by different, incompatible, theories count as the same. Well it might, since the question of token typing is simply a special case of this more general issue. Cf. Putnam (1962b).

cabulary. There is a large, though finite, stock of one-place predicate letters, $P_1^1, P_2^1, \ldots, P_k^1$, a somewhat smaller stock of two-place predicate letters, $P_1^2, P_2^2, \ldots, P_j^2$, a smaller still stock of three-place predicate letters, $P_1^3, P_2^3, \ldots, P_i^3$, and perhaps a smattering of four- and five-place predicate letters as well. There is also a finite stock of individual constants, $c_1, c_2, \ldots, c_m$, and a large stock of variables, $x_1, x_2, \ldots, x_n$. Finally, the language contains the usual quantifiers and truth functional connectives. The formation rules are just what one would expect, and among the symbol sequences they count as wffs are the following:

$$\sim P_3^1 c_2$$

$$(x_1)(x_2)P_8^2 x_1, x_2$$

$$(\exists x_1)(P_4^1 c_8 \supset P_6^1 x_1)$$

$$(x_1)(P_2^1 x_1 \& P_9^1 x_1) \supset (\exists x_1)(x_2)(P_2^3 c_2, x_1, x_2)$$

along, of course, with infinitely many others.

Since we are aiming to sketch an STM theory that sticks as closely as possible to folk psychology, let us suppose that the theory postulates two categories of states which interact to produce behavior: B-states (roughly analogous to beliefs) and D-states (roughly analogous to desires). The theory also hypothesizes that there is a mapping from B-state types to wffs and a mapping from D-state types to wffs. (To actually specify the mapping we would no doubt need some way of viewing most B- and D-states as compound entities, built from a limited number of primitives by a limited number of compounding operations. In short, we would have to view B- and D-states as having a structure which parallels the structure of wffs. But an STM theorist need say very little on all this, since he is merely postulating the existence of B- and D-states and the existence of the mappings.)

The substantive and empirically exacting part of the theory consists in a set of generalizations which detail causal interactions among stimuli, B- and D-states, and behavioral events by appeal to the syntactic structure of the wffs to which they are mapped. I do not propose here to offer generalizations with great psychological plausibility. But a few rough-and-ready examples may serve the dual purpose of illustrating what these generalizations may look like and facilitating the comparison with theories whose generalizations appeal to content. Here then are a few generalizations that might be part of a syntactic psychological theory, beginning with three which are the syntactic analogues of (1″)–(3″) of chapter 7.

(4)   For all subjects S, and all wffs A and B, if

S has a D-state mapped to A ⊃ B*

and if

S comes to have a B-state mapped to A,

then

S will come to have a D-state mapped to B.

(5)   For all subjects S, and all wffs A and B, if

S has a B-state mapped to A ⊃ B

and if

S comes to have a B-state mapped to A,

then

S will come to have a B-state mapped to B.**

(6)   For all subjects S, and all wffs A and B, if

S has a B-state mapped to A, and if this causes A to have the B-state mapped to B, and if subsequently, S ceases to have the B-state mapped to A,

then it is probably that

S will continue to have the B-state mapped to B.

Another generalization might go something like the following:

(7)   For all subjects S, and all wffs A and B, if

A syntactically entails B,

then

the probability that S will come to have the B-state mapped to B after coming to have the B-state mapped to A is significantly higher than the probability that S will come to have

---

*I.e., a D-state mapped to the wff consisting of A followed by '⊃' followed by B.
**This generalization claims, in effect, that the class of B-states is closed under modus ponens. If he wishes, the theorist might strengthen this to the claim that B-states are closed under entailment. To do this, he must first introduce the syntactic notion of entailment along the usual lines and then propose a generalization something like the following:

For all subjects S, and all wffs A and B, if

S has a B-state mapped to A,

and if

A syntactically entails B,

then

S has (will come to have?) a B-state mapped to B.

Needless to say, this is a singularly implausible claim.

the B-state mapped to B after coming to have the B-state mapped to $\sim\sim A$.

Many more examples might be offered, but these four should suffice to give the flavor of generalizations in a syntactic theory of the mind.

The next issue that we must address is the *testing* of a syntactic theory. Since the only states spoken of (4)–(7) are nonobservational posits of the theory, just how are these generalizations to confront behavioral data? The answer is twofold. First, of course, intratheoretic generalizations are not the only ones that an STM theorist may put forward. He may also advance generalizations that tie stimuli to B- and D-states or that link the latter to behavior. But commonly an STM theorist will not have nearly enough of the these generalizations to put his theory to the test, at least not in the early days of theory construction. And for the foreseeable future, all days will be early days. So if theory is to confront data, the syntactic theorist will have to make a significant number of ad hoc assumptions about causal links between B- and D-states on the one hand, and stimuli and behavior on the other. These will be assumptions which the theorist takes to hold reliably enough in the experimental setting and for the subjects on whom the experiments are being run. It will generally be clear that these assumptions do not hold for other quite normal subjects. Recall that a quite parallel set of special or ad hoc assumptions was required for the testing of cognitive theories whose generalizations were cast in folk psychological terms. Having said this much, let us turn to an example.

Consider a theorist who is trying to test (7) with typical English-speaking undergraduate subjects. One way to proceed would be to provide the subjects with some sentences putatively detailing facts about an unfamiliar domain, require them to memorize the sentences, then give them a quiz. The putative facts might include sentences like the following:

(8)   Among the Moa people of New Guinea, it is common for a man to have several wives and several separate dwellings.

(9)   Among the Moa people of new Guinea, it is not uncommon for a man to have several wives and several separate dwellings.

And the quiz might include a true-false question along the lines of:

(10)   Among the Moa people of New Guinea, it is common for a man to have several separate dwellings.

If the subjects perform as expected, those who have been given (8) will check the "true" box for (10) more frequently than those who have been given (9). For such data to count as confirming the generalization (7), the theorist must assume that there are wffs, A and B such that:

> on reading (8) the subjects commonly come to have a B-state mapped to A&B,

and

> on reading (9) the subjects commonly come to have a B-state mapped to $\sim \sim (A\&B)$,

and

> if a subject is given test question (10), then commonly he will check the "true" box if and only if he has a B-state mapped to B.

(I trust it goes without saying that I am oversimplifying in all sorts of ways.) Given these assumptions, the experimental results the theorist expects would indeed provide some confirmation for (7). And of course, if it should turn out that subjects who have been given (8) check the "true" box no more frequently than those who have been given (9), this is some reason to think that (7) is mistaken.

Analogously a theorist might use the belief perseverance experiment sketched at the end of chapter 7, section 1 as a test of generalization (6). However, the necessary ad hoc assumptions required would be syntactic analogues of the assumptions made by a theorist who couches his theory in terms of content. If the experiment is to serve as a test for (6), what must be assumed is that there are a pair of wffs, A and B, such that in the first part of the experiment, subjects commonly come to have the B-state mapped to A; that this commonly causes subjects to acquire the belief state mapped to B; that in the second part of the experiment (where subjects are told that they have been deceived) they commonly cease to have the belief state mapped to A; and that given the questionnaire in the last part of the experiment, subjects commonly check the "yes" box on the question about latent homosexual tendencies if and only if they have the B-state mapped to B.

Though I have been painting with a rather broad brush, I think we now have a sufficiently detailed sketch of syntactic theories. It is time to see how they compare to cognitive theories in the Strong RTM mold.

2. The Advantages of STM Theories

It is my contention that STM theories are a better choice for the cognitive theorist than those theories whose generalizations appeal to content, since syntactic theories can do justice to all of the generalizations capturable by quantifying over content sentences while avoiding the limitations that the folk language of content impose. Thus STM theories can capture generalizations which are beyond the reach of theories in the Strong RTM mold. A particularly handy way to highlight the advantages of STM theories is to return, for a moment, to figure 2 in chapter 5. Strong RTM theories take belief and other folk constructs seriously by generalizing over the content sentences that are used in ascribing folk psychological states. And, as depicted in figure 2, a subject's belief counts as the belief *that p* if it is content similar to the belief that would underlie *our own* normal assertion of 'p'. Content-similarity, in turn, resolves into causal-pattern similarity, ideological similarity, reference similarity, and perhaps some others. Now, to put the matter most simply, *the virtue of STM theories is that they eliminate the middleman.* The mental states postulated by an STM theory are not characterized by their content sentences but, rather, by the syntactic objects to which they are mapped. These can be selected by the theorist with an eye to giving the simplest and most powerful account of the causal links among stimuli, mental states, and behavior and without any concern for similarities or dissimilarities between the subject and the theorist. By eliminating the middleman, STM theories are able to characterize the cognitive states of a subject in terms appropriate to the subject rather than in terms that force a comparison between the subject and ourselves. And this eliminates the central problem of Strong RTM theories, since there is no risk of generalizations being lost when subjects are so different from us that folk psychology is at a loss to describe them. Further, by eliminating the appeal to various dimensions of *similarity* much of the vagueness that plagues content-based cognitive theories is eliminated as well.

Let me pin down these points by working through a few examples. In chapter 7, section 3 our focus was on ideological similarity, and the persistent problem was that as subjects became increasingly ideologically distant from ourselves, we lost our folk psychological grip on how to characterize their beliefs. For a syntactic theory, however, ideological similarity poses no problem, since the characterization of a B-state does not depend on the other B-states that the subject happens to have. A B-state will count as a token of a wff if its potential causal links fit the pattern detailed in the theorist's generalizations, regardless of the further B-states the subject may have or lack. Consider, for example, the case of Mrs. T. If we assume that before the onset of her disease the B-state which commonly caused her to say "McKinley was assassinated" obeyed generalizations like (4)–(6), then if the illness simply destroys B-states (or erases mental tokens) without affecting the causal potential of the tokens which remain, the very same generalizations will be true of her after the illness has become quite severe. In chapter 7 we imagined a little experiment in which, shortly before her death, we tell Mrs. T, "If McKinley was assassinated, then he is buried in Ohio," and she replies, "Well, then, he is buried in Ohio." This is readily explainable by (5) along with the very same ad hoc assumptions we would make in applying (5) before Mrs. T became ill. So if the generalization is there, it can be captured by a syntactic theory. But as we saw, there is no comfortable way to capture this generalization in the language of folk psychology. The ideological divide between Mrs. T and ourselves is too great. The story is essentially the same for the other two cases considered in chapter 7: the child naive about numbers and the subject with eccentric views about sex. In both cases the ideological oddity of the subject poses no problems for an STM theory. The very same generalizations apply to them and to people who are ideologically unproblematic. Thus a cognitive science that adopts the STM paradigm can aspire to broadly applicable developmental, clinical, and comparative theories, all of which are problematic for a content-based theory because of the constraints of ideological similarity.

In section 4 of chapter 7 we saw some examples of the way in which reference similarity impedes the statement of generalizations couched in terms of content. In the case of Mr. Binh, the causal history of his use of 'Jefferson' was so tangled that there was no saying what it referred to. And this, in turn, made it difficult to find comfortable characterizations of the content of the beliefs Binh expressed using the word. But for an STM theory, the odd causal history of Binh's Jefferson-concept poses no problem. As far as a syntactic theory is concerned, the B-state that causes Binh to say "Jefferson was a patriot" and the B-state that causes us to say it may both be treated as tokens of the same wff. Generalizations that apply to our B-state will apply equally to his. Thus (4) can be used straightforwardly to explain his performance on the imagined quiz, though its content analogue (1″) is problematic. In a similar fashion the vagueness illustrated with Burge's arthritis example simply does not arise for an STM theorist, since a syntactic theory ignores the subject's linguistic context. Regardless of how different linguistic practice may be in Bob's community, a syntactic theory will count the B-state underlying his utterance of "The arthritis is in my calves" and the B-state underlying the same utterance produced by a suitably similar person in our community as tokens of the same type. The taxonomy of cognitive states imposed by an STM theory is a narrow causal taxonomy, insensitive to those reference-fixing relations that extend beyond the cognitive states, stimuli, and behavior of the subject.

As we noted in section 5 of chapter 7, subjects who are markedly causal-pattern dissimilar from us create a rather different problem for

Strong RTM theories. The cognitive states of these subjects do not satisfy the same generalizations as our cognitive states. So what is needed is a separate set of generalizations descriptive of these subjects. However, the very causal-pattern divergences which lead us to seek a separate set of generalizations also undermine the content-based theory's capacity to express these generalizations. If our subjects are children, the problem is compounded by their ideological distance from us. But neither causal nor ideological distance poses any special problems for an STM theorist. To handle subjects whose basic cognitive processes differ from our own, the syntactic theorist may specify a distinct set of wffs (a different "mental language") and a distinct set of generalizations exploiting the syntactic structure of these wffs. Or, of course, it may suffice to keep the same set of wffs and simply fiddle with the generalizations, though if the generalizations are modified substantially, this will alter the implicit account of what is to count as a token of a wff. Having had some success with a theory about children at a given stage of development, an STM theorist may go on to seek diachronic or developmental generalizations which detail regularities in the sequence of mental languages-cum-generalizations that characterize children as they mature. For the theorist working in the Strong RTM mold, by contrast, the prospects for a developmental theory seem dim, since both causal pattern and ideological dissimilarity block any comfortable characterization of the content of cognitive states of young children.

3. Methodological Solipsism and the Autonomy Principle

Let me summarize where the argument of part II has taken us thus far. The question at hand is whether the notion of belief and related folk psychological notions will find a comfortable home in cognitive science. One view that urges an affirmative answer is the Strong Representational Theory of the Mind, which sees a mature cognitive science postulating representational states and adverting to content in its generalizations. However, in chapter 7 we assembled a number of arguments aimed at showing that the cognitive scientist is ill advised to adopt the Strong RTM paradigm. The cost in vagueness and in missed generalizations is very high. In the current chapter, I have been arguing that there is a better alternative available. The Syntactic Theory of the Mind, by avoiding any appeal to content in cognitive generalizations, sidesteps the difficulties that beset the Strong RTM. In this section I want to buttress the case in favor of the STM as an alternative to the Strong RTM by developing a pair of arguments. Each of these arguments works by defending a principle about what psychological theories should be like. The principles, *methodological solipsism* and the *principle of autonomy*, are very closely related, and each clearly entails that cognitive psychology should not aspire to couch its generalizations in terms of content. The arguments in favor of the principles are very different, however, both in their strategy and in their plausibility. Though neither argument pretends to be apodictic, I am inclined to think that the argument to be developed for the autonomy principle is significantly more persuasive than the argument for methodological solipsism. But perhaps this is because the former argument is mine. The latter is due to Jerry Fodor. I include it here not because I think it adds much weight to the case for the STM and against the Strong RTM, but because it has been so widely discussed that no consideration of these matters can ignore it. Let me begin with methodological solipsism.

The term 'methodological solipsism' was originally introduced by Putnam[2] to characterize a view he wished to disparage. On Putnam's account, there is a distinction between "psychological states in the wide sense" and "psychological states in the narrow sense."[3] Psychological states in the narrow sense do not presuppose "the existence of any individual other than the subject to whom the state is ascribed."[4] Psychological states in the wide sense do presuppose the existence of some other object or individual. Pain might be a natural example of a narrow psychological state, while being jealous of Henry is a prima facie example of a psychological state in the wide sense, since it entails the existence of Henry. (Strictly speaking, of course, it is not the state that entails Henry's existence; rather, the statement that the state obtains entails the statement that Henry exists.) The doctrine of methodological solipsism holds that psychology ought to be concerned exclusively with psychological states in the narrow sense. It is the burden of Putnam's argument that methodological solipsism is untenable since it excludes from psychology such states as knowing the meaning of a term.

Fodor, by contrast, urges that we adopt methodological solipsism as a research strategy in cognitive psychology. However, in Fodor's hands, the notion of methodological solipsism undergoes important elaboration. His central thesis is that mental states and processes, or at least those that cognitive psychology ought to concern itself with, are "computational."[5] "Computational processes are both *symbolic* and *formal*. They are symbolic because they are defined over representations, and they are formal because they apply to representations in virtue of (roughly) their *syntax*" (p. 226). Further, "what makes syntactic operations a species of formal operations is that being syntactic is a way of *not* being semantic. Formal operations are the ones which are specified without reference to such semantic properties of representations as truth, reference and meaning" (p. 227). Finally, it would appear that for Fodor, methodological solipsism is simply the doctrine that *cognitive psychology*

ought to restrict itself to postulating formal operations on mental states.
It ought not to postulate processes which apply to mental states in
virtue of their semantic properties. Fodor is quite forthright in conceding
that the doctrine of methodological solipsism is less than precise, since
he can provide neither a criterion nor a complete enumeration of what
is to count as a semantic property.

As should be clear, methodological solipsism is thoroughly congenial
to the Syntactic Theory of the Mind. It also entails the rejection of the
Strong RTM. For on any plausible account of what counts as semantic,
the theorist who couches his generalizations (his account of mental
processes) in terms of the *content sentences* used to characterize mental
states is surely postulating mental operations whose specification requires reference to semantic properties of these states. The case is clearest, I suppose, for reference, which is a semantic notion par excellence.
Since reference similarity is one of the features determining the propriety
of a content sentence, any mental operation whose specification turns
on the content sentences appropriate to the states involved will run
afoul of the methodological solipsist's scruples. By contrast, cognitive
theories in the STM mold are paradigm cases of the sort of theory a
methodological solipsist would endorse. So it would appear that a
sound argument for methodological solipsism would provide us with
another reason to prefer the STM over the Strong RTM.

For our purposes the essential part of Fodor's argument is his defense
of the formality condition which requires that semantic properties of
mental states play no role in the specification of psychological generalizations. Unfortunately, what Fodor says on this topic is none too
perspicuous. As I read him, he argues as follows. First, if a mental state
has semantic properties, these are presumably fixed by one or more
"organism/environment relations" (p. 244). Second, those psychologists
who would flout the formality condition and reject methodological
solipsism (Fodor calls them "naturalists") "propose to make science
out of the organism/environment relations which (presumably) fix semantic properties" (p. 244). Third, to do this the naturalist "would
have to define generalizations over mental states on the one hand and
environmental entities on the other" (p. 249). But, fourth, to define
such generalizations, the naturalist must have some "canonical way of
referring to the latter," and this way must make the generalizations
"law-instantiating" (p. 249) when the environmental entities are so
described. Put in another way, the characterization of the objects on
the environmental side of organism/environment interaction must be
"projectable" characterizations (p. 250), which "express nomologically
necessary properties" (p. 249) of the objects. As Fodor sees it, however,
this last point is the kicker. For, fifth, to get such projectable or law-

instantiating characterizations we must wait for appropriate develop-
ments in the science that studies that object. If the object is salt, then
the appropriate projectable characterization, viz. 'NaCl', will be "available only *after* we've done our chemistry" (p. 249). But since the objects
on the environment side might be anything we can think about or refer
to, we will not have appropriate characterizations for these objects until
all of the nonpsychological sciences have done their work. "The theory
which characterizes the objects of thought is the theory of *everything*;
it's all of science. Hence . . . naturalistic psychologists will inherit the
Earth, but only after everybody else is finished with it." (p. 248) We
ought not to attempt a naturalistic psychology, Fodor concludes, because
the attempt must wait on all of the other sciences to provide projectable
characterizations of the environmental objects interacting with the organism. "No doubt it's all right to have a research strategy that says
'wait awhile'. But who wants to wait *forever*?" (p. 248)

Though I would happily endorse the principle of methodological
solipsism, I am a bit wary about the reasoning that supports it. If I
have reconstructed Fodor's argument correctly, then there are two places
in which I suspect it is open to attack. The first is step three, which
claims that to "make science" out of those organism/environment relations which determine reference amounts to seeking *nomological generalizations* linking environmental entities and mental states. This is
surely *one* way in which a science concerned with reference-fixing
relations might proceed, and as Fodor points out it has typically been
what psychologists of a naturalistic bent have sought.[6] But, as best I
can see, there is no necessity for those who would make science of the
organism/environment interactions which underlie reference to do so
by seeking causal laws. There are, after all, many quite respectable
scientific domains, from descriptive botany, ethology, and paleobiology
to anthropology and linguistics, in which the quest for nomological
generalizations plays a relatively minor role. Focusing on the case at
hand, it is certainly true, as the second step of Fodor's argument suggests,
that if a psychologist couches his cognitive generalizations in terms of
the content sentences appropriate to various states, then his theory will
in one way or another *involve* those organism/environment relations
which contribute to determining the propriety of content sentences.
But without further argument, it is not at all clear that the psychologist
who pursues the Strong RTM strategy must seek *nomological generalizations about* those reference and content determining organism/
environment relations.

The second spot where I fear Fodor's argument is vulnerable is step
five, which claims that appropriate projectable characterizations of the
objects on the environment side of organism/environment interactions

will be forthcoming only from the sciences that study these objects. There is a strong suggestion in Fodor's essay that physics and chemistry are the appropriate sciences to look to for natural kinds like salt and water, and he expresses some puzzlement about "what science does uncles and umbrellas and undertakers."[7] Now perhaps Fodor has better antennae than I do for these delicate matters, but without further argument I am not convinced that such commonsense predicates as 'salt', 'uncle', and 'undertaker' are not perfectly respectable candidates for incorporation in nomological generalizations. They are, no doubt, not the ideal projectable predicates to be used in the generalizations of physics and chemistry. But those of us who take the special sciences seriously have come to expect that the classificatory schemes invoked in those sciences will cut across the classificatory grain imposed by physics. Physics and chemistry, presumably, will have no generalizations invoking 'uncle' or 'umbrella', but anthropology and economics might well find these terms rather more useful. Ironically, Fodor himself has been an eloquent defender of the scientific respectability of classificatory schemes which do not reduce smoothly to those of the physical sciences.[8]

Despite all this, I am a bit reluctant simply to dismiss Fodor's argument for methodological solipsism. Perhaps the argument can be fleshed out in a way which makes clear why the cognitive psychologist who would use folk psychological notions must seek the sorts of generalizations required by step three. And perhaps something more can be said to establish that workaday predicates like 'salt' and 'umbrella' are not suitable for formulating organism/environment generalizations. But absent these elaborations, I am not inclined to rest much weight on the argument.

Let me turn, now, to the principle of autonomy. The basic idea of the principle is that the states and processes that ought to be of concern to the psychologist are those that supervene on the current, internal, physical state of the organism. (One class of states and processes supervenes on another when, roughly speaking, the presence or absence of states and processes in the first class is completely determined by the presence or absence of states and processes in the second.[9]) What this amounts to is the claim that any differences between organisms which do not manifest themselves as differences in their current, internal, physical states ought to be ignored by a psychological theory. If we respect the autonomy principle, then the fact that a pair of organisms have different histories or that they are in significantly different environments will be irrelevant to a psychological theory except insofar as these differences make a difference to the organism's current, internal, physical state. Or, to put the matter the other way around, historical and environmental facts will be psychologically relevant only when they influence an organism's current, internal, physical state. So if a feature of the organism's history or environment might have been different without affecting the organism's current, internal, physical state, then that historical or environmental feature must play no role in the psychologist's theory.

Like methodological solipsism, the autonomy principle is incompatible with the explanatory strategy urged in the Strong RTM. The autonomy principle prohibits generalizations couched in terms of the content sentences that characterize mental states, since the propriety of a content sentence in characterizing a mental state is in part determined by reference similarity. Reference in turn is determined in part by the distant causal histories of a subject's term or concept and in part by the sociolinguistic environment in which the subject is embedded. But neither of these factors need leave their trace on the current, internal, physical state of the organism. Thus it is possible for a pair of subjects to differ in the reference of some term they use even though there is no corresponding difference in their current, internal, physical state. The formality condition urged by the methodological solipsist directly prohibits generalizations which turn on semantic properties of the states to which they apply. The principle of psychological autonomy accomplishes much the same goal by barring appeal to those external historical and environmental factors on which semantic properties like reference in part depend.

In the paper in which I proposed the autonomy principle, I offered no argument in its defense, since it seemed to have substantial intuitive plausibility.[10] But in subsequent discussion it has become clear that the intuitive appeal of the autonomy principle begins to pale when people see just what it entails about the use of folk psychological notions in scientific psychology. So plainly some argument is in order. I think the best defense of the autonomy principle begins with what might be called the *replacement argument*. Suppose that someone were to succeed in building an exact physical replica of me—a living human body whose current internal physical states at a given moment were identical to mine at that moment. And suppose further that while fast asleep I am kidnapped and replaced by the replica. It would appear that if the crime were properly concealed, no one (apart from the kidnappers and myself) would be the wiser. For the replica, being an exact physical copy, would behave just as I would in all circumstances. Even the replica himself would not suspect that he was an imposter. But now, the argument continues, since psychology is the science which aspires to explain behavior, any states or processes or properties which are not shared by Stich and his identically behaving replica must surely be irrelevant to psychology.

I think there is an important kernel of truth in the replacement argument. But as it stands, it plainly will not do. The problem is that in many circumstances my replica and I do not (indeed could not) behave in the same way, at least not as our behavior would ordinarily be described. An example will serve to make the point. One of my possessions is an old clunker of a car. If you were to offer me $1000 for it, I would delightedly sell it to you on the spot. But suppose that just prior to your offer I had been kidnapped and my replica sent out into the world in my place. Being quite unaware of the switch you offer the $1000 to my replica, and he agrees to the sale with the same sincere delight that I would exhibit. When it comes down to actually transferring ownership, however, my replica's behavior and mine diverge. He signs all the appropriate documents just as I would, and the signatures would convince a handwriting expert. Nonetheless, my replica does not sell you the old clunker. He can't, since he does not own it. I do. So it would appear to be just plain false that my replica and I would behave identically. I would sell you the car, and he wouldn't.

Now I think the right move to make in response to this objection is to grant the point. If we are willing to countenance the full range of commonsense descriptions of behavior, then it is false that a person and his replica will always behave identically. However, we should not expect a psychological theory to predict or explain behavior under any and every description countenanced by common sense. To see this more clearly, an analogy with chemistry is useful. It may be quite true that boiling a bottle of Chateau Lafitte causes a substantial reduction in its market value. But this is nothing that we expect chemistry alone to explain. Rather, we expect chemistry to explain the effects of boiling described in an appropriately delimited, proprietary chemical vocabulary. Moreover, there is not likely to be any antecedently obvious specification of the range of descriptions appropriate in chemical explananda. Elaborating or delimiting the language in which explananda are to be described is one aspect and often quite a fundamental aspect of theory construction in science.[11] To explain why boiling causes a decline in the market value of Chateau Lafitte we will have to supplement the chemical explanation of the effects of boiling with facts about the way chemical changes affect the sensory qualities of a wine and facts about the relation between sensory qualities and the market value of rare Bordeaux wines. The situation is similar in psychology. We cannot expect that a scientific psychology will explain behavioral events under all imaginable descriptions. Rather the psychologist must select or formulate an appropriate descriptive language for his explananda. And the formulation of such a vocabulary will be a fundamental part of psychological theory construction.*

Now where does this leave the autonomy principle? Well, the replacement argument maintained that an organism and its replica would behave identically and thus should be regarded as psychologically identical. But we then granted that an organism and its replica will not behave identically on some characterizations of behavior. Let me introduce the term *autonomous behavioral description* for any description of behavior which satisfies the following condition: if it applies to an organism in a given setting, then it would also apply to any replica of the organism in that setting. It would appear, then, that the issue before us reduces to the question of whether autonomous behavioral descriptions include all those that a psychologist will find useful in constructing systematic explanations of behavior. If the answer is affirmative, then the replacement argument leads to the desired conclusion, since replicas will behave identically in identical settings, when the behavior is described in the psychologists' proprietary behavioral-descriptive language. So let us ask whether there is any reason to think that autonomous behavioral descriptions include all those that a psychologist will find useful.

In thinking about this question it is helpful to reflect on the analogy between organisms and industrial robots. Both robots and organisms are complex, largely internally controlled systems which interact with their environments in systematic ways. Unless one is tempted by dualism, it is plausible to think that theories explaining the behavior of various sorts of robots and theories explaining the behavior of various sorts of organisms will be at least roughly analogous. So let us ask whether we would expect a theory of "robot psychology" to attempt

---

*Fodor gets this point just exactly right:

> It's worth emphasizing that the sense of "behavior" *is* proprietary, and that is pretty much what you would expect. Not every true description of an act can be such that a theory of the mental causation of behavior will explain the act under that description. . . . You can't have explanations of everything under every description, and it's a question for empirical determination which descriptions of behavior reveal its systematicity vis-à-vis its causes.[11]
> (Fodor (1980a), pp. 330–331)

Wilkes makes essentially the same point:

> Every science must devise a taxonomy of the events that fall within its domain of discourse, and hence has to devise a descriptive vocabulary of observational and theoretical predicates. Since events can be variously described, not every description of an action or a capacity for action will be a description in the domain of psychology.
> (Wilkes (1981), p. 150)

explanations of robot behavior under nonautonomous descriptions. As a beginning, we should note that there are many ways in which the doings of a robot might be described in nonautonomous language. For example, a given robot on the production line at General Motors might, on a certain occasion, successfully perform its millionth weld. Although 'performing its millionth weld' might be a correct description of what the robot does, it is clearly not an autonomous description. If, just prior to performing the weld, the robot in question had been replaced by a brand new replica robot, the replica would have performed a qualitatively identical weld. But it would be successfully performing its first weld, not its millionth. In performing a weld, a robot might also be falsifying Professor Hubert's prediction that no robot would ever perform a million welds, and simultaneously fulfilling a provision in the contract between General Motors and the robot's manufacturer. But again, neither of these descriptions of the robot's behavior is autonomous. It seems obvious that if we seek systematic generalizations to explain the robot's behavior, we should not expect our generalizations to explain the robot's behavior under *these* descriptions. The descriptions under which we expect a theory of robot behavior to explain that behavior are autonomous descriptions.

This is not to suggest that there is anything mysterious about the fact that the older robot performed its millionth weld, or that it falsified Professor Hubert's prediction, or that it fulfilled the contract. What it does suggest is that these facts and the descriptions which recount them are best viewed as logical or conceptual hybrids. To successfully perform its one millionth weld, a device must successfully perform a weld *and* it must have previously performed 999,999 other welds. The first element in this conjunct describes the behavior autonomously; it is just the sort of fact that we expect a theory of robot behavior to explain. The second element is a historical fact, and it is not at all what we expect a theory of robot behavior to explain. An analogous account can be given of the fact that the robot fulfilled a provision of the contract. Here again we have a conceptual hybrid, with one element being the occurrence of an autonomously described behavioral event and the other being the existence of a contract containing certain provisions about what the robot will or must do. If we are seeking a set of generalizations to explain robot behavior, it would be perverse to expect them to explain the latter fact or the hybrid into which it enters.

The view suggested by these examples is that all non-autonomous descriptions of robot behavior are conceptually complex hybrids. An explanation of the behavior they describe would naturally divide into two parts, the first being a theory of "robot psychology" which explains autonomously described behavioral events and the second being a heterogeneous collection of considerations from history, law, or what have you which collectively explain why the autonomously described event *counts* also as an event falling under the non-autonomous description. Now if the analogy between robots and organisms is a good one—and I think it is—it suggests that we should seek a parallel pattern of explanation in real psychology (as contrasted with "robot psychology"). We should expect to have our theory aim at explaining behavioral events autonomously described. Non-autonomous descriptions of behavioral events should be viewed as conceptually complex, resolvable into an autonomous component and a potpourri of other factors which explain why the autonomously described event *counts* as satisfying the non-autonomous description. Of course the other factors that enter into the analysis of non-autonomous behavioral descriptions will be rather richer and more complex when the subjects of our theory are people instead of animals or industrial robots. They may include the history of the individual in question, the history of the terms he uses, the linguistic, social, legal, and ritual practices that obtain in the society of which he is a part, and perhaps many other factors as well. So if our analogy is a good one, it is plausible to conclude that the descriptions of behavior that a psychological theory should use in its explananda will be autonomous descriptions. This is just the conclusion we needed to make a go of the replacement argument and thus to support the principle of autonomy.

On the view I have been urging, non-autonomous commonsense descriptions of behavior are typically conceptual hybrids. Sometimes there will be a readily available commonsense description of the autonomous conponent of a non-autonomous act. But this need not always be the case. It may be that substantial work needs to be done in forging appropriate autonomous behavioral descriptions for use in scientific psychology.[12] But this should come as no surprise, for, as we remarked earlier, the formulation of an appropriate terminology for describing the explananda is often an essential step in the growth of a new science. Note by the way, that there is no reason to expect that the autonomous behavior-descriptive terminology ultimately found to be most useful will be a purely physical description of movements of the sort that behaviorists sought but never found.

In evolving hybrid non-autonomous behavioral descriptions, common sense produces behavioral descriptions that are more fine grained than those that would be available if we restricted ourselves to autonomous descriptions. There is nothing unreasonable about this, since often enough our practical concerns demand some more fine grained description of behavior. But if I am right, then these practical concerns lead to a taxonomy of behavior which is ill suited to a systematic science aimed at explaining behavior. Folk psychology has followed the commonsense strategy by evolving a set of hybrid descriptions for *mental states* which build in various historical, contextual, and comparative features of the organism. Thus, as we saw in chapter 5, the folk notion of believing that p is an amalgam of historical, contextual, ideological, and perhaps other considerations. No doubt this way of slicing the mental pie proved itself to be efficient and useful in the day-to-day business of dealing with other people. Had it not, it surely would not have survived. The thrust of the autonomy principle, however, is that by building historical, contextual, and ideological features into mental state descriptions, folk psychology has taxonomized states too narrowly, drawing distinctions which are unnecessary and cumbersome when we are seeking a systematic causal explanation of behavior. To believe that p is to be in an autonomous functional state *and* to have a certain history, context, and ideological relation to the ascriber. These further factors can surely be studied by various disciplines. But they have no place in a science aimed at explaining behavior. By slicing the pie too finely, they impede the formulation of those generalizations which apply equally to an organism and its replica.

The Strong RTM would have us couch our cognitive generalizations in the hybrid language of content ascription. The Syntactic Theory of the Mind, on the other hand, requires purely formal generalizations which ignore those historical and environmental factors that may distinguish an organism from its replica in the eyes of folk psychology. If the argument for the autonomy principle is persuasive, then the STM strategy is the one to be preferred.

4. Do STM Theories Miss Important Generalizations?

In setting out my case for preferring the STM to the Strong RTM, the argument that Strong RTM theories are bound to miss important generalizations has played an important role. A number of people have attempted to establish just the opposite thesis, however, arguing that theories in the syntactic paradigm will miss generalizations that can be captured by theories following the Strong RTM strategy. According to these writers, there are regularities important for the explanation of behavior which can only be captured by generalizations which advert to the content or semantic properties of mental states. If they are right, then the view I have been defending is in trouble, and we shall have to reevaluate the virtues of content-based cognitive theories. In this section I shall consider three arguments aimed at showing that STM theories miss important generalizations. It is my contention that each of these arguments is mistaken. Unfortunately the advocates of these arguments have not yet developed them in the detail they deserve. Thus I shall have to do a fair amount of speculative amplification. But, of course, the prosecutor is not the best spokesman for the defense. Caveat emptor!

Pylyshyn's Argument

Of the several arguments aimed at showing that STM theories will miss significant generalizations capturable in terms of content, the one which has been developed in the greatest detail is due to Zenon Pylyshyn. Since Pylyshyn's argument admits of no easy summary, I will quote it at some length. Before doing so, however, I want to note a reservation about my interpretation. I shall be reading Pylyshyn as urging the advantages of what I have been calling the *Strong* RTM. However, Pylyshyn does distinguish the Strong RTM from the Weak RTM, which will make its appearance in the next chapter, and it is possible that he would prefer that his argument be taken as a defense of the Weak RTM. The reader is encouraged to reread Pylyshyn's argument after the Weak RTM has been explained. I do not think that Pylyshyn's argument is any more convincing when read as a defense of the Weak RTM, though I will not return to argue the point. With that by way of preface, here is Pylyshyn's argument:

> Stich takes an even stronger position on the separation of the problem of interpretation from the problem of function. He offers the interesting proposal that we ought to simply forget about the first of these and build functional models in which we do not bother to try to give expressions any interpretation as beliefs or goals (and hence as being representations). This would be in effect to abandon the goal of relating computational psychology to a folk belief-desire psychology. Tempting as such a radical break might be from certain perspectives. . . , I don't believe we could get away with it and still have explanatory theories. It simply will not do as an explanation of, say, why Mary came running out of the smoke-filled building, to say that there was a certain sequence of expressions computed in her mind according to certain expression-transforming rules. However true that might be, it fails on a number of counts to provide an explanation of Mary's behavior. It does not show how or why this behavior is related to very similar behavior she would exhibit as a consequence of receiving a phone call in which she heard the utterance "the building is on fire!", or as a consequence of her hearing the fire alarm or smelling smoke, or in fact following any event interpretable (given the appropriate beliefs) as generally entailing that the building was on fire. The

only way to both capture the important underlying generalizations (which hold across certain specific nonverbal inputs as well as certain classes of verbal ones, but only when the latter are in a language that Mary understands) *and* to see her behavior as being rationally related to certain conditions, is to take the bold but highly motivated step of interpreting the expressions in the theory as goals and beliefs. . . .

Of course, the computational model only contains uninterpreted formal symbols (that's what Fodor calls the "formality constraint"). The question is whether the cognitive theory which that model instantiates can refrain from giving them an intentional interpretation. In the above example, simply leaving them as uninterpreted formal symbols begs the question of why these particular expressions should arise under what would surely seem (in the absence of interpretation) like a very strange collection of diverse circumstances, as well as the question of why these symbols should lead to building evacuation behavior as opposed to something else. Of course, the reason the same symbols occur under such diverse circumstances is precisely that they represent a common feature of the circumstances—a feature, moreover, that is not to be found solely by inspecting properties of the physical environments. (E.g., what physical features do telephone calls warning of fire share with the smell of smoke?) What is common to all these situations is that a common interpretation of the events occurs—an interpretation that depends on what beliefs Mary has about alarms, smoke, and so on. . . . But what in the theory corresponds to this common interpretation? Surely one cannot answer by pointing to some formal symbols. The right answer has to be something like the claim that the symbols represent the belief that the building is on fire—i.e., it is a semantic interpretation of the symbols as representations of something. Otherwise the relevance of the other symbols stored in memory would have to be gratuitously stipulated. If they were interpreted, on the other hand, we would see that they are relevant because they constitute premises which sanction the inference from such conditions as the smell of smoke to the belief directly responsible for the action.[13]

It is clear that Pylyshyn thinks purely formal STM-style theories "simply will not do." There is something that, on his view, they fail to explain; there are "important underlying generalizations" that they fail to capture. But I must confess that I am not at all clear, either from this passage or from Pylyshyn's patient personal efforts to enlighten me, just what the missed generalizations are supposed to be. Perhaps the best strategy for clarifying the issue is to sketch in some detail the sort of explanations that are available for Mary's behavior if we follow the advice of the Strong RTM and attempt to build psychological theories which systematize and make more rigorous the content-based generalizations of commonsense folk psychology. We can then ask just what is missed if we drop the folk psychological strategy of identifying mental states via content sentences and view them, instead, simply as tokens of syntactic objects. Here is the folk psychological explanation of Mary's behavior:

Why did Mary come running out of the building? Well, it's a long story. First, she had a number of long-standing desires, one of which was the desire to leave the building she is in if the building is on fire. (Or perhaps this was not a long-standing desire; perhaps it was itself derived from the long-standing desire not to be hurt and the belief that if one does not leave a building that is on fire then one will be hurt. But let us ignore this complication.) At this point the story branches into several versions, depending on just how it was that Mary learned the building was on fire.

Version 1: Mary began to inhale smoke. This caused her to believe that the building was on fire. The causal connection here is complex and indirect. The direct consequence of inhaling the smoke was that Mary came to believe that she was inhaling smoke. From this belief, and the long-standing belief that if one is inhaling smoke then there is a fire nearby, she inferred that there was a fire nearby. Next, from the belief that if there is a fire nearby, then (probably) the building is on fire, she inferred that the bulding was on fire. (All of these inferences of course were exceedingly fast, and there is no need to assume that the intermediate steps were available to Mary's introspection. The folk psychological story cannot be told plausibly unless we assume that most of our inference making is unconscious.) This last belief—the belief that the building was on fire—interacted with the long-standing conditional desire mentioned above and led Mary to acquire the desire to leave the building. The desire to leave the building in turn interacted with the belief that if one runs out the door then one will leave the building. The result was the desire to run out the door.

Version 2: When Mary picked up the phone, an utterance of the sentence, "The building is on fire!" was heard. This caused her to believe that the building was on fire. In this case too the causal connection was indirect and complex. The sound impinging on her ear caused Mary to believe that she was hearing an utterance of "The building is on fire!" And this belief led, via some version of the celebrated Gricean path,[14] to the belief that the building was on fire. From here the story rejoins version 1 and leads again to Mary running out the door. Various other versions of the story could be told, with Mary learning of the conflagration by hearing the fire alarm, seeing flames, and so on. There are also versions on which there is no fire: what Mary smells is actually soot dislodged by a chimney sweep; a flashing red strobe light leads her to believe that there are flames in the next room, etc. Of course the inferential chains in these various accounts do not tell the whole Strong RTM story about Mary's behavior. A Strong RTM explanation would not only tell us which beliefs and desires lead to which others, it would also tell us why. The explanations proffered would invoke generalizations which specify the pattern of interactions among beliefs and desires in terms of the content sentences we use to characterize them. Thus for example, a Strong RTM explanation might tell us that Mary's belief that the building is on fire, along with her conditional desire (to leave the building if it is on fire) lead to the desire to leave the building, in virtue of a generalization like (1″) in chapter 7.

Let us consider, now, the sort of explanation of Mary's behavior that might be offered by a theorist who adopts the STM paradigm. Perhaps the easiest way to tell the story is to assume that each of the distinct content sentences used to characterize beliefs and desires in the Strong RTM explanation corresponds to a distinct syntactic string. The correspondence being assumed cannot of course be a type-type correspondence, since, as I have been at pains to point out, tokens of a single syntactically characterized state type may in different subjects have radically different folk characterizations. All that is being assumed is a token-token correspondence: each of Mary's beliefs and desires (i.e., each token) corresponds to a token of a syntactic type, and the syntactic tokens are type distinct when and only when the corresponding belief or desire is accorded a distinct content sentence. This is, I should note, far from a trivial assumption. For we might well discover that what folk psychology characterizes as the belief that p is, *within a single subject*, subserved by several functionally or syntactically different states. In chapter 11 we will ponder the implications of such a result. But since Pylyshyn's argument seems to be raising a general objection against any purely formal STM explanation of Mary's behavior, the token-token correspondence assumption is a fair one here, for this is certainly one way an STM theory might look. Here then is a sketch of a purely formal or syntactic explanation of Mary's behavior:

Why did Mary come running from the building? It's a long story. First, she had a long-standing D-state whose syntactic form was that of a conditional, viz. $F \supset L$ (corresponding to the desire to leave the building if it is on fire),* where F and L are themselves syntactically well-formed strings. F and L should be thought of as syntactically complex, and thus Mary is likely to have many further B- and D-states which involve various parts of F or L, compounded with other symbols into other wffs. But none of these "background" B- and D-states will function in the explanation of her behavior, save of course for those mentioned below. At this point the story branches into several versions.

In version 1, Mary began to inhale smoke. This caused her to have the B-state F. The causal connection here is indirect and complex. The direct consequence of inhaling the smoke was that Mary came to have a B-state I (corresponding to the belief that she was inhaling smoke). From this B-state and the long-standing B-state $I \supset N$ (corresponding to the belief that if one is inhaling smoke then there is a fire nearby) she inferred (i.e., was caused to add to her B-store) a token of N. And from N and the long-standing B-state $N \supset F$ she inferred the B-state F. This last B-state, F, interacted with the conditional D-state $F \supset L$ to produce a D-state L. The D-state L in turn interacted with the B-state $R \supset L$ (corresponding to the belief that if one runs out the door, then one will leave the bulding) to produce the D-state R. And the D-state R, finally, led Mary to run out the door.

In version 2, when Mary picked up the phone an utterance of "The building is on fire!" was heard. This caused her to have the B-state H (corresponding to the belief that she was hearing an utterance of "the building is on fire!"). That B-state led her, via a syntactic version of the Gricean path, to have the B-state F. From here the story rejoins version 1, and leads again to Mary running out the door.

On various other versions, the B-state F is caused by hearing the sound of the fire alarm, smelling soot, and so on. Of course the inferential chains in these various accounts do not tell the whole syntactic story about Mary's behavior. An STM explanation will not only tell us which B- and D-states lead to which others, it will also tell us why. Thus for example, the interaction of the B-state F and the D-state $F \supset L$ to yield the D-state L is subsumed under a generalization like (4) in section 1.

Given the close parallelism between the content-based Strong RTM explanation and the purely formal STM explanation, it is a bit puzzling that Pylyshyn sees the latter as missing important generalizations. Let us attend with some care to what he has to say on this score. First he claims that the purely syntactic explanation "does not show how or why [Mary's behavior in the inhaling-smoke version] is related to very

---

*These parenthetical remarks about what various B- and D-states correspond to are no part of the STM explanation. They are inserted to underscore the parallelism between STM and Strong RTM explanations.

similar behavior she would exhibit as a consequence of receiving a phone call in which she heard the utterance 'the building is on fire!' or as a consequence of her hearing the fire alarm. . . ." But on the face of it, this charge seems just plain false. What the various versions have in common, according to the content-based Strong RTM explanation is that they all lead Mary to *believe that the building is on fire,* and this belief plays an essential role in the etiology of her fleeing behavior. On the purely syntactic explanation, there is a prima facie perfect parallel. What the various versions have in common is that they all lead Mary to have the B-state F, and this B-state plays an essential role in the etiology of her fleeing behavior.

Pylyshyn perhaps anticipates this move. For he says that if we leave the psychological states invoked in our theory as uninterpreted formal symbols, we beg the question "of why these particular expressions should arise under what would surely seem (in the absence of interpretation) a very strange collection of diverse circumstances, as well as the question of why these symbols should lead to building evacuation behavior as opposed to something else." Presumably the symbols to which Pylyshyn is referring are those that comprise the B-state F (i.e., the state which subserves Mary's belief that the building is on fire). What the STM explanation leaves unexplained, according to Pylyshyn, is why F should arise under such diverse circumstances, and why F should lead to building evacuation behavior. Well, what sort of explanation would a *content-based* account have to offer? Here is what Pylyshyn says: "Of course, the reason the same symbols occur under such diverse circumstances is precisely that they represent a common feature of the circumstances—a feature, moreover, that is not to be found solely by inspecting properties of the physical environments. . . . What is common to all these situations is that a common interpretation of all these events occurs—an interpretation that depends on what beliefs Mary has about alarms, smoke, and so on." If I understand him, Pylyshyn is claiming that various diverse stimuli (smoke, phone call, etc.) lead to the same symbols because Mary *interprets* them in the same way. Just what does this amount to? The answer Pylyshyn gives is that these diverse stimuli, along with other beliefs that Mary has, lead her to infer that the building is on fire. But surely *this* is no explanation at all. It simply begs the question. If we want to know why diverse stimuli lead to the same belief, it is no help to be told that they are all interpreted in the same way, when the notion of interpretation itself is unpacked in terms of the beliefs to which the stimuli, in collaboration with other beliefs, lead. Obviously there is a parallel syntactic story to be told, and it is equally vacuous. Diverse stimuli lead to the same B-state (F in our example) because, in collaboration with preexisting B-states, all of them begin inferential chains which lead to the B-state F.

There is one final move in Pylyshyn's argument:

> What in the [syntactic] theory corresponds to this common interpretation? Surely one cannot answer by pointing to some formal symbols. The right answer has to be something like the claim that the symbols represent the belief that the building is on fire—i.e., it is a semantic interpretation of the symbols as representing something. Otherwise even the relevance of the other symbols stored in memory would have to be gratuitously stipulated. If they were interpreted, on the other hand, we would see that they are relevant because they constitute premises which sanction the inference from such conditions as the smell of smoke to the belief directly responsible for the action.

The core of this argument is the claim that without semantic interpretation we could not see the "relevance" of other symbols stored in memory. However, I think that a careful look at the syntactic accounts elaborated above shows this to be quite wrong. Among the "other symbols stored in memory" were the long-standing B-states I $\supset$ N and N $\supset$ F. In asking why these particular symbols are relevant to the inference from I to F, I assume Pylyshyn is asking why these particular symbols should causally interact as sketched above, while others stored in memory do not interact with I to produce F. But surely there is no mystery here. These symbols are relevant because of their *syntactic form* and of course because of generalizations like (5) in section 1, which detail the causal interactions among symbol sequences that are syntactically related in this way.

On Pylyshyn's view, what is crucial to seeing how symbols stored in memory are relevant to each other is "a semantic interpretation of the symbols as representing something." But I think his own example can be extended a bit to illustrate that this is exactly wrong. For suppose that in building an STM account of Mary's cognitive states we ran across some symbols to which we could *not* assign any semantic interpretation. Suppose, for example, that there is a symbol sequence, W, such that the syntactically conditional sequence W $\supset$ F appears among Mary's long-standing B-states. Given what we already know about Mary, it would be natural to try interpreting this as a conditional belief, ascribable with a content sentence of the form:

If _____, then the building is on fire.

But now suppose that our best efforts at assigning a semantic interpretation to W end in failure. We might find, for example, that W is added to Mary's belief store under a variety of perceptual circumstances that strike us as having nothing whatever in common and that some of the components of W enter into a network of B-states which have no near analogue in us. What I am sketching of course is an ideologically exotic subject, one who has concepts and beliefs sufficiently different from our own that we cannot provide the sort of semantic interpretation Pylyshyn favors. Though it would cripple any attempt to apply content based generalizations like (1″)–(3″) in chapter 7, the impossibility of interpretation poses no problem for a purely syntactic account of the sort I have been advocating. It is a "semantic" or content-based theory of the sort advocated by the Strong RTM that stands to miss important generalizations, not a syntactic theory of the sort advocated by the STM.

Patricia Churchland's Argument

A second argument purporting to show that content-based theories can capture generalizations missed by STM theories was suggested to me by Patricia Churchland. As will emerge in chapter 10, Churchland is hardly a defender of the Strong RTM. Her argument was offered in the spirit of devil's advocacy. I have chosen to discuss it at some length because I think it captures in an acute way the misgivings of those who suspect that somehow the STM is throwing out the baby with the bath water.

Churchland's argument focuses on the inputs and outputs of an STM-style theory—i.e., on the links between sensory stimulation and belief on the one hand and between desire and behavior on the other. One of the ways in which a content-based theory may specify connections between stimuli and behavior is by linking specific stimulus types to specific belief types; thus:

(11)   For all subjects S, when an elephant comes into view, S will typically come to believe that an elephant is in front of him.

This sort of generalization can be mimicked easily enough by a syntactic theory:

(12)   For all subjects S, when an elephant comes into view, S will typically come to have a sequence of symbols, E, in his B-store.

But, Churchland points out, the content-based version of the generalization looks to be an instance of a much more powerful generalization, since both occurrences of the word 'elephant' could be replaced by 'rabbit' or 'avacado' or 'policeman' and the generalization would remain true. We can exploit the fact that the same words occur both in the characterization of the stimulus and in the characterization of the belief by proffering a generalization like:

(11′) For all subjects S and all noun phrases N, if a sentence of the form

n comes into S's view

is true, then typically S will acquire a belief ascribable by a sentence of the form

S believes that n is in front of him,

where 'n' throughout is replaced by N.

No such generalization is available for (12), however, since nothing in the syntactic characterization of the B-state that S acquires duplicates the description of the stimulus causing the belief.

An entirely analogous point can be made on the output side. Individual generalizations like

(13) For all subjects S, if S desires that he raise his arm now and if S has no stronger incompatible desires, then S will raise his arm.

can be readily mirrored in a purely syntactic theory, by simply replacing the description of the desire with a description of the syntactic state which subserves it. The result will be a generalization with the following form:

(14) For all subjects S, if S has D-state R (i.e., if S has the sequence of symbols R in his D-store), and if S has no stronger incompatible D-states, then S will raise his arm.

But once again there appears to be a broader generalization of which (13) is an instance—a generalization which exploits the fact that the same embedded sentence (give or take a few grammatical transformations) occurs both as content sentence and as action description. Thus (13) may be generalized to something like:

(13′) For all subjects S and all declarative sentences P, if S has a desire ascribable with a sentence of the form

S desires that p

where 'p' is replaced by P, and if S has no stronger incompatible desires, then P will come to be true.

On first blush Churchland's argument is rather plausible. It does indeed seem that in forsaking content-based generalizations, STM theories are left with nothing but *arbitrary* connections between stimulus and belief on the one side and between desire and behavior on the other. Moreover, by identifying beliefs and desires via content sentences, Strong RTM theories do seem able to capture important systematic relations, both between stimulus and belief and between desire and behavior. However, I think that when we look a bit more closely, it turns out that the advantages afforded by content-sentence character-izations of cognitive states are an illusion. The generalization they facilitate are either false or vacuous.

Let me begin on the input side, where the argument is clearest. What Churchland alleges is that there is some regular and systematic con-nection between the stimulus causing a belief and the content sentence we would use to characterize a belief; if an N comes into view, then S will typically come to believe there is an N before him. But the bold version of this claim advanced in (11′) is surely false. To see this we need only let the noun phrase be something like 'the child who will grow up to be the fiftieth president of the United States,' or 'the next winner of the Belmont Stakes'. The typical subject does not come to believe that the next winner at Belmont is before him when that horse comes into view. Nor would it help much to restrict N so as to exclude complex definite descriptions. Noun phrases like 'a bachelor' or 'a burglar' are equally problematic.

It might be thought that (11′) could be rescued by insisting that N be an *observation term*. We might, for example, define an 'observation term' to be any term such that a belief attributable by using the term arises whenever an object satisfying the term comes into view. But of course restricting (11′) to observation terms defined *this* way reduces it to a vacuous tautology. Another thought is to seek some independent, non-question-begging characterization of what is to count as an ob-servation term. I am inclined to think that this quest is doomed to failure, however. One of the lessons of chapter 5 was that the propriety of a content sentence in ascribing a belief to a subject depends both on the network of further beliefs the subject has and on the causal and social factors which enter into the determination of reference. A belief simply will not count as the belief that p unless the subject has a suitable set of further beliefs, an appropriate linguistic environment, and concepts with an appropriate history. It follows that *no* sort of stimulus will be causally sufficient to produce the belief that p, since to end up with that belief the subject must be ideologically and ref-erentially prepared for it. So, for example, a subject who is sufficiently ideologically or referentially exotic from our point of view (a young child, say, or a Dani tribesman) will *not* acquire the belief that an elephant is in front of him when an elephant comes into view. Nor will he even acquire the belief that a red thing comes into view. (The Dani, a Stone Age agricultural people of New Guinea have a language with only two basic color terms: *mili* for dark, cold hues and *mola* for bright, warm ones.)[15] If 'red' and 'elephant' won't do as observation terms in Churchland's argument, it is hard to think that anything will. To summarize, the problem with (11') is that it is false, and the only obvious way to patch it would be to restrict its domain of application to observation terms. No characterization of observation terms has been offered, however, which does not turn (11') into a vacuous tautology, nor is there much hope that one will be forthcoming.

Let us turn, now, to the other sort of generalizations that Churchland's argument envisions, those linking desires with behavior. Obviously (13'), like (11'), is *false* in the form first stated. Among my desires are the desire to inherit a million dollars, the desire to travel around the world, and the desire to convince Zenon Pylyshyn of the virtues of the STM. In no case do I have a stronger incompatible desire. But, alas, it does not follow that these things will come to pass. Plainly (13') needs some patching, and two thoughts suggest themselves. First, we must place some restriction on the sort of sentence over which the generalization ranges. A natural idea is to restrict P to sentences describing *actions*, thus eliminating the desire to inherit a million dollars. And while we are at it, we had better insist that they be so-called *basic* actions, in contrast with "generated" actions like convincing Pylyshyn.[16] Second, even if we restrict P to sentences describing basic actions, there must be some provision guaranteeing that S is *able to perform* the action in his current situation. No matter how much I may want to raise my arm, it will not move if it is anesthetized or strapped securely to a 1000-kg weight.

If we try to patch (13') along these lines, however, the problem of vacuity looms once again. What we need this time are characterizations of a *pair* of notions: *basic action*, and *ability to perform* an action. And, as before, the definitions offered for these notions must be non-question-begging; they must not turn (13') into a tautology. It is easy to be skeptical about the prospects for such non-question-begging definitions. However *would* one define *ability to perform* an action apart from saying that a person has the ability if he actually would perform it when he wanted to, given that he had no stronger competing desires? A rhetorical question is not an argument of course. Nor do I propose to attempt an argument showing that any definition which would rescue (13') from falsehood would also render it vacuous. There are notorious swamps along that path. But I am inclined to think that no such argument is really called for. The burden of proof rests on the critic of the STM to show that (13') *can* be patched in a non-question-begging way. In the absence of any indication that this can be done, I think it is plausible to conclude that there is no generalization here to be missed.

Fodor's Argument

A third argument contending that Strong RTM theories capture generalizations missed by syntactic theories is one we have already seen. Chapter 7, section 1 began with several quotes from Fodor, the first of which was taken from a passage in which he was arguing that advocates of the STM have "rather lost track of the state of play."[17] Cognitive psychology, according to Fodor, was founded on the hope that the generalizations of commonsense psychology "can be systematized and made rigorous." And since all of these generalizations "apply to mental states in virtue of their contents," you cannot save the generalizations without appealing to the notion of content.

There are several points in Fodor's argument that I do not wish to dispute. He is, I think, quite right in claiming that the generalizations of commonsense psychology ("literally all of them") are couched in terms of content. Moreover, it is clear that if we follow the STM strategy of ignoring content and formulating generalizations in purely syntactic terms, then content-based generalizations will be unstatable. In contrast with Fodor, however, I am not inclined to view this loss with much alarm. The thrust of my argument throughout this chapter has been that STM theories can do all the explanatory and predictive work of content-based theories, *and they can do it better*. For syntactic theories are not encumbered with the intrinsic vagueness and the built-in expressive limitations that plague Strong RTM theories. If we assume (rather implausibly, I think) that the best STM theory will follow the general contours of commonsense psychology, then the content-based generalizations of folk psychology will turn out to be special cases of syntactic generalizations, gerrymandered to fit the vague and idiosyncratic class of syntactic mental states to which commonsense content descriptions can be assigned. Folk generalizations will coincide with STM generalizations in the theoretically uninteresting class of cases in which the subjects are similar to us. But folk generalizations will not extend to the mental states of young children, or primitive folk, or senile people, even when these people can be described by the same syntactic psychological generalizations that apply to our own mental states. What is more, there will be no way within an STM theory of demarcating that special class of subjects and mental states to which folk generalizations apply. But this inability of STM theories to capture the vague and observer-relative distinctions embedded in folk psychology is, I would argue, all to the good. There is no reason why a scientific psychology should respect the Protagorean parochialism of common sense.

Fodor is clearly right that cognitive science began with the hope that content-based generalizations could be systematized and made more rigorous. As this effort has progressed, however, it has become increasingly clear that the most interesting and theoretically powerful generalizations are formal or syntactic ones which simply cannot be stated in the aboriginal language of content. If this is right, then surely the sane scientific strategy is to accept the STM paradigm and drop the attempt to characterize the interactions of mental states in terms of their content. It is, after all, a venerable tradition to kick away ladders once we have climbed them.

Chapter 9

The Weak Representational Theory of the Mind

1. Syntactic Generalizations and Semantically Interpreted States

The issue we have been pondering is whether the concept of belief and other intentional folk psychological concepts have any role to play in cognitive science. Thus far that question has been cast as a dispute between the Strong Representational Theory of the Mind, which gives an affirmative answer, and the Syntactic Theory of the Mind, whose answer is negative. There is, however, a third view that must be reckoned with, which also gives an affirmative answer. This is the view I shall call the *Weak Representational Theory of the Mind*. The Weak RTM positions itself midway between the Strong RTM and the STM, by keeping the Strong RTM's claim that mental states are relations between organisms and contentful or semantically interpreted mental sentences but dropping the Strong RTM's insistence that nomological generalizations which describe the interactions among mental states apply to them in virtue of their contents. It was that last claim, recall, which made the Strong RTM strong. In its place the Weak RTM adopts the STM view, which holds that the generalizations of cognitive science will be purely formal, applying to mental states not in virtue of their semantic properties, but rather in virtue of their syntax.

Since much of the argument of this chapter will focus on the relative merits of the Weak RTM and the STM, it is important to be as clear as possible on exactly how these two doctrines differ. The STM views mental states as relations to tokens of purely syntactic objects. Generalizations detailing the interactions of mental state tokens describe them in terms of their syntactic types. On the matter of content or semantic properties, the STM is officially agnostic. It does not insist that syntactic state types have no content, nor does it insist that tokens of syntactic state types have no content. It is simply silent on the whole matter. But to put the point this way is perhaps a bit misleading, for in remaining agnostic on questions of content, the STM is in effect claiming that psychological theories have *no need* to postulate content or other semantic properties, like truth conditions. It sees no psychological work to be done by the hypothesis that mental state tokens or types have semantic properties. The Weak RTM agrees with the STM in viewing mental states as relations between organisms and syntactic objects. Unlike the STM, however, the Weak RTM insists that these syntactic objects *must have content or semantic properties*. This last doctrine can be unpacked in two ways, one of which is considerably stronger than the other. The weak version claims only that every token mental state to which a cognitive theory applies has *some* content or *some* truth condition. This view is far from trivial, since it rules out cognitive theories which apply to mental state tokens to which no content or truth conditions can be ascribed. The stronger version of the doctrine agrees with the weaker version in requiring all mental state tokens to have content or truth conditions. But it goes on to claim that these semantic features are correlated with the syntactic type of the token. Thus on the stronger reading of the doctrine, if a pair of mental state tokens are of the same syntactic type, then they must have the same content or truth conditions as well. Since the Weak RTM agrees with the STM that the syntactic type of a mental state token determines its interactions with other tokens, the view that content is correlated with syntactic type entails that mental states which behave in the same way (i.e., mental states which are "functionally identical") must have the same content. Advocates of the Weak RTM generally presuppose the correlation thesis, and I will take this to be an integral part of the Weak RTM. However, much of what I have to say against the Weak RTM applies as well to the version which does not insist that semantic properties are correlated with syntactic types.

When it is construed as accepting the correlation thesis, the Weak RTM pretty clearly supports the view that folk psychological posits like belief will find a comfortable home in cognitive science. If the state types recognized by cognitive science are syntactic state types all of whose tokens have the same content or truth conditions, then it would be natural enough to identify these cognitive state types with folk psychological state types. The B-state type all of whose tokens have the content that snow is white (or all of whose tokens are true if and only if snow is white) is plausibly identified as the belief type *that snow is white*. State types, recall, are properties. So another way of putting this point is that the property of believing that snow is white is to be identified with the B-state type whose tokens have the content that snow is white. Without the correlation thesis on the other hand, it is much less clear whether the Weak RTM portrays cognitive science as making serious use of folk psychological constructs. If there is a B-state type some of whose tokens are true if and only if snow is white and some of whose tokens have quite different truth conditions, we would not want to identify that B-state type with the property of believing that snow is white. But that property (and of course endlessly many like it) are the fundamental constructs of folk psychology. It is in terms of these properties that folk psychology builds its generalizations. If there is nothing in the cognitive scientist's theory with which believing that snow is white can be identified, then things look grim for those who think that cognitive science will embrace the psychological constructs of common sense.[1] All of this provides another sort of motivation for construing the Weak RTM as committed to the correlation thesis, since without this commitment the Weak RTM would offer little encouragement to those who hope that the concepts of folk psychology will find a respectable home in scientific psychology.

2. Interpreting Fodor and Interpreting the Weak RTM

Since I have already alerted the reader that Fodor turns up on various sides of these issues, it should come as no surprise that Fodor is among the principal defenders of the Weak RTM. In the following two sections we will look at a pair of arguments Fodor has advanced in defense of this view. But before doing that, I want to spend some time pondering the paradox that Fodor's views present. How is it possible to endorse *both* the Strong RTM (which claims that the generalizations of cognitive science advert to content) and the Weak RTM (which claims that the generalizations of cognitive science do not advert to content), sometimes within the confines of a single article? Thinking about this puzzle will provide some useful clues on how Fodor's arguments are to be interpreted. It will also help us to say rather more clearly what the Weak RTM is claiming when it asserts that syntactic mental tokens have content.

Since I have made the unfriendly allegation that Fodor is at least prima facie inconsistent, let me begin by substantiating that charge. Chapter 7, section 1 began with three quotes, all of them quite insistent on the point that the generalizations of cognitive science must appeal to the notion of content. The reader is urged to review these passages, and contrast them to the three that follow.

4.

This is the theory [propounded in the following essays]:

(a)   Propositional attitude states are relational.

(b)   Among the relata are mental representations. . . .

(c)   Mental representations are symbols: they have both formal and semantic properties.

(d)   *Mental representations have their causal roles in virtue of their formal properties. . . .*[2]

5.

It is very characteristic of current versions of RTM—indeed it is one of the few respects in which they differ significantly from classical formulations of the doctrine—to be explicit in requiring that only *non*-semantic properties of mental representations can figure in determining which mental operations apply to them. . . . I take [this] to be part and parcel of the idea that mental processes are computational, and I take the idea that mental processes are computational to be among the central tenets of cognitive science.

The upshot is that one can do quite a lot of cognitive science without ever raising foundational—or, indeed, any—issues about the semanticity of mental representations. In a certain sense you can do the whole theory of mental processes without raising such issues, what with mental operations being computational and mental processes being causal sequences of mental operations. That is, in fact, pretty much what has happened in the cognitive science literature. . . .[3]

6.

What we're all doing [in AI, procedural semantics, linguistics, cognitive psychology, and psycholinguistics] is really a kind of logical syntax (only psychologized); and we all very much hope that when we've got a reasonable internal language (a formalism for writing down canonical representations), someone very nice and very clever will turn up and show us how to interpret it; how to provide it with a semantics.[4]

How is it possible for Fodor to have it both ways, for him to urge *both* that cognitive generalizations apply to mental states in virtue of their content and that "only *non*-semantic properties of mental representations can figure in determining which mental operations apply to them"? One way to take the bite out of this apparent contradiction would be to endorse the correlation thesis which holds that differences in content are mirrored by differences in syntax. If this were true, then generalizations couched in terms of content would, so to speak, be co-extensive, with generalizations couched in terms of syntax. And although strictly speaking it might be their syntactic properties which account for causal interactions among mental state tokens, there would be no harm in talking as though semantic properties were causally relevant, since if they were, the system would behave in exactly the same way. In Dennett's colorful terminology, the mind would be portrayed as a "syntactic engine" which mimics a "semantic engine." In support of this benign reading one could cite a number of passages in which Fodor seems to endorse the correlation thesis. Here are two:

The computational theory of the mind requires that two thoughts can be distinct in content only if they can be identified with relations to formally distinct representations.[5]

That taxonomy in respect of content *is* compatible with the formality condition, plus or minus a bit, is perhaps *the* basic idea of modern cognitive theory.[6]

We cannot get Fodor off the hook simply by assuming that he accepts the correlation thesis, however. For there are also places in which Fodor seems to *reject* the correlation thesis. In chapter 5, section 6, we saw Fodor endorsing the view that a pair of computers might be running the same machine language program, though one was simulating a chess game while the other was simulating the Six Day War. Thus a pair of mental sentence tokens might be syntactically or functionally identical though one is about Moshe Dayan and the other is about the king's bishop. Consider also the following quote:

> Searle is certainly right that instantiating the same program that the brain does is not, in and of itself, a sufficient condition for having those propositional attitudes characteristic of the organism that has the brain. . . .
>
> [However] given that there are the right kinds of causal linkages between the symbols that the device manipulates and things in the world . . . it is quite unclear that intuition rejects ascribing propositional attitudes to it. . . .
>
> It seems to me that Searle has misunderstood the main point about the treatment of intentionality in representational theories of the mind. . . . For the record, then, the main point is this: intentional properties of propositional attitudes are viewed as inherited from semantic properties of mental representations (and not from the functional role of mental representations, unless "functional role" is construed broadly enough to include symbol-world relations).
>
> It is entirely reasonable (indeed it must be true) that the right kind of causal relation is the kind that holds between our brains and our transducer mechanisms (on the one hand) and between our brains and distal objects (on the other). . . .
>
> Some necessary conditions are more interesting than others. While connections to the world and symbol manipulations are both presumably necessary for intentional processes, there is no reason (so far) to believe that the former provide a theoretical domain for a science; whereas there is considerable a posteriori reason to suppose that the latter do.[7]

Here Fodor grants that the functional properties of a system, the way it manipulates symbols, is not sufficient to determine the intentional or semantic properties of the symbols manipulated. Both functional properties and "connections to the world" are necessary to endow mental representations with semantic properties. But those connections to the world include causal relations "between our brains and distal causal objects," and such connections are hardly likely to correlate with functional properties. (Indeed on Fodor's view, even if they did correlate, it is hard to see how we could ever know this, since "there is no reason to believe that [connections to the world] provide a theoretical domain for a science.")

It now looks as though we have traded one puzzle for another. We tried to explain away Fodor's endorsement of both the Strong and the Weak RTM by supposing that he accepts the correlation thesis, which makes the difference between those two views look less significant. But now we find that his commitment to the correlation thesis is at best a sometime thing. How is *that* inconsistency to be explained? At about this point some readers may feel an inclination to throw up their hands and mutter something about how even the best of philosophers are sometimes inconsistent. However, I am inclined to think that there is an explanation which is both more charitable and substantially more interesting. As I see it, in both endorsing and rejecting the correlation thesis, Fodor has fallen victim to an endemic ambiguity in discussions of content. Let me elaborate.

In chapter 5 we saw that commonsense ascriptions of content behave like multidimensional similarity judgments. One of the factors that is relevant to these folk ascriptions and judgments is the functional profile, or what we earlier called the *narrow causal pattern*, of the state in question—i.e., its pattern of causal interactions with stimuli, behavior, and other mental states. When mental states are viewed as tokens of syntactic types, the functional profile exhibited by a mental state can be equated with what we have been calling its formal or syntactic properties. Thus the syntactic properties of a state are one among several sorts of features determining its "content." Moreover content judgments, like other similarity judgments, exhibit a pronounced context sensitivity. What counts as a suitable content ascription in one conversational context may be quite unacceptable in another. Within these two facts lie the seeds of considerable confusion. For there are conversational contexts where a modicum of causal-pattern similarity is similarity enough to sustain a content judgment, despite substantial divergences in ideology, reference, and other factors. In short, there are conversational contexts where nothing more than a loose causal-pattern similarity *counts* in assessing content. To make matters worse, I think that often when cognitive psychologists use content sentences to describe mental states, the conversational context requires no more than rough causal-pattern similarity.

Now the upshot of all this is that there is what might be called a *minimal functional* reading of content ascriptions and claims about content, a reading on which nonfunctional factors are systematically ignored. And of course on the minimal functional reading the correlation thesis is tautologous. If all that is required for a pair of state tokens to share the same content is that they are suitably similar in their functional or syntactic properties, then it must be the case that content correlates with syntactic type. There is also, however, a reading of content ascriptions and of claims about content on which nonfunctional factors like reference and ideological similarity are relevant. Let us call this reading the *non-minimal* reading. On the non-minimal reading, the correlation thesis is false, for the reasons alluded to by Fodor and elaborated in some detail in chapters 4 and 5. Now it is my hunch that when Fodor endorses the correlation thesis and embraces the Strong RTM, he is conceiving of content in minimal functional terms. However, when he is urging the Weak RTM, puzzling over the "semanticity" of mental representations and denying the correlation thesis, he is construing content along non-minimal lines. Though the equivocation between minimal and non-minimal readings of content talk is encouraged by the context sensitivity of our commonsense notion of content, I think it is clear that when he is most serious about the semanticity of mental states, Fodor must cleave to the full-blooded non-minimal reading. Otherwise it would make no sense to scold procedural semantics, as Fodor is wont to do, for failing to do real semantics, and it would be pointless to hope that after we have succeeded with our "psychologized logical syntax" some clever person will turn up to show us how to provide it with a semantics.

There is an important moral here. In talking about content, semantic properties, and the like, the minimal functional construal of these notions is to be avoided. For on that construal the differences between the Syntactic Theory of the Mind, the Weak Representational Theory, and the Strong Representational Theory collapse. What is more, on the minimal functional reading of content, neither the Strong nor the Weak RTM provides much encouragement to those who hope that folk psychological concepts will find a place in cognitive science.*

---

*Shortly before this manuscript went to press I received a pair of interesting letters from Fodor, detailing how he would have his writing interpreted. If I understand him properly, Fodor agrees that there is a systematic ambiguity in his talk about content. When he is endorsing the correlation thesis and when he appears to accept the Strong RTM, he has one notion of content in mind. However, when he denies the correlation thesis and

3. The Argument from Cognitive Psychology

Of the various arguments that have been offered in favor of the Weak RTM, I think the most influential has been Fodor's contention that it is "presupposed by the best—indeed the only—psychology we've got."[8] If this is right then any arguments against the Weak RTM must certainly be viewed with considerable suspicion. For there is a strong presumption, on my part at least, that scientists generally have good reasons for building their theories as they do. And although this presumption may occasionally be mistaken, I am inclined to agree with Fodor that "a working science is *ipso facto* in philosophical good repute."[9] In contrast with Fodor, however, I do not think that contemporary cognitive psychology presupposes the Weak RTM. Rather, I contend, it is the Syntactic Theory of the Mind that cognitive psychology presupposes.

The *locus classicus* for the argument that cognitive psychology presupposes the Weak RTM is chapter 1 of Fodor's *The Language of Thought*. However, when viewed as a defense of the Weak RTM, that argument is very curious indeed. Fodor summarizes the argument as follows:

> 1. The only psychological models of cognitive processes that seem even remotely plausible represent such processes as computational.
> 2. Computation presupposes a medium of computation: a representational system.[10]

Most of the argument of the chapter is devoted to defending the first of these claims, and that defense is entirely successful. In a number of carefully dissected examples, Fodor shows that cognitive psychological theories construe mental processes as computations or symbol manipulations and that the principles governing these processes must be sensitive to the form or syntax of the symbolic structures involved in the computations. All of this of course is thoroughly congenial to the Syntactic Theory of the Mind. Fodor devotes considerably less effort to defending the second of his claims; one gets the impression that he

---

when he insists that content should play no role in the generalizations of cognitive science, he would be read as invoking the other notion of content. All of this squares well with the interpretation I have just given. Fodor does not accept my characterization of the two readings of content-talk as a *minimal functional* reading and a *non-minimal* reading, however. Rather, he urges, there are "narrow" and "wide" senses of content. This is no mere terminological difference, since Fodor concedes that ordinary English typically cannot express the narrow content of a belief state. On the minimal functional construal, by contrast, it is all too easy to find a content sentence to characterize most beliefs. No matter how ideologically or referentially peculiar a subject's belief state may be, if it is passingly causal-pattern similar to a potential belief state of ours, the sentence we would use to express our belief will serve as a (minimal functional) content sentence for the exotic belief. Fodor promises a paper explicating the notion of narrow content. Since it is plainly not a commonsense notion, it is to be hoped that Fodor will also explain why the cognitive scientist should think he needs any such notion.

takes it to be obvious. And there is a sense in which it *is* obvious. Computation—symbol manipulation—does require a system of symbols to be manipulated. As Fodor would have it, "No representations, no computations."[11] What makes Fodor's second claim both controversial and puzzling is his insistence that these "representations" are not simply uninterpreted syntactic objects. Rather, Fodor claims, "such familiar semantic properties as truth and reference are exhibited by formulae in the representational system."[12] However, it is not at all clear why Fodor thinks that formulae in the computational medium (or "representational system") must have semantic properties. Since he insists that "one wants the rules of computation to apply formally to the objects in their domains,"[13] the semantic properties are presumably not alluded to in the cognitive theory's generalizations, as they would be in a Strong RTM theory. Moreover, we saw that in defending the Weak RTM elsewhere Fodor was ready to concede that "you can do the whole theory of mental processes" without attending to the "semanticity" of mental representations, and that "that is, in fact, pretty much what has happened in the cognitive science literature."[14] But if cognitive psychologists can and do develop the theory of mental processes without attending to the semanticity of formulae in the mental code, it will be impossible to show that they (or their theories) presuppose the Weak RTM simply by examining those theories. The most that can be shown— and I think Fodor has succeeded in showing this beyond any serious doubt—is that the best cognitive theories we have presuppose the STM. What the Weak RTM adds to the STM is the semanticity of mental sentences, and this, Fodor concedes, has played no role in the cognitive science literature.

Although the theories advanced by cognitive psychologists do not exploit the semanticity of mental sentences, it might still be suggested that they do or should *presuppose* it. To defend this view it would have to be shown that there would be some *point* to the move, some advantage to be gained by insisting that mental sentences have content, or truth conditions, or some other semantic properties. In the following two sections we will consider a pair of attempts to say what that point might be. Before attending to these arguments, however, I want to note briefly one motive for requiring that mental sentences have content which should be rejected. We noted earlier that if the syntactic states postulated by cognitive theories have content (and if the content correlates with syntactic types), then the intentional states posited by folk psychology will have been vindicated by scientific psychology. Thus one might be tempted to require that mental sentences have semantic properties precisely in order to ensure that the posits of commonsense psychology are compatible with theories in cognitive science. It is my guess that deep down some such motive is behind Fodor's insistence that mental sentences must be semantically interpreted, despite his acknowledgment that semantic interpretation does no work in cognitive theories.

It is easy to sympathize with this speculative reconstruction of Fodor's motivation. One cannot but hope that *some* vindication of propositional attitudes will be forthcoming, since without them we hardly know where to begin in thinking about ourselves, our institutions, our history, and our values. But surely our desire to vindicate the intentional states of folk psychology cannot be used as a reason for imposing the semantic constraints of the Weak RTM on cognitive theorizing, for this would be to put the cart before the horse. If propositional attitudes are to be vindicated by showing that they can be identified with states postulated by cognitive science, then the states in question must be something that the cognitive theorist has independent reason to postulate. It is no vindication at all to identify propositional attitudes with semantically interpreted mental sentences, if the only reason the theorist has for postulating semantically interpreted (rather than purely syntactic) mental sentences is to vindicate the propositional attitudes. If there is a legitimate point to imposing the restrictions of the Weak RTM, we will have to look elsewhere to find it.

4. Interpreting Internal States to Explain Interpreted Behavior

The question now before us is whether there would be any reason for the cognitive theorist to adopt the more restrictive constraints of the Weak RTM in preference to the more permissive STM paradigm. Is there anything to be gained by insisting that the mental sentences postulated by a cognitive theory must have content or truth conditions? One argument that might be construed as speaking to this issue is reported by Pylyshyn, though attributed to Fodor.

> As Jerry Fodor has pointed out to me, one can hardly escape the interpretation problem entirely. For suppose that we accepted Stich's insistence that when his daughter thought about sums, her thoughts should simply be viewed as uninterpreted symbols. Now what are we to say about the case in which his daughter actually says "five"? Are we to take that as an uninterpreted symbol as well? Are we to maintain that linguistic tokens are uninterpreted? Surely nobody would agree to that. But now the point is that so long as we need to interpret some of the organism's behavior, we need to interpret the internal symbols to which it is causally connected (although an uninterpreted state X could cause an event in

some equivalence class, such as that which corresponds to uttering a sound of a certain sort, we can only explain why it leads to saying the number "five" by interpreting X as having something to do with numbers). We must, as Haugland has argued, carry the intentional interpretation inward in order to explain the output under that particular interpretation.[15]

As Pylyshyn depicts him, Fodor is making a pair of claims: first that utterance tokens are semantically interpreted, and second that we can explain why an internal state leads to an interpreted utterance only by interpreting the internal state itself. I am inclined to think that both of these claims are correct, but I do not think they provide any serious support for the Weak RTM. My argument turns on a pair of considerations. First, although Fodor and Pylyshyn are surely right that much linguistic behavior can be described in intentional or semantic terms, it is far from clear that cognitive psychology ought to aim at explaining this behavior *described in this way*. Second, even if it is necessary to "carry the intentional interpretation inward" in order to explain behavior described in semantic terms, this does not justify requiring that *all* mental sentences be semantically interpreted, nor does it justify requiring that all tokens of the same mental sentence type have the same semantic interpretation. To explain the production of a semantically interpreted utterance, it suffices to assume that the belief state *token* underlying the utterance admits of a semantic description. Let me take up these points in turn.

Commonly, utterances can be characterized with the aid of a content sentence. When my daughter, having mastered elementary arithmetic, utters the words, "Seven plus five equals twelve," she is saying that seven plus five equals twelve. This much is beyond dispute. But of course there are many ways of describing any bit of behavior, and as Fodor himself has noted very clearly, we cannot expect a psychological theory to explain behavior under any and every description.[16] So let us reflect on whether behavioral descriptions of the form 'S said that p' are suitable explananda for psychological theory. In chapter 8 we argued that psychology should aim at explaining behavior only under autonomous descriptions. If that is correct then, generally, 'S said that p' will not be an appropriate psychological explanandum.* The analogy with selling a car should be borne in mind. Plainly people sometimes

---

*Oddly, 'S said that seven plus five equals twelve' may be an exception, since if 'said that seven plus five equals twelve' is true of my daughter then, as best I can tell, it will be true of her replicas as well. But this is a quirk of content sentences which refer to abstract objects like numbers. 'S said that Nixon is not a crook' or 'S said that Ouagadougou is the capital of Upper Volta' clearly are not autonomous behavioral descriptions.

do sell cars. But it seems clear that this is not the sort of behavioral description under which a systematic cognitive theory ought to attempt to explain their behavior. For to actually sell a car various legal preconditions must obtain. And, not to put too fine a point on it, these are just none of psychology's business.

From the fact that a psychological theory cannot explain why I sold my car (that is, cannot explain my behavior under that description), it should not be concluded that my selling the car cannot be explained at all. The right conclusion to draw is that my selling the car is a conceptually hybrid act. Explanations of such acts require several components. First we need an explanation of the behavior I exhibited while selling my car, *autonomously described.** Second, we need an account of why that behavior, in those circumstances, constituted the act of *selling my car.* This second component of the story will marshal historical facts, legal facts, and perhaps other sorts of facts as well. There is an important analogy between this case and the case of saying that Ouagadougou is the capital of Upper Volta. In the latter case, as in the former, psychological theory alone cannot be expected to explain the behavior under the folk description at hand. Rather, psychology can explain the behavior under an appropriate autonomous description. A second component of the explanation will detail why that behavior, in those circumstances, constituted the act of saying that Ouagadougou is the capital of Upper Volta. This second component will invoke facts about the history of the language, facts about patterns of usage in the speaker's linguistic community (both of these being relevant to the determination of reference), and no doubt other sorts of facts as well.

I think this point is of the utmost importance. The explanation of human action as it is described in the everyday language of human affairs is a complex and variegated business. Many different disciplines have a legitimate part to play in this endeavor, including jurisprudence, sociology, linguistics, anthropology, history, philosophy and others. Among cognitive psychologists one sometimes runs across the conviction that psychology alone can explain human action under the full range of commonsense action descriptions. But this disciplinary imperialism does no service to cognitive science. The explanation of human action under commonsense action descriptions is not an endeavor that can be confined within a single intellectual domain.

The second claim of the Pylyshyn/Fodor argument is that to explain the production of a semantically interpreted behavior we must carry

---

*I am not at all sure just what an appropriate autonomous description of this behavioral event would be. Indeed, perhaps an appropriate autonomous behavioral descriptive language does not yet exist. But no one said psychology was supposed to be *easy.*

the interpretation inward to the mental state which causes the behavior. The idea here is that an utterance does not *count* as saying that Ouagadougou is the capital of Upper Volta unless it is *caused by* the belief that Ouagadougou is the capital of Upper Volta. A necessary condition of being an utterance with a certain semantic characterization is being caused by a mental state with the same semantic characterization.* Indeed Fodor and Pylyshyn might add that the situation is similar for behaviors like selling my car. Presumably a bit of behavior does not count as selling my car if it is not caused by the intention to sell my car. If I sign the papers with the intention of giving you the autograph you have requested, then I have not sold you my car, even if what I have autographed is a bill of sale.

Now I am inclined to think that, details aside, all of this is basically right. What it shows is that we must assign content or semantic interpretations to mental states if we are to explain behavioral episodes under commonsense descriptions. But this does not constitute an argument for the Weak RTM. For the Weak RTM, recall, is a view about what theories in cognitive psychology should be like, and we have just argued that it is no part of the business of cognitive psychology to explain behavioral episodes under these descriptions. Even waiving this point, however, the Pylyshyn/Fodor argument would not lend support to the Weak RTM. For what Pylyshyn and Fodor have shown is that to explain the occurrence of a semantically interpreted utterance *token* we must assign a content or semantic interpretation to the belief *token* that causes it. What they have not shown is that all belief tokens of the same syntactic type must be assigned the same content, or indeed any content at all. It is entirely possible for a pair of subjects to have syntactically identical B-state tokens, and for these B-state tokens to lead to the production of phonetically identical utterance tokens, though both the utterance tokens and their respective underlying B-state tokens differ from one another in content or truth conditions. That, recall, was the moral to most of the examples marshaled in chapter 4, section 2. It is also entirely possible for a pair of subjects to share B-states of the same syntactic type, leading to utterances of the same phonetic type, though content can be ascribed to one subject's utterance and underlying B-state but not to the other's. The case of the child whose arithmetic knowledge is quite primitive illustrates this possibility, as does the case of the immigrant whose words have hopelessly tangled reference. The

---

*Actually this is a bit too simple. I need not believe that Ouagadougou is the capital of Upper Volta in order for my utterance to count as saying it. Rather, I must have some suitably involuted Gricean intention, part of which gets the same semantic interpretation as my utterance. But such complications are irrelevant to the present argument, and I shall ignore them.

Weak RTM, however, requires that *all* mental sentences in the purview of a cognitive psychological theory have content or truth conditions, not merely that some tokens of some mental state types do. Moreover, the interesting version of the Weak RTM requires that all tokens of a mental sentence type have the *same* content or truth conditions. Nothing in the Pylyshyn/Fodor argument shows that there would be any point to imposing such constraints on theories in cognitive psychology. Indeed our recent reflections indicate that there is good reason not to accept these constraints, since if the cognitive theorist restricts his theory to mental sentences which have content or truth conditions, then the mental processes of many subjects will be beyond its reach.

In contrast with the Weak RTM, the STM seems perfectly suited to handle the situation. The STM does not deny that some mental state tokens may have content or truth conditions. Rather, by its silence on the matter, it suggests that this is none of psychology's business. Also, the STM is prepared to countenance both contentless mental tokens and mental types whose tokens differ in content. So theories in the STM mold need not ignore the mental states of people who are very young, very ill, or very confused.

5. The Arguments from Reliability and Limited Knowledge

The Weak RTM makes a pair of claims: first, that cognitive processes are to be viewed as sequences of formal or syntactic operations on the formulae of an internal mental code, and second, that these formulae have content or semantic properties. It is this second claim that distinguishes the Weak RTM from the Syntactic Theory of the Mind. The question we have been pondering is what point there might be to imposing the requirement of semanticity, given that the semantic properties of mental states play no role in the generalizations of the theory. Why not simply view cognitive processes as formal or syntactic processes and let it go at that? During the last few years, an answer to this question—actually a cluster of distinct but similar answers—has been suggested by a trio of philosophers at the University of Southern California: Hartry Field, Brian Loar, and Stephen Schiffer. In this section I propose to take a critical look at the USC proposal. I will focus my discussion on the extended, non-technical version of the view developed by Schiffer.[17]

To begin, some amplification is in order on just how these philosophers understand the requirement that the sentences of the mental code have semantic properties. On Schiffer's view the very least that is required for mental formulae to have semantic properties is for them to have *truth conditions*.[18] To suppose that each formula in the internal code has a truth condition is to suppose that there is some theory which entails, for every formula F in the mental code, a theorem of the form

F is T if and only if S

where 'S' is replaced by a metalanguage sentence. Schiffer calls such a theory a "Tarski-theory" and the predicate 'T' implicitly defined by such a theory a "Tarski-predicate." As Schiffer points out, not just any Tarski-theory for the formulae of the internal code can be accepted as a genuine semantics or truth theory for those formulae since there are indefinitely many alternative Tarski-theories, which assign radically different T-conditions. It might be thought that the obvious advice here is to accept the Tarski-theory whose T-conditions are also genuine truth conditions, i.e., the one that assigns to each formula the conditions under which it is in fact true. But this doesn't help much, for it assumes there is some independent fact about each formula in the mental code, a fact which specifies what its truth condition really is. And, on Schiffer's view, it is not at all clear what sort of fact might this be, nor how we are supposed to gain access to it.

The central strategic move in Schiffer's paper is to suggest that in viewing the problem of selecting among Tarski-theories in this way we have picked up the wrong end of the stick. Instead of looking for some independent set of facts which determine the truth conditions of sentences in the mental code, we should ask what we want an assignment of truth conditions *for*. As Schiffer puts it, "the question 'What are the truth conditions of the sentences [in the mental code]?' can have no sense for us, no cash-value, that is over and above the question, 'Which Tarski-predicate on [the mental code] *should* we employ?' " (p. 213) Once the issue has been cast in this way, Schiffer's concerns link up neatly with our own. What troubled us was why a theorist should want to postulate or assign semantic properties like truth conditions to the formulae of a mental code. And this is precisely what Schiffer proposes to tell us.

As a heuristic aid to his argument, Schiffer invites us "to consider a rather unusual individual" whom he calls 'Hilarious Meadow'.

> We shall suppose that Hilarious has beliefs and desires in whatever sense we have them, although initially we do not know what they are, and that he thinks in a system of internal representation. We shall also suppose that he has quite a large transparent head, and that the sentences of his internal system are clearly visible to us; but, as we do not know what the sentences mean, they look to us like the orthographic inscriptions of some totally unfamiliar

> language, which, of course, is exactly what they are. Nevertheless, we *will* suppose that we do know (a) which strings are sentences of Meadow's internal system, (b) what the conceptual role of each sentence is . . . , and (c) exactly which sentences he believes and desires. As regards this last supposition, we might suppose that within Hilarious's transparent head there are two large transparent boxes, one marked 'B', the other 'D', and that Hilarious believes just those sentences that are stored in B, and, likewise, desires just those that are stored in D. . . . Let us refer to Meadow's internal system of representation as 'M'. . . . (pp. 212–213)

By the "conceptual role" of a sentence, Schiffer means "its role in theoretical and practical reasoning; a theory of conceptual role . . . would tell us how sensory stimulation influences what sentences we believe, how our beliefs influence one another, and how beliefs and desires lead to further desires, and eventually to bodily movement." That is, a theory of conceptual role would be what we have been calling a syntactic theory of mental processes. And Schiffer is willing to grant that, in principle, "an adequate conceptual role psychological theory plus all relevant environmental facts" would be entirely adequate for the explanation of behavior (p. 218). In light of this, the question at hand is "why we should need to employ *any* Tarski-predicate for M, why, in other words, we should need a semantical characterization of M" (p. 214).

Schiffer proposes a pair of interconnected answers to this question, the first centering on the utility of "head-world reliability correlations," and the second on the prediction of behavior in the absence of detailed knowledge about the environment. Here is his account of "head-world reliability":

> If Hilarious is like us, and we are supposing that he is, then the fact that he believes a certain sentence will often be a very reliable index of how the world is. For example, we might haphazardly discover of a certain sentence S that the fact that Hilarious believes S is extremely reliable evidence that Hilarious had left-over Chinese food for breakfast.
>
> We are about to see that we may well wish systematically to exploit these reliability correlations, and the crucial point as regards the justification of the truth predicate is that we *can* systematically exploit these reliability correlations by defining Tarski-predicates on M. Given a Tarski-predicate T, we can speak of a sentence's T-condition, and they may be categorized in various ways so that we can form generalizations of the form:
>
> For any sentence S of M, if S's T-condition is of kind K, then

the probability of S being T given that Hilarious believes (desires, intends, etc.) S is such and such.

Thus, if we can find reasons for the systematic exploitation of head-world reliability correlations, then we shall be in a position to justify the employment of a Tarski-predicate on M.

One obvious reason for wanting systematically to exploit head-world reliability correlations is that we have an interest in gaining information about the world; and given a suitable reliability theory for M we should be able to exploit Hilarious as a source of information about the world. (pp. 216–217)

Whatever the defects of Schiffer's argument may be, it is certainly the right kind of answer to the question that confronts us. What troubled us was why a theorist should want to postulate that the syntactic objects of his computational psychological theory have semantic properties. Schiffer's answer is that by doing so the theorist would be able to exploit his subjects as a source of information about the world. If this is correct, then surely it is a perfectly reasonable justification for the postulation of semantic properties. However, for two rather different reasons I am inclined to think that semantically interpreting the formulae of the mental code in the way that Schiffer suggests will not in fact facilitate the use of subjects as sources of information about the world. First, there is reason to doubt the very possibility of constructing a truth theory for the formulae of an internal mental code which will do the kind of work Schiffer requires of it. Second, I am dubious about the prospect of building a reliability theory of the sort Schiffer's account requires. I will take up these points in turn.

The conjuring of Hilarious Meadow is a clever and useful device for clarifying the issue of semantic interpretation, but a certain ambiguity is introduced by focusing the discussion on a single individual. Schiffer labels Meadow's system of internal representation 'M', and the problem he poses is "why we should need a semantical characterization for M" (p. 214). What is unclear here is whether the semantical characterization we seek is supposed to apply only to the tokens that occur within Hilarious's head, or whether it is supposed to apply to tokens of the same functional or syntactic type that occur within other heads. Suppose for example that Hilarious has a twin brother, Ridiculous, who uses the same syntactic system of internal formulae. Ridiculous and Hilarious need not have just the same formulae in their B and D boxes, but they do share the same "conceptual role psychology." Is a semantical characterization of M also a semantical characterization for Ridiculous's system of internal representation? Or might we require very different semantic theories for Hilarious and Ridiculous? Nothing that Schiffer says entails a clear answer to this question. But since the prospect of a different semantic theory for each individual would surely be noteworthy, I am inclined to infer from Schiffer's silence that he thinks a single semantic theory will do for all subjects who share the same conceptual role psychology.

If he does think this, however, he is certainly mistaken. To see this we need only recall some of the examples, which show that states with the same narrow causal profile are often about quite different things. Tom and his Victorian counterpart had beliefs that were identical by the narrow causal standard, though Tom's belief was about Eisenhower, while Dick's was about Angell-James. Similarly John and Robin had beliefs which were identical on the narrow causal standard though John's were about chicory and Robin's were about endive. To tie these examples to our present concern we need a pair of observations. First, the narrow causal standard of individuation is just the standard that would be applied by what Schiffer calls a "conceptual role psychology." So a conceptual role theory would count Tom's belief and Dick's as tokens of the same syntactic type, and similarly for John's belief and Robin's. Second, the referential difference that conceptual role psychology ignores *makes a difference* when our aim is to use a subject's beliefs as sources of information about the world. Dick might be a passingly good source of information about Angell-James. But it better not turn out that we can exploit him as a source of information about Eisenhower, since Dick died before Eisenhower was born.

What we have shown so far is that there can be no single truth theory for the formulae of the human internal code. Rather, we shall need many different truth theories, even assuming that we all share the same conceptual role psychology. Still, this does not completely undermine Schiffer's proposed justification for seeking a semantics for mental syntax. We might still hope to use subjects' beliefs as a source of information about the world with the help of personalized semantics. To do this we must supplement our semantics with a theory of reliability which, as Schiffer portrays it, details the probability that a subject's belief will be T as a function of the category into which its truth condition falls. The prospects of constructing such a theory strike me as singularly bleak.

Part of the reason for my skepticism is that a reliability theory, like a truth theory, will have to be personalized. Perhaps the fact that Hilarious believes S is a reliable indicator that Hilarious had leftover Chinese food for breakfast. But the same sentence in Ridiculous's B box might be a much less reliable indicator that Ridiculous had leftover Chinese food for breakfast. Why? Well here are just a few of the possible reasons:

1. Hilarious knows his oriental cuisines well; Ridiculous doesn't. There is a good chance that Ridiculous would mistake leftover Thai food for leftover Chinese food, though Hilarious would never make such a mistake.

2. Hilarious and Ridiculous are equally poor at telling Chinese food from other sorts of oriental food, but Ridiculous lives in San Francisco, where all manner of oriental restaurants abound, while Hilarious lives in Little Rock, where the only oriental food available is Chinese. Thus the probability that Hilarious might *encounter* any leftover oriental food which is not Chinese is close to zero.

3. Ridiculous believes that any food in a doggie bag from Ming's is Chinese. Hilarious knows that Ming's serves a variety of oriental cuisines. Thus when Ridiculous eats oriental food from a Ming's doggie bag he comes to believe S. Under the same circumstances, Hilarious does not come to believe S. Since Hilarious lacks the false belief which sometimes leads Ridiculous to believe S when he hasn't eaten Chinese food for breakfast, S is a more reliable indicator in Hilarious's head than in Ridiculous's. Note the theoretical point underlying this example. Hilarious and Ridiculous are ideologically different; one has a belief that the other lacks. What this example shows is that even minor ideological differences can have a major impact on the reliability of a belief. So a personalized theory of reliability would have to take careful account of just about all a subject's beliefs. Not an inviting prospect.

The need to personalize reliability theory is not the only reason to doubt that such a theory could be built. There is a further worry, even within a personalized theory, about finding appropriate ways to categorize T-conditions. The needed categories are the ones which will play a role in generalizations of the form Schiffer indicates. Though Schiffer does not tell us what these categories might be like, one might assume that what he has in mind are broad categories like T-conditions dealing with one's perceptual environment, or T-conditions dealing with one's past history. But this plainly will not do. Ridiculous may be very *un*reliable when the belief in question is that he had Chinese food for breakfast but very *reliable* when the belief is that he had French food. Indeed if we take seriously the idea of building personalized theories of reliability, it may well turn out that we will have to assess the reliability of a subject's beliefs in categories as slim as a single belief each.

What I would conclude from all this is that the prospects are very dim indeed for exploiting subjects as sources of information about the world by building a truth theory for their mental code and plugging this into a systematic theory of reliability. If this is the best reason we have for seeking a semantics for the mental code, then surely we are better off to forget about semantics and seek our information about the world directly. This conclusion should not be misconstrued as claiming that we do not, or ought not, use other people as sources of information. As Schiffer rightly notes, we do this all the time; it is the very raison d'être of linguistic communication. It would be out of place here to attempt a detailed account of how we pull it off, and that is a bit of luck, since I have no worked-out account to offer. Part of the story, I suspect, is that we ascribe content to some tokens of some mental states of some people, more or less as recounted in chapter 5. Another part of the story must involve inference to the best explanation. If Schiffer believes that there were small pink spots on his desk last night, I would be inclined to believe it too. If what he believes is that there were small pink elephants on his desk, however, I am not much inclined to believe it. The difference surely has everything to do with inference to the best explanation. But whatever the correct account might be, it certainly is not the case that we now do it Schiffer's way. We couldn't, since we do not know what the internal code is, we do not have a semantics for it, and we have no theory of reliability. On the last two counts, if my recent remarks have been on target, we are not likely to see much improvement.

I noted earlier that Schiffer offers a second reason why a theorist might want a truth-theory for formulae in the internal code, a reason that centered on predictions of behavior under conditions of limited information. Here is how Schiffer makes the point:

> We may refer to the conjunction of our reliability theory and our conceptual role psychological theory as our *extended psychological theory of Hilarious*. The essential points now are these.
>
> (1) The conceptual role theory together with our knowledge of what sentences of M Hilarious believes, desires, and intends at a given time can only lead us to predictions of the bodily movements caused by such states.
>
> (2) However, the *extended* psychological theory together with the same knowledge of Hilarious's thoughts will also lead us to predictions about the impact of his bodily movements on the environment; that is, more intuitively put, it will lead us to predictions of bodily movements *under descriptions which ascribe to them effects on the environment*.
>
> (3) The extended theory would be superfluous to our understanding of Hilarious if we had the conceptual role theory plus easy access to all relevant environmental facts; but we do not have such access, and, as things are, the extended theory is crucial to such understanding. . . .

[I] want to illustrate [these points] by reference to two hypothetical cases.

Case 1. We are given that Hilarious intends a certain sentence S, and that he believes and desires certain other sentences. Our conceptual role psychological theory of Hilarious does not directly associate any bodily movement with his intending S, but it does enable us to predict, on the basis of this intention together with the aforementioned concomitant beliefs and desires, that he will presently, perhaps instantly, intend a certain sentence S', and that this intention will result in the contraction of his right index finger. That, of course, is the *limit* of what *can* be yielded by the conceptual role theory with respect to the particular sequence of thoughts in question. However, it happens that, quite apart from the deliverances of our conceptual role theory, we also know that there is a gun in Hilarious's hand, that the gun is loaded, that the safety catch is off, that his right index finger is firmly planted against the trigger, and that the gun is pointing directly at the midsection of someone who is standing 10 feet in front of Hilarious. Now, on the basis of the deliverance of our conceptual role theory together with what we know independently about the immediate environment, we should be able to predict that Hilarious will shoot the person standing before him.

Case 2. As before, Hilarious intends S, and has the other concomitant beliefs and desires. But, unlike before, we now have no knowledge of Hilarious's circumstances; we know, initially, nothing about the gun in his hand, the proximity of another person, etc. Yet we do have our extended psychological theory for Hilarious, which incorporates a certain reliability theory, which incorporates a certain Tarski-predicate on M, and it further happens that: (a) the Tarski-predicate, T, is such that our Tarski-theory for M has as a theorem the sentence ⌐σ is T iff Hilarious shoots the person standing before him⌐, where σ is a structural description of S, the already mentioned sentence Hilarious intends; and (b) our reliability theory enables us to compute the probability of S being T, given that Hilarious intends S, is quite high. In the event, we should again be able to predict that Hilarious will shoot the person standing before him, even though this time we knew nothing initially about Hilarious's circumstances.

On the basis of this example, and the remarks preceding it, this much should now be obvious: from the point of view of our *practical interests* in having a psychological theory of Hilarious's behavior, the extended psychological theory is absolutely indispensable, and the mere conceptual role theory, unsupplemented by a reliability theory, would be next to useless. (pp. 218–219)

Several points must be granted to Schiffer. First, it is quite true that to predict behavior under the descriptions that are likely to be of the most practical interest to us—that is, under descriptions which ascribe environmental effects to them—a conceptual role (or purely syntactic) theory would have to be supplemented by a great deal of environmental information, information of a sort we sometimes will not have. Second, if we had a reliability theory of the sort Schiffer describes, we could predict behavior under these interesting environmental-effect descriptions, even without detailed information about the environment. What I find wildly implausible about all of this is the thought that we could ever have a reliability theory that does what Schiffer requires. Indeed it is less than clear that it even *makes sense* to talk about the probabilities that Schiffer's reliability theory must specify. Consider what the reliability theory must do. It must tell us what the probability is that Hilarious will shoot the person standing before him, given that Hilarious intends to shoot the person standing before him. What is more, it must tell us what this probability is *in general*, not merely in the particular circumstances that Hilarious now finds himself in. To do this, I should think, we must know the conditional probability (given only that he has the intention) that Hilarious will have a gun in his hand, that the safety will be off, that the gun will be in good working order, that the gun will be loaded, that he will know how to use it, that his aim will be true, that the victim will not duck, and that no one will interfere. Now I submit that in most instances we have no serious idea how to go about determining such a conditional probability. Whatever would we measure to determine the likelihood that an unspecified intended victim might successfully duck? Moreover in those few cases where we might make some headway toward establishing an empirical reliability estimate, the information needed would be, if anything, more difficult to obtain than the environmental information whose occasional absence leads Schiffer to seek a theory of reliability. What this shows, I think, is that Schiffer's second reason for seeking a semantics for the mental code is no better than his first. A truth theory for mental syntax will be of no help in predicting behavior unless we can supplement it with a theory of reliability, and the prospects for the latter sort of theory are simpiy hopeless.

A basically sound perception underlies Schiffer's second argument for mental code semantics. From the point of view of our practical interests, a mere conceptual role (or syntactic) psychology would be next to useless unless it is substantially supplemented by facts about the environment in which the subject finds himself. This ought not to be construed as a criticism of the STM paradigm however, for very much the same is true of just about any sophisticated empirical theory. Classical physics will not tell us what we want to know about the trajectory of a spacecraft unless we know a great deal about the environment through which the spacecraft is traveling, and organic chemistry is often next to useless in predicting the pharmacological properties of a new compound because we do not know enough about the environment in which it will be active. I conclude that Schiffer's discussion has given us no reason to seek a semantics for the mental code and thus that he has provided no justification for preferring the Weak RTM to the less restrictive STM paradigm.

6. The Case Against the Weak RTM

Thus far in this chapter I have bent over backward to give the Weak RTM the benefit of the doubt, and I have politely refrained from pointing out just how curious a view it is. In this concluding section I propose to be a bit less delicate. The Weak RTM begins with the concession that semantic properties play no role in the generalizations of cognitive science. Nonetheless it insists that the cognitive theorist must assume or postulate that all the mental states to which his theory applies *have* truth conditions (or content) and thus that he must refrain from constructing theories which apply to states which cannot be assigned content or truth conditions in any natural way. Our discussion has been devoted to pondering what justification there might be for imposing what seems, at first blush, to be a quite pointless restriction.

What has so far hardly been mentioned is that, quite apart from its apparent pointlessness, there are good reasons *not* to accept the restrictions imposed by the Weak RTM. If the Weak RTM is construed as committed to the correlation thesis, then the best reason for rejecting it is that it is *false*. It simply is not the case that the content or truth conditions of those mental state tokens to which content or truth conditions can be ascribed correlate with the syntactic type or narrow causal profile of the tokens. The point was argued at length in chapters 4 and 5, and as we have seen, it is sporadically conceded by advocates of the Weak RTM.

Even if we ignore the embarrassment over the correlation thesis, however, there is abundant reason not to accept the Weak RTM's restraints. Indeed the case against the Weak RTM can be built by borrowing some of the arguments offered against the strong version of the representational theory. In chapter 7, I argued that cognitive theories which couch their generalizations in terms of content would find ideologically, functionally and referentially unusual subjects beyond their reach. Thus the Strong RTM impedes the quest for developmental, comparative, and clinical cognitive theories. But much the same argument applies mutatis mutandis to the Weak RTM. For although the Weak RTM does not insist that a cognitive theory's generalization advert to content, it does insist that the states postulated by a cognitive theory can be assigned content in some natural way. Recall that the central point in the argument against the Strong RTM was that there is no comfortable way to assign content to the mental states of young children, exotic folk, brain-damaged patients, and others. So the Weak RTM, like the Strong, promises to cripple developmental, comparative, and clinical cognitive theorizing. Even if we had found some reason in favor of imposing the Weak RTM on cognitive science, this would surely count heavily against doing so. Since all of the proposed justifications of the Weak RTM have been found wanting, I think we have an overwhelming case for adopting the Syntactic Theory of the Mind over either version of the Representational Theory.

Chapter 10

Will the Concepts of Folk Psychology Find a
Place in Cognitive Science?

Let me summarize the argument of part II thus far. The question with which we began was whether the folk psychological notion of belief was likely to find a comfortable place in cognitive science. Two conceptions of cognitive science were proposed which promised an affirmative answer, viz. the Strong and the Weak Representational Theories of the Mind. But I have argued that neither of these views is tenable. To replace them, I have urged the adoption of the Syntactic Theory of the Mind, which construes cognitive mental states as relations to purely formal or syntactic mental sentences. If as I have argued, cognitive science is and should be adhering to the STM paradigm, then it would appear that there is no place for the folk concept of belief in cognitive science. This conclusion follows from three related observations. First, the mental state tokens postulated by cognitive theories in the STM mold need not and often will not admit of any comfortable ascription of content. Second, an STM theory may view mental state tokens to which content *can* be ascribed as type identical to tokens with quite a different content. Thus, third, it will generally not be possible to correlate the state types postulated by STM theories with any truth condition or content sentence. But it is of the essence of folk psychological belief state types that they have content or truth conditions. Folk psychology individuates beliefs and specifies the causal relations among them in terms of their content. Thus we cannot identify folk psychological belief state types with mental state types as they are conceived in STM theories. The folk psychological property of *believing that snow is white* cannot be identified with any property recognized by an STM cognitive theory.

To the best of my knowledge, this strategy of arguing against the scientific utility of folk psychological concepts is quite new in the literature. Not so the conclusion it supports. A number of other writers have argued that folk psychology and serious science are ill suited to one another, and this chapter will be devoted to a survey of their arguments. I am inclined to think that each of the arguments I will recount lends some further support to the conclusion, though none of them is free from problems. It will perhaps come as no surprise that among the arguments to be reviewed, the one I find most persuasive anticipates some of the themes that occupied us in the previous three chapters.

1. Folk Psychology Is a Degenerating Research Program

In a number of places[1] Patricia and Paul Churchland have argued that folk psychology "is a stagnant or degenerating research program, and has been for millennia."[2] Underlying this claim is the view that folk psychology constitutes "an empirical theory, with all the functions, virtues, *and perils* entailed by that status."[3] The function of folk psychology, qua theory, is to explain behavior, and its most conspicuous virtue is that it enables us to "explain, and even predict, the behavior of other persons with a facility and success that is remarkable."[4] The peril alluded to is that folk psychology might "constitute a radically false theory, a theory so fundamentally defective that both the principles and the ontology of that theory will eventually be displaced."[5] On the Churchlands' view, it is at least a good bet that the concepts and ontology of folk psychology will not find any place in the scientific canon of the future.

The argument for this conjecture consists of three observations. First, for all its workaday utility, folk psychology has some very notable shortcomings.

> Its comprehension both of practical and of factual reasoning is sketchy at best; the kinematics and dynamics of emotions it provides is vague and superficial; the vicissitudes of perception and perceptual illusion are, in its terms, largely mysterious; its comprehension of the learning process is extraordinarily thin; and its grasp on the nature and causes of mental illness is almost nil.[6]

> Consider our utter ignorance of the nature and psychological functions of sleep, that curious state in which a third of one's life is spent. Reflect on the common ability to catch an outfield fly ball on the run, or hit a moving car with a snowball. Consider the internal construction of a 3-D visual image from subtle differences in the 2-D array of stimulations in our respective retinas. . . . Or consider the miracle of memory, with its lightning capacity for relevant retrieval. On these and many other mental phenomena, [folk psychology] sheds negligible light.[7]

From all of this Churchland would have us conclude that folk psychology is "*at best* a highly superficial theory, a partial and unpenetrating gloss on a deeper and more complex reality. Having reached this opinion," he writes, "we may be forgiven for exploring the possibility that [folk psychology] provides a positively misleading sketch of our internal kinematics and dynamics, one whose success is owed more to selective application and forced interpretation on our part than to genuine theoretical insight on [folk psychology's] part.[8]

The second observation is historical. The story of folk psychology is "one of retreat, infertility, and decadence."[9]

> The [folk psychology] of the Greeks is essentially the [folk psychology] we use today, and we are negligibly better at explaining human behavior in its terms than was Sophocles. This is a very long period of stagnation and infertility for any theory to display, especially when faced with such an enormous backlog of anomalies and mysteries in its own explanatory domain. . . . [Folk psychology's] failure to develop its resources and extend its range of success is therefore darkly curious, and one must query the integrity of its basic categories.[10]

The Churchlands' third observation is that folk psychology comports poorly with those other, better developed sciences whose explanatory domains overlap to a greater or lesser extent with that of folk psychology. The point is an important one since it bears on the degree of tolerance we should extend in the face of folk psychology's failings. "A troubled or stagnant theory may merit patience and solicitude on other grounds; for example, on grounds that it is the only theory or theoretical approach that fits well with other theories about adjacent subject matters, or the only one that promises to reduce or to be explained by some established background theory whose domain encompasses the domain of the theory at issue."[11] But, Churchland argues, "it is just here, perhaps, that [folk psychology] fares poorest of all."[12]

> If we approach *homo sapiens* from the perspective of natural history and the physical sciences, we can tell a coherent story of his constitution, development, and behavioral capacities which encompasses particle physics, atomic and molecular theory, organic chemistry, evolutionary theory, biology, physiology, and materialistic neuro-science. That story, though still radically incomplete, is already extremely powerful, outperforming [folk psychology] at many points even in its own domain. And it is deliberately and self-consciously coherent with the rest of our developing world picture. In short, the greatest theoretical synthesis in the history of the human race is currently in our hands, and parts of it already provide searching descriptions and explanations of human sensory

input, neural activity and motor control.

> But [folk psychology] is no part of this growing synthesis. Its intentional categories stand magnificently alone, without visible prospect of reduction to that larger corpus.[13]

Churchland offers the following eloquent summary of his argument:

> What we must say is that [folk psychology] suffers explanatory failures on a epic scale, that it has been stagnant for at least twenty-five centuries, and that its categories appear (so far) to be incommensurable with or orthogonal to the categories of the background physical science whose long-term claim to explain human behavior seems undeniable. Any theory that meets this description must be allowed a serious candidate for outright elimination.[14]

Although I have considerable sympathy with some of the claims the Churchlands are urging, I am inclined to think that this is the weakest of the arguments to be considered in this chapter. It is clear that folk psychology leaves a great deal to be desired as a science, and that it has not made much progress since the time of Sophocles.[15] Still, there are at least three objections to the Churchland argument which undercut a fair amount of its persuasive power.

The first is the observation, lately stressed by Wilkes[16] that folk psychology is not properly viewed *merely* as a crude explanatory, scientific theory, since the terms of folk psychology have more work to do than do scientific terms.

> Although they share with the latter the tasks of describing, explaining and predicting, they have countless other roles as well: to warn, threaten, assess, applaud, praise, blame, discourage, urge, wheedle, sneer, hint, imply, insult . . . and so on. The conceptual apparatus of common-sense psychology stands to that of scientific psychology as a multi-purpose tool stands to a spanner.[17]

Wilkes actually argues for a much stronger thesis, viz., that "there is no useful sense of the term 'theory' whereby everyday psychological explanation suggests or contains a theory of the mind."[18] But this seems to me to overstate the case quite seriously. Our everyday use of folk psychological concepts to explain and predict the behavior of our fellows clearly presupposes some rough and ready laws which detail the dynamics of belief and desire formation and connect these states to behavior. These presupposed laws can with a bit of effort be teased out and made explicit.[19] Collectively they surely count as a commonsense theory. But to make the point against the Churchlands' argument we need only the weaker, and hardly controversial, observation that commonsense psychological notions are pressed into service in many ways besides explaining and predicting behavior. Given the many and varied uses of folk psychological notions, the failure of folk psychological theory to make any serious progress in the last two millenia seems less surprising. Since folk concepts served well in their non-proto-scientific roles, and since (as Churchland concedes) folk assumptions were not recognized as protoscientific theories, there was little pressure for them to evolve into better theories.

A second objection to the Churchlands' argument is that it exaggerates the importance of the stagnation in the history of folk psychology. True enough, our commonsense psychology has changed but little since Sophocles. But during most of the intervening millennia the very idea of doing empirical science and of evolving and elaborating concepts to meet the needs of a developing science was quite unknown. If folk psychology scored no major gains in the two thousand years after Aristotle, the same must be said for biology, chemistry, and economics. Those latter disciplines, or at least the first two, have fared rather better in the last few centuries. But this progress can be traced in substantial measure to the fact that their domains have become the subject matter of increasingly professionalized experimental sciences. Psychology, by contrast, has barely a century of history as an experimental discipline. What is more, though the earliest experimental psychologists—Wundt, James, and others—often attempted to exploit the conceptual apparatus of folk psychology, this strategy was largely extinguished in experimental psychology during the decades when behaviorism dominated the scene. It is only with the flourishing of the cognitive paradigm during the last decade or two that the idea of exploiting folk psychological notions in experimental psychology has regained respectability. So those who would defend the conceptual apparatus of folk psychology might plausibly protest that the program of exploiting these notions in serious science has barely begun. The charge of stagnation is thus, perhaps, premature.

A final objection to the Churchlands' argument focuses on the prospects for integration with other sciences. Though the Churchlands are surely correct in their contention that the conceptual apparatus of folk psychology comports poorly with the growing body of theory in the physical sciences, just the opposite is true if we look to the social sciences. Economics, political science, sociology, and anthropology are up to their ears in the intentional idiom that is the hallmark of folk psychology. If all talk of beliefs, desires, expectations, preferences, fears, suspicions, plans, and the like were banished from the social sciences, those disciplines as we know them today would disappear. We simply have no way of recounting our knowledge of social, political, and economic processes without invoking the intentional language of folk psychology. Of course, this observation might be viewed as a two-edged sword, indicating not that folk psychology is more respectable than the Churchlands maintain, but rather that the social sciences which share its conceptual apparatus are themselves targets for elimination from the growing canon of science. But, absent further argument, it is tempting to dismiss this move as no more than a crass physicalist prejudice. If, as Laudan urges, we choose between theories largely on the basis of the problems they solve, then for all their evident difficulties, the social sciences will be around for the foreseeable future.[20] For there are simply no serious competing theories which address problems in the social domain and which do not invoke the intentional concepts of folk psychology.

2. The Infralinguistic Catastrophe

A second argument due to Patricia and Paul Churchland turns on the fact that many creatures, including very young members of our own species, are not plausibly described as having beliefs at all.[21] There are no content sentences which are serious candidates to characterize the mental states of these creatures. Still, there is reason to suppose that the cognitive processes operative in ourselves are not fundamentally different from those in young children and nonlinguistic animals. Thus if the cognitive processes in infralinguistic creatures are not appropriately characterized in folk psychological terms, there is reason to think that the best theory characterizing our own cognitive activity will not characterize it in folk psychological terms either.

Here is how Paul Churchland elaborates the argument. The first premise is that

> the behavior of an infant during the first several months after birth invites description/explanation in terms of specific perceptions, beliefs and reasonings no more than does the (more leisurely) behavior of many plants, or the (more frantic) behavior of many microscopic protozoa. The apparently chaotic economy of an infant's behavior—and there is plenty of behavior if one looks closely—is not rendered transparent or coherent by any such projection of familiar categories. The relevant organization in its behavioral economy has yet to develop. Were it not for the fact that infants resemble and eventually develop into thinking adults, whereas plants and protozoa do not, we would not even be much tempted to ascribe propositional attitudes and our usual cognitive concepts to them.[22]

As Churchland notes, an opponent might insist that despite appearances very young children do have propositional attitudes, though "the particular propositions that would express the infant's attitudes are inexpressible in our language, the infant's ideas or concepts being primitive ones quite different from our own."[23] But he rightly dismisses this move as "a near paradigm of an untestable hypothesis."[24] Indeed without some better account of just what sort of entities propositions are supposed to be and what it is for a psychological state to "express" a proposition or to "have" one as its content, I am inclined to think that the "inexpressible propositions" move is worse than untestable; it is incomprehensible.

The second premise in Paul Churchland's version of the argument is that

> the basic parameters of rational intellectual activity are the same whatever its stage of development, notwithstanding the increasing degree to which that activity becomes "comprehensible" in terms of propositional attitudes as we consider the later stages of its development.[25]

More particularly Churchland claims that there are conspicuous continuities between infants and older, language-using children along "three dimensions of human development: the behavioural, the structural, and the functional."[26] Under the first heading, there is a "steady articulation of the infant's behavioural repertoire—from the stage where our usual cognitive concepts simply fail to find adequate purchase to a stage where they find paradigmatic application. . . . If there is any basic change or shift in the infant's mode of intellectual activity during that first year, it does not show itself in any characteristic change in the development of its behaviour."[27] Under the heading of "physiological or structural considerations, the situation with respect to continuity appears, at least at a gross level, much the same."

> The major brain cells or neurons are already formed some months before birth. Development from there consists most noticeably in such things as the branching growth of dendrites, the lengthening of axons, and the progressive myelinization of these interconnective impulse-carrying fibres. . . . All of these processes begin very early (prenatally, in fact), develop continuously, and continue to develop through infancy, childhood, and well into adult life. This apparent continuity of structural development speaks in favour of [the second premise].[28]

Finally, under the heading of functional continuity, what little we do know again speaks in favor of the second premise:

We know that the network of neurons/axons/dendrites generates and conducts nervous impulses, and that the conductive/generative dispositions of that network can be modified by the successive impulses to which it is subject. We know that the gross structure of that network is of a kind that fits it for the processing of information, and for evolving in the manner in which it does so . . . . And we know that the structural development that the brain undergoes fits it for processing information in more and more complex ways. But nervous activity in a network of this kind is a characteristic of the brain at *all* stages of its development, even to some degree of its immature, pre-natal stage. The brain, in short, is a self-modifying information processor from its inception to its death.[29]

The conclusion that Churchland would draw from these two premises is as follows:

As a general approach to what rational intellectual development consists in, the [folk psychological] approach is pursuing what must be superficial parameters. That is, sentential parameters cannot be among the primitive parameters comprehended by a truly adequate theory of rational intellectual development, and the relevance of sentential parameters must be superficial or at best derivative even in the case of fully mature language-using adults.[30]

In contrast with the previous "degenerating research program" argument, this argument is one I am inclined to endorse with little reservation. Indeed, it is very similar in spirit, if not in detail, to the argument I developed in chapter 7. Among my basic themes there was that in opting for a cognitive psychology built from folk notions we are likely to lose important generalizations, since folk psychology cannot characterize the mental states of young children or "exotic" folk. So if there are generalizations which apply equally to their cognitive processes and to our own, a cognitive theory couched in the language of folk psychology will be unable to articulate them. Churchland has given us some positive reasons to suspect that there are generalizations which encompass the cognitive processes of both infants and familiar adults. And he agrees with my contention that folk psychological descriptions have no comfortable purchase on the cognitive states of infants. The theory about our commonsense notion of belief developed in chapter 5 might in fact be a welcome supplement to Churchland's argument, since it explains why it is that the behavior of infants does not invite "description/explanation in terms of specific perceptions, beliefs and reasonings." Note, though, that Churchland's fulminations against "superficial sentential parameters" are justified only when they are directed toward theories which take cognitive states to be contentful or semantically interpreted mental sentences. Nothing Churchland says casts any suspicion on the purely syntactic theories that I have been urging. Churchland gives us no reason to think that the cognitive processes of infants cannot be characterized in purely syntactic terms. Thus if we attempt to extend his argument against "sentential parameters" to mental states conceived as they are in the STM paradigm, the first premise of the argument will go without support.

3. The Multiplicity of Mental States

For all its length and complexity, there is one important respect in which the account of our folk psychological notion of belief that I developed in chapter 5 was oversimplified. As I portrayed it, folk psychology deals with only a *pair* of basic mental categories—*beliefs*, which represent the world as we take it to be, and *desires*, which represent the world as we wish it would be. But this does not begin to capture the actual diversity of mental states recognized by common sense. In addition to *believing* that p, a person may *suspect* that p, *think* that p, *feel* that p, *assume* that p, *remember* that p, *recall* that p, *anticipate* that p, or *take p for granted*. With a modicum of effort this list of belief-like states would be easy to extend. And, of course, there is a parallel list for desire-like states. It was Wittgenstein who first focused philosophical attention on the diversity of mental state concepts expressible in ordinary language, and Wittgenstein too who first stressed the many and complex ways in which these concepts interrelate with one another as well as with various social and linguistic practices. Without an appropriate background of practices, we quickly lose our grip on the subtle distinctions embedded in our commonsense conceptual framework. In extreme cases the whole folk psychological conceptual network can seem awkward or inapplicable. Thus as Hacking notes, enthnographers often find themselves quite unable to locate familiar mental states in alien cultures.

> As soon as you get to interesting concepts, things go poorly. You may find that hoping or expressions of anger or joy don't have a place in that culture, thanks to a lack of the same array of practices that we have in ours. Likewise for *their* important concepts. Moreover, having grasped "hope," the other people needn't by analogy grasp our "joy" or "anger," for each is embedded in its own web. This may even be true for speech acts, like promising or even stating, that are sometimes held out as neutral between cultures.[31]

What Hacking reports about joy, anger, and hope is also apparently true of belief and its conceptual cousins. Needham gives a painstaking analysis of various more or less belief-like mental states recognized by a variety of societies and concludes that in many cases there just is nothing that matches up with our own notion of belief.[32] The practices of stating, reporting, avowing, accepting, defending, and so on, which form the backdrop for our own notion of belief, are unrecognizable in those societies. Thus to the extent that these practices constitute a necessary prerequisite for belief, persons in these societies simply do not have any beliefs.

All of this poses some obvious difficulties for the cognitive scientist who tries to press the folk notion of belief into service in his theory. The nuance and subtlety built into our folk notions serve a host of practical purposes in facilitating communication, analysis, and social relations. But they are unlikely to be of much interest to the cognitive scientist. What he needs is a broad cover term which embraces indifferently a wide range of subtly different folk notions in the belief family. The presupposed background of practices built into our folk notion of belief is problematic in another way for the cognitive scientist, since it threatens him with Needham's problem: in many societies the background practices are sufficiently different that there just isn't anything looking all that much like prototypical cases of belief.

Confronted with this difficulty, the obvious move for the theorist to make is to patch and trim the folk notion of belief, blotting out the fine distinctions that divide believing that p from thinking that p, remembering that p, feeling that p, suspecting that p, etc., and ignoring many of the conceptual ties that bind the folk notion of belief to various background practices or "language games." But once this conceptual surgery is complete, we might well wonder whether the resulting notion has much more than a label in common with the folk notion of belief. On Wilkes's view, the modifications needed to eliminate the "riotous overlap, alluring vagueness, categorial ambiguity, and rich shades of nuance"[33] in our folk notions are so drastic that we are left with a quite new concept.

> Once ordinary-language concepts have been adopted, they then have to be adapted—modified, tidied up, extended or restricted— in short, denaturalized: baked in the theoretical kiln until they bear as little resemblance to their parent concepts as do the physicists' notions of force, mass and energy.[34]

The curious thing about these conceptual contortions is that people making them do not take themselves to be twisting common concepts beyond recognition. Psychologists who adopt terms like 'belief' or 'memory' occasionally note that their technical usage departs a bit from ordinary language, but they clearly do not think they are doing violence to ordinary notions. A possible explanation of this fact is simply a lack of sensitivity to the richness and complexity of commonsense notions. But an alternative and equally plausible explanation is that in ordinary language the term 'belief' already serves as a broad general purpose cover term. Pursuing this idea Morton argues that while we sometimes use 'believes' in such a way that it contrasts with 'think', 'conjecture' and the rest, "we also use 'believes' as a particularly neutral member of the list." It is almost, though not quite "a neutral core for an accretion of further specifications."[35] If Morton is right, then the modifications mandated by the cognitive scientist's "theoretical kiln" might be viewed as relatively modest ones along lines already partly anticipated by everyday usage.

I do not propose to take sides in this dispute, for I suspect that the truth lies somewhere in the middle. The sort of broad nuance-neglecting use of 'believes' that would be required in a psychological theory would probably leaven distinctions to a greater extent than does the neutral use that Morton recounts. Whether these changes would be substantial enough to qualify as a change in the underlying concept is a question without an answer. Perhaps the best place to leave this issue is with the observation that if the arguments of the previous three chapters are correct, then the question is moot. The best strategy for cognitive science is the one advocated by the Syntactic Theory of the Mind, and by the time folk concepts have been modified *that* drastically, there can be little question that they no longer merit their ancestral titles.

Chapter 11
The Future of Folk Psychology

1. A Modified Panglossian Prospect

In part I my concern was to characterize the commonsense concept of belief that we invoke in describing and explaining ourselves and our fellows. The burden of part II has been that this folk notion of belief ought not to be invoked in the emerging discipline of cognitive science. More specifically, I have argued that neither the Strong nor the Weak Representational Theory of the Mind provides a suitable paradigm for the development of cognitive theories. For the remainder of this volume I shall take that conclusion as established. What I wish to ponder in this last chapter are the consequences of this result for the broader issues broached at the outset.

We began, recall, with the observation that if the more virulent strains of behaviorism had proved to be viable, then our commonsense world view, the "manifest image" of what we are like, was in serious trouble. For Watson and others, the mental states postulated by common sense— beliefs among them—are the superstitious posits of our savage past. In the sober light of science we can see that there *are* no such things, just as there are no gods to throw thunderbolts, nor witches to poison wells. Now, though the ghost still rattles its chains here and there, virulent behaviorism is a dead issue in psychology. It was done in by the cognitivist revolution whose partisans currently dominate the scientific study of mental states and processes. But if I am right in my contention that contemporary cognitivism makes no use of the folk psychological notion of belief and its intentional kin, then the status of the manifest image of mind is once again a live issue. For if the best science of the mind we now have does not mention the contentful states of folk psychology, is that not ample reason to conclude that the states posited by common sense do not exist and that statements of the form 'S believes that p' are uniformly false? Have we not perhaps shown that the behaviorists were *right* about the status of commonsense psychological posits, albeit for the wrong reason?

It is possible to be encouraged along this line of thought by a naive reading of Quine's doctrine on what there is.[1] For Quine the entities we are committed to are simply those quantified over in our best scientific theories. Thus if our best theories fail to quantify over putative entities of a certain sort, we should conclude that there are no such things. And since (ex hypothesis) cognitive science does not invoke the language or concepts of folk psychology, the states of folk psychology are not among the entities over which it quantifies. So these putative states do not exist.

I am quite sure that it is possible to be tempted by this argument, since I was so tempted, and for rather longer than I would like to admit. But I am now convinced that the temptation is one which must be resisted. For even if we accept the view that science alone is the arbiter of what exists and what does not,* we cannot infer from the fact that a term does not occur in the vocabulary of a theory to the conclusion that the theory does not quantify over the putative entities in the extension of the term.[2] So it is plainly mistaken to infer from the fact that a term occurs nowhere in science to the conclusion that the entities putatively denoted by the term do not exist. Consider, for example, such terms as 'favored by Elizabeth I', 'slept in by George Washington', or 'looks like Winston Churchill'. Surely none of these terms occurs in any currently received scientific theory. Nor is it likely that they will find a place in the scientific canon of the future. But it would be simply perverse to deny, on these grounds, that there are any beds slept in by George Washington or any men (or statues) that look like Winston Churchill. It would be comparably perverse to deny the existence of people who believe that p on the grounds that 'believes that p' is not invoked in cognitive science, or to deny the existence of beliefs that p because '(is a) belief that p' is ill suited to cognitive theory building.

Let us pursue this analogy a bit further. What we want to say, in the 'looks like Churchill' case is that our science does quantify over *human beings*; men and women are among the values of the variables of anthropology, physiology, etc. And, as it happens, some of those human beings look like Churchill; that is, they are entities which satisfy the predicate 'looks like Churchill'. Before attempting to tell an analogous story about beliefs, let me introduce an assumption that will substantially simplify our discussion. The assumption is that the correct cognitive theory is an STM theory which cleaves reasonably closely to the general pattern presupposed by folk psychology. Such a theory will postulate belief-like states which interact with desire-like states,

---

*In fairness to Quine, it is far from clear that he ever held such a view. The argument of the previous paragraph was billed as being inspired by a *naive* reading of Quine.

with perception, and so on along the lines sketched in figure 2.[3] The tokens of these states are particulars, which may have all sorts of properties in addition to those in virtue of which they count as syntactic states of a certain type. And it would seem perfectly plausible to say that certain of these syntactic state tokens are, as it happens, beliefs that p—that a certain current syntactic state token of mine, for example, happens to be a belief that Ouagadougou is the capital of Upper Volta. The analogy with 'looks like Churchill' is in some respects quite a good one, since if the analysis in chapter 5 is on the right track, then for a syntactic state token to count as a belief that Ouagadougou is the capital of Upper Volta, it must be *similar* to the state that typically underlies our own normal utterance of the content sentence. And it is certainly plausible to think that there are such belief-like state tokens, just as there are men and statues which look like Churchill, despite the fact that neither 'looks like Churchill' nor 'is a belief that Ouagadougou is the capital of Upper Volta' is a predicate to be taken seriously by science.

One way of construing the view I have been sketching is as a sort of token identity theory for beliefs: Each token of a belief that p is identical with some syntactic state token. I am not entirely happy about this way of putting the matter, however, because it suggests that 'token of the belief that p' specifies some well-defined class or category. But of course this is not the case. Since belief ascriptions behave like similarity judgments, whether or not a person can appropriately be said to believe that p, and thus whether or not one of his syntactic states can appropriately be described as the belief that p, will depend on the context in which the description is offered. So rather than talking of belief tokens being identical with syntactic state tokens, it would be less misleading, though more long-winded, to say that anything which, in a given context, may be appropriately described as a belief that p is identical with some belief-like syntactic state token. We will shortly see another reason for resisting talk of belief tokens.

It is important to note that while anything which can be described as a belief that p is identical with some syntactic state token, the converse of this identity claim is false. It is not the case that every belief-like syntactic state token can be described as a belief that p. For to count as a belief that p, a state must suitably resemble the state which typically underlies the production of some content sentence in our language. And if the correct cognitive theory does indeed posit a category of belief-like states, then almost certainly there are some belief-like state tokens among the very young, the very ill, or among exotic folk which do not much resemble the belief-like states giving rise to any of our own utterances.

This chapter began with the worry that our manifest image of the mind might be in conflict with the scientific image urged by cognitive science. But now it is beginning to look as though a much more optimistic conclusion is in order. It is not quite the Panglossian picture sketched in chapter 1, which portrayed cognitive science as adopting the language and concepts of folk psychology. Rather, the picture that is emerging is of a cognitive science that does not invoke the concepts of commonsense psychology but nonetheless postulates states many of whose tokens turn out to be describable as the belief that p, the desire that p, and so on. If this view can be sustained, then perhaps we need not worry about our scientific psychology undermining the humanities, the social sciences, and the many social institutions which are so intimately interwoven with the conceptual framework of folk psychology. To borrow a phrase from Fodor, such a conclusion would surely justify at least "modified rapture."[4] In the remaining pages of this section, I want to examine this cheerful view more carefully, looking first at what it has to say about the belief state *types* of folk psychology, second at what it entails about the generalizations of folk psychology, and finally at the account it suggests about the relation between cognitive science and the social sciences. Lest the reader be overcome by modified rapture, I should warn that like most silver linings, this one has its cloud. It will appear in the following section.

On the view we have been considering, my belief that Ouagadougou is the capital of Upper Volta is identical to some belief-like syntactic state token. But what about *believing that Ouagadougou is the capital of Upper Volta*, the property or state type which I share with other geographically knowledgeable people? What, if anything, is the property of believing that p to be identified with? The obvious suggestion is to identify folk psychological belief types with syntactic state types. But this simply won't do, since the proposed identification would entail what we earlier called the correlation thesis, and the correlation thesis is false.[5] Because of the role of reference and ideological similarity in determining whether a given state token counts as a belief that p, it is possible for a pair of syntactic state tokens to share the same syntactic state type even though one of those tokens would be a belief that p while the other would not. Conversely it is possible for a pair of belief-like syntactic state tokens both to count as beliefs that p in a given context even though the syntactic state tokens in question are different in syntactic type. This would be the case, for example, if the context emphasizes ideological or reference similarity, while requiring no more than a very rough causal-pattern similarity. It would also be the case in those contexts which require only a rough similarity in all dimensions. I am inclined to think that most of our attributions of beliefs to animals illustrate this sort of misfit between folk psychological and syntactic taxonomies. It would be quite remarkable if cats turned out to have cognitive states which are syntactically type identical with any of ours. But despite the fact that Tabby and I share no syntactically type identical states, it is often quite appropriate to describe one of her belief-like states as "the belief that her food is in the dish." (As we noted in chapter 8, section 1, there is a certain vagueness inherent in the notion of a syntactic state type. However, the range of variability here is bound to be less than the causal-pattern differences countenanced in some contexts by folk psychological belief ascriptions.) Since the property of believing that p is not in general coextensive with any syntactic state type, the property of believing that p cannot be identified with a syntactic state type.

But now if commonsense belief properties cannot be identified with syntactic state properties, just where do they fit into the ontological scheme of things? One proposal that seems to be suggested by our analysis of belief sentences is that the property of being a belief that p is simply the property of being similar to the syntactic state which typically underlies our normal utterance of 'p'. But I am inclined to think that this answer will not do either, since on any reasonable account of what a property is, it will turn out that there is no such thing as the property of being similar to the syntactic state . . . etc. The problem is that properties are the sorts of things which either are or are not possessed by an entity in a given possible world. But because of the context sensitivity of similarity, it is not the case that a syntactic state either is or is not similar to the one underlying our normal utterance of 'p'. In one conversational context it may be perfectly appropriate to describe a syntactic state in this way, while in another context the description may be utterly inappropriate. It is simply a mistake to assume that every meaningful predicate or open sentence corresponds to or expresses a property.

All of this still leaves us with no account of the property of believing that p. But, on reflection, perhaps that is just where we want to be. For in chapter 5 it was argued that a predicate of the form 'is a belief that p' can be analyzed as a predicate making a similarity claim. And, as we have just seen, such predicates typically do not express properties at all. What this suggests is that *there is no such thing as the property of believing that p*. The predicate 'is a belief that p' does not express or correspond to a property. If this is right, then we have yet another reason for not thinking of folk psychological beliefs as state tokens, since a state token is the instantiation of a property by an individual during a time interval, and if there is no property, then there can be no state token. It is important to realize, however, that the nonexistence of belief *properties* and belief *state tokens* does not entail that *predicates* of the form 'is a belief that p' are meaningless or never apply to anything, just as the nonexistence of the property of being similar to the USSR does not entail that 'is similar to the USSR' is meaningless or that it never applies to anything. In both cases the predicates in question apply to things quite unproblematically, though in different contexts they may apply to quite different things. A question I have often encountered in setting out my views about belief is whether I think there are any such things as beliefs. But the question is less than clear. If it means: Are statements of the form 'S believes that p' or 'x is a belief that p' ever true, the answer is plainly *yes*, at least on the modified Panglossian view we are currently exploring. However, if the question is construed as asking whether there are belief state tokens or belief state types (i.e., properties), then the answer is negative.

As Dennett has rightly noted, much recent work in the philosophy of mind can be construed as attempting to say what a pair of organisms or systems have in common when the same folk psychological predicate is true of each.[6] Often this question turns into a quest for some *property* that subjects share when they are thinking of Vienna or when they believe that Ouagadougou is the capital of Upper Volta. What our recent reflections make plain is that this quest is bound to end in failure. It is not in virtue of sharing some property that subjects both believe that p. So there is a sense in which Needham's painstaking Wittgensteinian survey of belief in various cultures came to just the right conclusion: There is no such thing as believing that p.[7] But putting the point in this way suggests a paradox which is not there. In denying that believing that p is a property, we need not deny that statements of the form 'x is a belief that p' are often unproblematically true.

Let us turn our attention, now, to the generalizations of folk psychology, generalizations like (1), (1″), (2) and (2″) in chapter 7. What status do they have on the modified Panglossian view I am elaborating? I have already argued at length that such generalizations have no role to play in a serious cognitive science. But nothing in those arguments nor anything in the arguments of the current section suffices to show that these generalizations might not turn out to be *true*. They are, to be sure, *vague* claims, since they inherit all the intrinsic vagueness of the folk psychological language of content. But no matter; vagueness is not incompatible with truth. Even if the generalizations turn out to be empirically false, as the rather crudely formulated examples in chapter 7 surely will, it is reasonable to think that they can be hedged into truths by adding some folk psychological qualifications and making clear that the regularities they aver, although they generally obtain, are not without exception. These generalizations might be thought of as analogous to rule-of-thumb generalizations in cooking. Consider, for example, the generalization that separated mayonnaise can usually be repaired by beating a bit of it into dry mustard, then gradually beating in the rest.[8] This generalization, like the generalizations of folk psychology, suffers from a certain vagueness. It is not clear just what counts as separated mayonnaise, nor is it clear where mixing gives way to beating and beating to whipping. Another point of analogy between the generalizations of cooking and those of folk psychology is that neither sort of generalization will find a place in a serious explanatory science. But nonetheless many of the generalizations known to good cooks are *true*, and wonderfully useful. A final analogy between folk psychological and culinary generalizations is that in both cases it is plausible to suppose that serious science will be able to explain why the rough-and-ready folk generalizations are generally true, and perhaps even explain why they are sometimes false. In the case of mayonnaise, I would guess that the explanation will come from the physical chemistry of colloids along with some detailed investigation of what, from the physical chemist's point of view, a separated mayonnaise actually is. And in the case of belief, the explanation will come from an STM cognitive theory along with some detailed investigation of what syntactic state or states are generally describable as beliefs that p. I am not at all clear about what is required to *reduce* one science or set of generalizations to another. But I suppose that if the term is used in some suitably loose sense, the prospect we are envisioning could be described as the reduction of folk psychology to STM cognitive theory.

To conclude our discussion of the modified Panglossian prospect, let us consider how the humanities and social sciences would fare if the view we are considering should prevail. In chapter 1, we worried that if the posits of folk psychology should turn out not to exist, then the descriptive claims of historians, literary critics, and others would turn out to be false. If the notion of believing that p is no more scientifically respectable than the notion of being bewitched, then any account of what Henry VIII believed Pope Clement would do is bound to be false. But on the modified Panglossian view, the historian's pronouncements are perfectly respectable and have a fair shot at being true. To say 'Henry VIII believed that Pope Clement would allow the annulment' is to claim that Henry was in a belief-like state similar to the one that would underlie our own normal utterance of the content sentence. And that may well be true. Even the vagueness of belief sentences need not be much of a problem to the historian, since it is generally reduced by context. And historians have context to spare. Of course historians often use the language of folk psychology to make *causal* claims in addition to purely descriptive ones. Thus for example it might be claimed that Henry decided to remarry *because* he believed that Catherine would not produce an heir to the throne. These causal claims, too, may well turn out to be true. If Henry's belief is some syntactic state token and if the facts turn out right, then this state could well be among the causes of his decision and his subsequent actions.

The social sciences often do more than make singular causal claims invoking the language of folk psychology; they try to formulate generalizations or laws. These attempts are a bit more problematic for the modified Panglossian, since economic or sociological generalizations cast in the language of folk psychology will suffer from the same vagueness and the same limitations that afflict the attempt to state psychological generalizations in folk psychological language. But I think the Panglossian might well persevere in his upbeat outlook by viewing these generalizations as rough-and-ready, rule-of-thumb generalizations, rather like those invoked by the experienced cook. When suitably hedged, the economist's or the sociologist's generalizations may be both true and useful, just as the chef's are. When (or if) a social science matures to the point where the vagueness and limitations of folk psychology become problematic, social scientists can begin to recast their theories about the relation between mental states and social processes in the content free language forged by the STM cognitive theorist. The modified Panglossian can take much the same line about philosophical theories cast in folk psychological terms. If the vagueness and limitations of folk language are problematic at a given stage of inquiry and if cognitive science has forged a less troublesome vocabulary, then by all means the philosopher should use it.[9]

2. Could It Turn Out That There Are No Such Things as Beliefs?

The modified Panglossian prospect that I have been sketching is a thoroughly attractive vision. It promises the best of both worlds: a serious cognitive science and a respectable folk psychology whose vocabulary can be invoked in good conscience to write history, literary criticism, and even social science. The optimist in me very much hopes that this vision can be sustained. But in more pessimistic moods I am inclined to think that the future will be rather less cheerful. Underlying my pessimism is the fact that the modified Panglossian story makes essential use of a pair of empirical assumptions. And the truth of these assumptions is very much an open question. If either of them should turn out to be mistaken, the proposed reconciliation between cognitive science and folk psychology would collapse. Let me focus on these assumptions one at a time.

The first was made quite explicitly in the previous section. In order to tell the story we did, we had to assume that "the correct cognitive theory is an STM theory *which cleaves reasonably closely to the pattern presupposed by folk psychology*. Such a theory will postulate belief-like states which interact with desire-like states, with perceptions, etc., along the lines sketched in figure 2." But now suppose that this assumption should turn out to be false. Suppose that the best theory of the mind we can come up with is not an STM theory at all. Or, rather more plausibly, suppose that it *is* an STM theory, but one whose general organization or gross functional architecture is *significantly* different from the functional architecture presupposed by folk psychology. If this should turn out to be the case, then we could no longer say that belief sentences stand a good shot at being true. For in saying 'S believes that p' we are saying that S is in a belief-like state similar to the one that would underlie our own ordinary utterance of the content sentence. And if it turns out that the overall structure of the human cognitive system is significantly different from the structure postulated by folk psychology, then this claim will be false. There will *be no* belief-like states, and thus S will be in none. (Nor, of course, will there be one underlying our own normal utterance of 'p'.) If folk psychology turns out to be seriously mistaken about the overall organization of our cognitive economy, then there will be nothing to which the predicate 'is a belief that p' applies.

Is there any reason to take this possibility seriously, any reason to think that folk psychology *might* turn out to be quite radically wrong about the general organization of our cognitive system? I want to propose two rather different lines of argument suggesting that the answer is yes, there is a real possibility that folk psychology might turn out to be quite radically wrong.

The first argument, the less serious of the pair, is an inductive generalization from the sorry history of folk theories in general.[10] It starts with the observation that folk psychology really is a *folk* theory, a cultural inheritance whose origin and evolution are largely lost in prehistory. The very fact that it is a folk theory should make us suspicious. For in just about every other domain one can think of, the ancient shepherds and camel drivers whose speculations were woven into folk theory have a notoriously bad track record. Folk astronomy was false astronomy and not just in detail. The general conception of the cosmos embedded in the folk wisdom of the West was utterly and thoroughly mistaken. Much the same could be said for folk biology, folk chemistry, and folk physics. However wonderful and imaginative folk theorizing and speculation has been, it has turned out to be screamingly false in every domain where we now have a reasonably sophisticated science. Nor is there any reason to think that ancient camel drivers would have greater insight or better luck when the subject at hand was the structure of their own minds rather than the structure of matter or of the cosmos. None of this constitutes an argument for the *falsity* of the folk theory about the general structure of the mind. But that is not the question at hand. The issue before us is whether we should view the possibility of folk psychology being false as anything more than a mere logical possibility. And I think the general failure of folk theories is reason enough to think that folk psychology might suffer the same fate.

At this point it might well be protested that casting aspersions on the origins and family history of a theory carries little weight once the theory has been fleshed out and pressed into service as a serious empirical hypothesis. If the functional architecture posited by folk psychology is useful in explaining the results of psychological experiments, then we should take the posit seriously no matter how disreputable its origins. And if some other account of the functional architecture of the mind does a better job, then we have reason enough to be skeptical of the folk story without insulting its parentage. The protest is one with which I have considerable sympathy. Ultimately questions about the general organization of the mind will have to be settled by building and testing theories embodying different organizational assumptions. What is more, optimists who think that the gross architecture of folk psychology will stand up to scientific scrutiny have plenty of ammunition in their arsenal. A great deal of the recent work in cognitive science has, tacitly or explicitly, assumed very much the picture of mental organization that folk psychology proposes. There are other straws in the wind, however. There are findings and theories suggesting that something is seriously wrong with the simple belief-desire structure implicit in commonsense wisdom. It would be out of place here to attempt any general census of the literature, tallying up those studies that presuppose folk structures and those that do not. Nor do I think there would be much point in the exercise, since the field is too new and too much in flux. But I do want to argue that the tenability of the folk conception of mental organization is very much an open empirical question. And to that end I will briefly review some work which seems to suggest that our cognitive system is organized along lines quite different from those posited by folk psychology.

The work I wish to review is drawn from the experimental social psychology literature on dissonance and self-attribution. Before considering this work, however, I want to focus attention on the fundamental feature of folk psychology which, I think, the work to be reviewed calls into question. For folk psychology, a belief is a state which can interact in many ways with many other states and which can be implicated in the etiology of many different sorts of behavior. A pattern of interaction which looms large in our commonsense scheme of things is the one linking beliefs to their normal, sincere linguistic expression. It is via this link that folk psychology describes belief. A belief *that p* is a belief-like state similar to one which we would *normally express by uttering 'p'*. But, of course, the belief that p does much more than merely contribute to the causation of its own linguistic expression. It may interact with desires in many ways, some of which will ultimately issue in nonverbal behavior. It is a fundamental tenet of folk psychology that *the very same* state which underlies the sincere assertion of 'p' also may lead to a variety of nonverbal behaviors. There is, however, nothing necessary or a priori about the claim that the states underlying assertions also underlie nonverbal behavior. There are other ways to organize a cognitive system. There might, for example, be a cognitive system which, so to speak, keeps two sets of books, or two subsystems of vaguely belief-like states. One of these subsystems would interact with those parts of the system responsible for verbal reporting, while the other interacted with those parts of the system responsible for nonverbal behavior. Of course it might be the case that the two belief-like subsystems frequently agreed with each other. But it might also be the case that from time to time they did not agree on some point. When this situation arose, there would be a disparity between what the subject said and what he did. What is striking about the results I shall sketch is that they strongly suggest that *our* cognitive system keeps two sets of books in this way. And this is a finding for which folk psychology is radically unprepared. If it is true, then states similar to the one underlying our own ordinary utterance of 'p' do *not* also participate in the production of our nonverbal behavior. In those cases when our verbal subsystem leads us to say 'p' and our nonverbal subsystem leads us to behave as though we believed some incompatible proposition, there will simply be no saying which we believe. Even in the (presumably more common) case where the two subsystems agree, there is no saying which state is the belief that p. If we really do have separate verbal and nonverbal cognitive storage systems, then the functional economy of the mind postulated by folk theory is quite radically mistaken. And under those circumstances I am strongly inclined to think that the right thing to say is that *there are no such things as beliefs*.

With this by way of stage setting, let me turn to a quick review of the salient studies from the attribution and dissonance literature. The central idea of attribution theory is that people attempt to explain their own physical, emotional, and behavioral responses by invoking relatively crude theories or rules of thumb. As the jargon would have it, they "attribute" their responses to the hypothesized causes suggested by their theory about how they work. What is more, this attribution itself has a host of further mental and behavioral effects.[11] A typical attribution experiment will attempt to focus on the attributional processes by leading a subject to make the *wrong* inference about the cause of his response. The subject will then be led to behave as though this mistaken attribution were correct. An example will serve to give the flavor of this work. Storms and Nisbett[12] asked insomniac subjects to record the time they went to bed and the time they finally fell asleep. After several days of recordkeeping, one group of subjects (the "arousal" group) was given a placebo pill to take fifteen minutes before going to bed. They were told that the pill would produce rapid heart rate, breathing irregularities, bodily warmth, and alertness, which are just the typical symptoms of insomnia. A second group of subjects (the "relaxation" group) was told that the pills would produce the opposite symptoms: lowered heart rate, breathing rate, body temperature, and alertness. Attribution theory predicts that the arousal group subjects would get to sleep *faster* on the nights they took the pills, because they would attribute their symptoms to the pills rather than to the emotionally laden thoughts that were running through their minds. It also predicts that subjects in the relaxation group will take *longer* to get to sleep. Since their symptoms persist despite having taken a pill intended to relieve the symptoms, they will infer that their emotionally laden thoughts must be particularly disturbing to them, and this belief will upset them further, making it all that much harder to get to sleep. Remarkably enough, both of these predictions were borne out. Arousal group subjects got to sleep 28 percent faster on the nights they took the pill, while relaxation subjects took 42 percent longer to get to sleep.

The core idea of dissonance research is that if subjects are led to behave in ways they find uncomfortable or unappealing and if they do not have what they take to be an adequate reason for enduring the effects of this behavior, then they will come to view the behavior or its effects as more attractive. Conversely if subjects are given some special reward for engaging in behavior they take to be intrinsically attractive, they will come to view the behavior as less attractive than if they had not received the special reward. The explanation offered for the "inadequate justification" phenomenon is that subjects note they have done something they thought to be unpleasant without any adequate reason and explain this prima facie anomalous behavior with the hypothesis that the behavior or its consequences are not so unpleasant as they had thought. The "overjustification" phenomenon is explained by supposing that subjects note they were rewarded to engage in the behavior, and they infer that, since they were motivated by the reward, the behavior itself must have played less of a role in motivating them. From this they infer that it must not be quite so intrinsically attractive. Once again an example will give the flavor of the work in this area. In a classic study, Zimbardo et al. asked subjects to endure a series of electric shocks while performing a learning task.[13] When the learning task was completed, they asked the subjects to repeat it. Some subjects were given adequate justification for repeating the task (the research was important, and nothing of value could be learned from the experiment unless the task was repeated). Other subjects were given insufficient justification (the experimenter was just curious about what would happen if they did it again). The prediction was that subjects in the inadequate justification group would come to think that the shocks were not all that unpleasant. This prediction was borne out in a startling way. Subjects in the insufficient justification group performed better in the second round of the learning task than did subjects in the adequate justification group. They also exhibited significantly lower galvanic skin responses in response to the shocks than did the subjects in the adequate justification group.

So far the work I have been recounting does not bear directly on the hypothesis that verbal and nonverbal behavior are subserved by different belief-like cognitive subsystems. To join that issue we must look at the work of Nisbett and Wilson. These investigators noted that the experimentally manipulated effect (or "dependent variable") in attribution and dissonance studies was generally some nonverbal indicator belief or attitude. However, when the nonverbal behavior of subjects under different experimental conditions seemed clearly to indicate that they differed in belief or attitude, their verbal behavior often did not indicate any difference in belief or attitude. Moreover when subjects' attention was drawn to the fact that their behavior indicated some change had taken place, they denied that the experimentally manipulated cause (or "independent variable") had been at all relevant to the change. Rather, they constructed some explanation of the change in their behavior in line with socially shared views about what sorts of causes are likely to produce the behavior in question. The picture this suggests is that subjects' verbal reporting systems have no access to the processes actually underlying their nonverbal behavioral changes. What the verbal reporting system does is to hypothesize explanations of the behavioral changes that have been noted, invoking relatively crude socially shared theories about how such behavior is to be explained. To use Nisbett's and Wilson's apt phrase, when we are called upon to explain why we acted in a certain way, we often respond by "telling more than we can know."

To see in a bit more detail what led Nisbett and Wilson to this view, let us return to our two illustrative studies. After the completion of the insomnia studies it was pointed out to arousal group subjects that they had gotten to sleep more quickly after taking the pill and to relaxation group subjects that they had taken longer to fall asleep. Subjects were asked why this had happened.

> Arousal subjects typically replied that they usually found it easier to get to sleep later in the week, or that they had taken an exam that had worried them but had done well on it and could now relax, or that problems with a roommate or girlfriend seemed on their way to resolution. Relaxation subjects were able to find similar sorts of reasons to explain their increased sleeplessness. When subjects were asked if they had thought about the pills at all before getting to sleep, they almost uniformly insisted that after taking the pills they had completely forgotten about them. When asked if it had occurred to them that the pill might be producing (or counteracting) their arousal symptoms, they reiterated their insistence that they had not thought about the pills at all after taking them. Finally, the experimental hypothesis and the postulated attribution process were described in detail. Subjects showed no recognition of the hypothesized process and . . . made little pretense of believing that *any* subjects could have gone through such processes.[14]

Analogous results were reported in the shock experiment.

> We pointed out to experimental subjects that they had learned more quickly the second time. A typical response would have been, "I guess maybe you turned the shock down."

> I don't remember any subject who ever described anything like the process of dissonance reduction that we knew to have occurred.[15]

In the Nisbett and Wilson paper the focus was on cognitive *processes*. Their central thesis was that subjects' reports about their own cognitive processes were not accurate introspective reports from an internal font of knowledge. Instead they proposed that

> when people are asked to report how a particular stimulus influenced a particular response, they do not do so by consulting a memory of the mediating process, but by applying or generating causal theories about the effects of that type of stimulus or that type of response. They simply make judgments, in other words, about how plausible it is that the stimulus would have influenced the reponse. These plausibility judgments exist prior to, or at least independently of, any actual contact with the particular stimulus embedded in a particular complex stimulus configuration.[16]

In support of their contention that verbal reports about underlying cognitive processes are often grounded in socially shared theories, Nisbett and Wilson cite numerous studies which indicate that a subject's verbal reports about the stimuli affecting his behavior and his reports about the processes mediating between stimulus and response correlate well with the predictions offered by nonparticipant "observer" subjects who were simply read verbal descriptions of the experiments and asked to predict what stimuli would affect the subject's behavior and what the processes would be. The most plausible explanation for this correlation is that both participant and observer subjects are basing their verbal reports on a shared set of theories about the processes underlying behavior.

Nisbett and Wilson are less clear on the status of verbal reports about mental *states*. Indeed in the final section of their paper they go out of their way to acknowledge that, while verbal reports about our own mental processes are typically rooted in commonsense theory rather than in accurate introspective access, verbal expressions of beliefs, emotions, evaluations, and plans probably do reflect access to "a great storehouse of private knowledge." As a number of critics have noted, however, it is extremely implausible to suppose that verbal reports of states are generally accurate if verbal reports of processes are not, since in many instances the inferential processes which the investigators attribute to the subjects involve the generation of new states from previously existing ones, from stimuli, etc.[17] And it would be anomalous indeed for subjects with no verbalizable access to their cognitive processes to be able to verbalize the various states invoked or produced in the intermediate stages of these processes. Quite apart from such a priori considerations, it is often clear from the evidence that subjects are not able to report on the various states invoked in attribution and dissonance processes. Consider, for example, the subjects in the Storms and Nisbett insomnia experiment. The attribution theory explanation requires that subjects undergo a reasoning process something like the following:

> I am alert, warm, breathing irregularly, and have a rapid heart rate; I have just taken a pill which should alleviate all of these symptoms; since the symptoms are as severe as ever, the troubled thoughts or emotions which cause the symptoms must be even more severe than usual tonight.

However, subjects resolutely deny that they had any such thoughts and they find it thoroughly implausible that anyone could have gone through such a thought process.

In a recent paper Wilson acknowledges that when the issue at hand is the accessibility to verbal reports, the distinction between states and processes is untenable.[18] Instead he proposes a model which hypothesizes two relatively independent cognitive systems. One of these systems "mediates behavior (especially unregulated behavior), is largely unconscious, and is, perhaps, the older of the two systems in evolutionary terms. The other, perhaps newer, system is largely conscious, and its function is to attempt to verbalize, explain, and communicate what is occurring in the unconscious system."[19] This second system, which Wilson calls the "verbal explanatory system," does not generally tap into the system mediating behavior. Rather, it proceeds by "making inferences based on theories about the self and the situation."[20]

In support of this hypothesis Wilson describes a number of experiments aimed at showing that the behavior controlling system and the ¡verbal explanatory system can be manipulated independently. An example will illustrate how these experiments work. Wilson, Hull, and Johnson induced subjects to agree to visit senior citizens in a nursing home.[21] For one group of subjects overt pressure from the experimenter was made salient as a reason for agreeing to make the visit. For a second group of subjects pressure from the experimenter was not made salient. It was hypothesized that in subjects in the second (no pressure) group the behavior controlling system would infer that the subject had agreed because he or she was a helpful person; no such inference was expected in the first (pressure) group. A behavioral test of this hypothesis was included in the experiment. A second experimenter, as part of what was supposedly a second study, asked subjects if they would volunteer to help former mental patients. As expected, subjects in the no-pressure group were significantly more likely to volunteer to help former mental patients.

Crosscutting this manipulation of the hypothesized behavior controlling system was an attempt to manipulate the verbal explanatory system. Immediately after agreeing to visit the nursing home, half of the subjects in each group were asked to list all of the reasons they could think of that might explain why they agreed to go, and to rate the relative importance of the reasons. (This group of subjects will be referred to as the "reasons analysis" group.) Some time later all subjects were given a questionnaire, again administered by a second experimenter and supposedly as part of a second study. In the questionnaire, subjects were asked to rate themselves on various traits relevant to helpfulness. The hypothesis was that the reasons analysis manipulation would not affect the subjects' nonverbal behavior, i.e., that it would not affect their willingness to volunteer to help the former mental patients. It was further hypothesized that the reason analysis manipulation would prime the verbal explanatory system and thus that it would affect subjects' reports about how helpful they were. Both predictions were borne out. When induced to think about reasons, subjects in the no-pressure group rated themselves as significantly more helpful than did subjects in the pressure group. These results are just what we would expect if there are indeed separate behavior controlling and verbal explanatory systems which can be manipulated independently. Thus the results provide some intriguing evidence in favor of the model which postulates two more-or-less independent cognitive systems.*

Wilson is careful to stress the tentative and rather speculative status of the dual systems hypothesis. He urges that we view the model "more as a heuristic for generating research than as a theory with firm empirical underpinnings."[22] Given the fragmentary nature of the evidence and the rather rudimentary state of the model, his caution is certainly appropriate. But for our current purposes, even a tentative model suffices to establish the point. My thesis is not that the presuppositions of folk psychology have been shown to be false. My claim is only that the jury is still out. Much important work is being done in a framework compatible with the folk psychological picture of the structure of the mind. However, as Wilson's model illustrates, there is also much serious work which does not comport comfortably with that folk psychological picture.

The modified Panglossian story of the previous section makes a pair of empirical assumptions. Thus far we have been focusing on the assumption about the general organization or "gross architecture" of our cognitive system. I want to turn, now, to the second assumption. This one, unlike the first, will require some effort to tease out of the story we have told about folk psychology. To simplify matters, I will begin by assuming that the folk psychological account of our cognitive architecture is correct, though this assumption too is often challenged by the models which cast doubt on the second assumption.

When we invoke a content sentence to attribute a belief to someone, we are characterizing that person's belief by comparing it with a potential belief of our own. We are saying that the subject has a belief state similar to the one which would play the central causal role if our utterance of the content sentence had had a typical causal history. This assumes a certain degree of what I shall call *modularity* in the organization of our belief or memory store.[23] A belief or memory storage

---

*For another line of argument in support of a dual system model, see Wason and Evans 1975. To forestall a possible objection, it might be worth noting that neither of the dual systems postulated by Wilson would count was a "module" as Fodor (1983) uses that term. What Wilson is proposing is a quite radical cleavage in what folk psychology encourages us to think of as the central store of beliefs. Neither of the two resulting subsystems of states can comfortably be regarded as a system of beliefs.

system is *modular* to the extent that *there is some more or less isolatable part of the system which plays (or would play) the central role in a typical causal history leading to the utterance of a sentence.* There is no a priori guarantee that our belief store is organized in this way. It might be the case that there is no natural or segregatable part of the belief store which *can* be isolated as playing a special role in the production of individual speech acts. If this turns out to be the case, however, typical belief attributions will misfire in a quite radical way. They assume that there is some isolable belief state which plays a central role in the production of speech acts, and they assert that the subject has a state similar to the one which would play this role were the content sentence uttered in earnest. If the assumption turns out to be false, belief ascriptions will typically lack a truth value. They will in effect be invoking definite descriptions ('similar to *the belief state which would play the central causal role . . .* ') which fail to denote.

Perhaps the best way of seeing what is involved in the modularity assumption is to look at some mental models which are plainly compatible with it. Many workers in cognitive psychology and artificial intelligence are interested in the structure or organization of human memory. Some models of memory organization postulate a distinct sentence or sentence-like structure for each memory. On these models, memory may be viewed as a list of sentence-like structures, with each one corresponding to a separate belief. The best known advocate of these sentential models of memory is John McCarthy.[24] If the memory or belief store is organized in this way, then it is a relatively straightforward matter to locate the belief state underlying an utterance. It will be a separate sentence or formula, one of many on the memory list. The modularity assumption is clearly satisfied. Note that the sentential theorist need not and should not claim that to believe that p is *merely* to have a certain formula on the memory list. To count as a belief that p, a formula must be embedded in a suitable doxastic neighborhood; there must be many other related beliefs on the memory list in addition to the formula that leads to the utterance of 'p'. This after all is the lesson to be learned from our discussion of holism and ideological similarity. Still a McCarthy-style sentential model of memory is a paradigm case of what I am calling a modular organization. Given a suitable background, there is a straightforward way to say which part or element of the memory store would underlie a sincere assertion of the content sentence.

From the point of view of the memory-model builder, sentential models have a number of advantages. Perhaps the most conspicuous is that they are easy to modify. If we assume an appropriately rich set of background beliefs, then to add a new belief requires only the addition of a single new formula. Thus, for example, if we have a model of my current memory and if tomorrow I come to believe that my son will star in his school play, we can add this belief to the model by adding the appropriate formula. But sentential models also have some much discussed disadvantages. The most notorious is that their relatively unstructured format makes it difficult to locate information which is *relevant* to the task at hand. If the model is supposed to explain how subjects recover information from memory in, say, answering questions, then as the size of the memory increases, the task of locating the answer gets harder. The problem is compounded if the answer is not explicitly represented in the memory but is entailed by formulae which are explicitly represented. For in that case no simplistic matching search will suffice, and complicated heuristics are required to locate premises which may be relevant to answering the question.

In an effort to deal with these problems, a number of different proposals have been explored. One idea is to model memory as a complex network of nodes and labeled links, where the nodes represent concepts and the links represent various sorts of relations among concepts.[25] The network structure provides a systematic way to search through the memory when hunting for information relevant to a certain concept or set of concepts. Network models are still quite far over to the modular end of the spectrum, however. For in a network model it is generally unproblematic to isolate the part of the network which would play a central role in a normal utterance of a given content sentence. There will be a distinct fragment of the network which represents the belief that the hippie touched the debutante. The belief that the policeman touched the hippie will be represented by another fragment sharing various nodes with the first.

In recent years a number of theorists have expressed considerable skepticism about highly modular models. Part of their skepticism can be traced to the suspicion that sentential and network models cannot explain our ability to locate relevant information in memory quickly and efficiently. But added to this is a growing concern about modeling non-deductive inference. It has grown increasingly clear that language use and comprehension require enormous amounts of non-deductive inference.[26] Information relevant to the subject matter of the discourse, the intentions of the speaker, the setting of the conversation, and more must all be brought into play in reaching an interpretation of simple, everyday discourse. And much of the needed information is not logically entailed by anything the hearer believes. It is at best plausibly suggested by the information he has stored in memory, plus the information conveyed by the utterances to be interpreted. Thus models which aim at explaining our ability to interpret a discourse must propose a memory structure which will facilitate the efficient use of memory in non-deductive inference. Similar problems confront theorists concerned to model thinking, problem solving, or creative thought.

There is certainly no consensus on how these problems are best attacked. What is important for our purposes, however, is that a number of leading theorists have urged that the best way to tackle them is to build models in which no single component or naturally isolatable part can be said to underlie the expression of a belief or a desire. Winograd for example notes that in early artificial intelligence models of language use and memory structure, it was typically assumed that "there is a systematic way of correlating sentences in natural language with the structure in the representation system that corresponds to the same facts about the world."[27] He adds, quite rightly, that a model incorporating this assumption "corresponds quite closely to the model of language and meaning developed by philosophers of language like Frege, drawing on ideas back to Aristotle and beyond."[28] It is in short an assumption that early models borrowed from folk psychology. Winograd, however, describes his work as a progressive departure from this assumption. He cites with approval Maturana's observation that many phenomena which *"for an observer* can be described in terms of representation" may nonetheless be understood as "the activity of a structure-determined system with no mechanism corresponding to a representation. As a simple example," Winograd continues,

> we might watch a baby successfully getting milk from its mother's nipple and argue that it has a "representation" of the relevant anatomy, or of the activity of feeding. On the other hand, we might note that there is a reflex that causes it to react to a touch on the cheek by turning its head in that direction, and another that triggers sucking when something touches its mouth. From the viewpoint of effective behavior, it has a "correct representation," but it would be fruitless to look for neurophysiological mechanisms that correspond to reasoning that uses facts about breasts or milk.[29]

Winograd suggests that we should explore the same idea in modeling higher cognitive functions. We would be modeling the cognitive processes of subjects whose behavior tempts us to describe them in terms of beliefs and desires, representations, and so on, though the models themselves would have nothing "either physical or functional" which correlates in any straightforward way with the beliefs, desires or representations. Comparing the situation to programing in a rather different domain, Winograd notes:

> If I say of a program, "It has the goal of minimizing the number

of jobs on the waiting queue," there is unlikely to be a "goal structure" somewhere in memory or a "problem solving" mechanism that uses strategies to achieve specified goals. *There may be dozens or even hundreds of places throughout the code where specific actions are taken, the net effect of which is being described.*[30]

It is interesting to note that the philosopher D. C. Dennett has used a very similar illustration in arguing that beliefs and desires need not correspond in any systematic way to distinct functional states.

> In a recent conversation with the designer of a chess-playing program I heard the following criticism of a rival program: "It thinks it should get its queen out early." This assigns a propositional attitude to the program in a very useful and predictive way, for as the designer went on to say, one can usually count on chasing that queen around the board. But for all the many levels of explicit representation to be found in that program, nowhere is anything roughly synonymous with "I should get my queen out early." explicitly tokened. The level of analysis to which the designer's remark belongs describes features of the program that are, in an entirely innocent way, emergent properties of the computational processes that have "engineering reality". I see no reason to believe that the relation between belief-talk and psychological-process talk will be any more direct.[31]

Another major figure in artificial intelligence who has long been urging non-modular approaches to memory storage is Marvin Minsky. In his widely discussed "Frames" paper he urges that we move away from theories which try "to represent knowledge as collections of separate, simple fragments."[32] On Minsky's view, "the strategy of complete separation of specific knowledge from general rules of inference is much too radical. We need more direct ways for linking fragments of knowledge to advice about how they are to be used."[33] In a more recent paper Minsky elaborates what he calls a "Society of Mind" view in which the mechanisms of thought are divided into many separate "specialists that intercommunicate only sparsely."[34] On the picture Minsky suggests, none of the distinct units or parts of the mental model "have meanings in themselves"[35] and thus none can be identified with individual beliefs, desires, etc. Modularity—I borrow the term from Minsky—is violated in a radical way since meaning or content emerges only from "great webs of structure" and no natural part of the system can be correlated with "explicit" or verbally expressible beliefs.[36]

At this point the optimal strategy would be to supplement the programmatic and often rather metaphorical views I have been reporting with the description of a few up-and-running non-modular models of memory and language use. Unfortunately the optimal strategy is not one I can follow, since to the best of my knowledge there are no such up-and-running models. The absence of well-developed non-modular alternatives would be a real deficit in my argument if my goal were to show that modular theories of memory structure are *false*. But my goal has been the more modest one of establishing that the falsity of modular models is a possibility to be taken seriously. And to show this, I think it suffices to demonstrate that serious theorists take the prospect very seriously indeed.

Let me summarize the argument of this section. We began by asking whether it might turn out that there are no such things as beliefs. Might it be the case that ordinary folk psychological belief ascriptions will turn out, quite generally, not to be true? The answer I have been urging is that this is indeed a serious possibility, since ordinary belief ascription makes a pair of empirical assumptions, both of which might turn out to be false. On my view, then, it is too early to say whether folk psychology has a future. The modified Panglossian prospect sketched in the previous section promises a welcome reconciliation between the scientific and the manifest images of the mind. But if it turns out that either the modularity or the gross architecture presupposed by folk psychology is mistaken, the proposed reconciliation will crumble.

3. The Instrumentalist View of Folk Psychology

I think it would be appropriate to bring this volume to a close with some brief reflections on the views of a philosopher who has struggled, perhaps more persistently than anyone else, to come to grips with the possibility that folk psychology may turn out to be false psychology. The philosopher is D. C. Dennett, and from his earliest work to his most recent he has sought some way to insulate our commonsense attributions of belief and desire from the possibility that scientific advances may show them all to be mistaken. Underlying Dennett's concern is a pair of convictions with which I have considerable sympathy. The first is that folk psychology is intimately interwoven with our view of ourselves as persons and as moral agents. If we had to renounce folk psychology, we should probably have to reject the notions of personhood and moral agency as well. But to do this is to plunge into the abyss, since the concept of personhood stands at the very center of our conception of ourselves and our place in the universe. Dennett's second conviction is that folk psychology is almost certainly not going to mesh very well with a mature cognitive science. Though he is prepared to admit that the issue is an empirical one, and still far from settled, he is not optimistic about the Panglossian vision of cognitive science, in either its original or its modified form. Thus as Dennett sees it, some other way must be found to protect our conception of ourselves from the ravages of science.

The central doctrine in Dennett's effort to insulate folk psychology from potential scientific falsification maintains that folk notions like belief and desire either are or can be reinterpreted as *instrumentalistic* concepts. On this view, attributions of belief and desire are to be construed as part of an idealized predictive calculus, and the states attributed are not taken to correspond to any actual physical or functional state within the organism or system. As Dennett puts it, "the beliefs and other intentions of an intentional system need [not] be *represented* 'within' the system in any way for us to get a purchase on predicting its behavior by ascribing such intentions to it."[37] Rather, these "putative . . . states" can be relegated "to the role of idealized fictions in an action-predicting, action-explaining calculus."[38] Beliefs and desires are not what Reichenbach calls "illata—posited theoretical entities." Instead, as he sees it, they are "abstracta—calculation bound entities or logical constructs."[39] Their status is analogous to the lines in a parallelogram of forces.[40] The virtue of this view is that it shields ascriptions of belief and desire from most sorts of scientific falsification. Since beliefs and desires are explicitly relegated to the status of instrumentalistic fictions, they are compatible with *anything* we might discover about the physiological or functional organization of the human cognitive system, so long as the instrumentalistic calculus does indeed provide a useful predictive device.

Dennett tends to waffle a bit on whether he views our *actual* folk psychological concepts as instrumentalistic or whether he is proposing that these concepts might be *replaced* by instrumentalistic substitutes.[41] In what follows, I will attend to these alternatives in turn. First let us consider the suggestion that the folk psychological notions we actually use are instrumentalistic and thus make no substantive commitments about underlying internal mechanisms. Is this true? Two lines of argument point toward a negative answer.

The first begins with the fact that we often talk about beliefs and desires as though they had *causal* properties. Suppose for example that you have been accused of giving false information to the police. They asked you where Harry was on the day of the crime, and you reported that he was in Chicago. Later evidence has made it clear that he could not possibly have been in Chicago on that day, and the false report has landed you in considerable trouble. On hearing of your plight, I ask with some puzzlement, "Whatever caused you to say that to the police?" And you reply, "I really believed Harry was in Chicago." For a second example suppose that Otto, a notorious stick-in-the-mud, has recently quit his job and is now spending most of his time planning an extended trip around the world. On hearing of this, I ask you, "What caused the radical change in Otto's behavior?" and you reply, "Oh, he has always had a strong desire to travel, though he could never afford it. But recently an uncle died leaving him almost a million dollars." Now there are two things to note about these little dialogues. The first is that they are prefectly natural; we say things like that all the time. The second is that they appear to be ascribing causal properties to beliefs and desires. It may of course be that these surface appearances are deceptive and that the remarks must be analyzed in some way which does not ascribe causal properties to folk psychological states. But without a persuasive argument to this effect, I am inclined to take commonsense discourse about beliefs and desires at face value. Beliefs and desires, as they are conceived by folk psychology, do have both causes and effects. If this is right, however, it is a problem for the instrumentalist view, since only real entities, "illata," can have causes and effects. "Abstracta" or calculational fictions cannot. It makes no sense to ask about the causes or effects of a line in a parallelogram of forces.

A second argument against the view that folk psychology conceives of beliefs and desires instrumentally rests on our intuitions about various cases in which the innards of an apparent intentional system turn out not to be what we expected. If Dennett is right, there is nothing we *could* find out about the inner workings of a person which would convince us that he did not have beliefs and desires, so long as he behaved in a way which was compatible with the instrumentalistic belief-desire calculus. But surely there are things we might find out which would convince us that a "person" who behaved normally enough did not really have beliefs. Ned Block has conjured the case of a chess-playing computer which, though it plays a decent game of chess, has no internal representation of rules or goals or strategy. Rather, this computer's memory contains an *enormous* multiply branching tree represention of every possible chess game up to, say, 100 moves in length. At each point in the game, the computer simply plays the appropriate prerecorded move. Watching the play of such a machine, we might be tempted at some point to say, "It believes I am going to attack with my queen." But on learning just how the machine works we are much less inclined to say this. Analogously, if we were to run across (what appeared to be) a person whose conversations, chess play-ing, and other behaviors were controlled by an enormous, prepro-grammed branching list of what to do when, I think our intuition would rebel at saying that the "person" believed that I was about to attack with my queen—or indeed that he believed anything else! Entities with innards like that don't have beliefs.

In one of his papers Dennett in effect concedes the point that the inner workings of an organism which behaves like an intentional system *are* relevant in determining whether it has beliefs and desires. "In a science fiction mood," he writes, "we can imagine startling discoveries (e.g., some 'people' are organic puppets remotely controlled by Martians) that would upset any home truths about believers and moral agenthood you like."[42] But once this has been granted, it can no longer seriously be maintained that our folk psychological notions of belief and desire are instrumentalistic. If belief and desire ascriptions were simply elements of a predictive calculus, then the transceivers inside these organic puppets should be quite irrelevant to the truth or falsity of such ascriptions.

As I mentioned earlier, it is not clear whether Dennett really thinks that ordinary folk psychological ascriptions of belief and desire are intended instrumentalistically. As often as not, he appears to be arguing that our notions of personhood, moral agency, and the like can be preserved by *replacing* folk notions with suitably similar concepts, reconstructed explicitly to avoid any possible clash with scientific psychology. Dennett and I have made something of a sport out of debating whether the ersatz notions he proposes would sustain our view of ourselves as rational, free, moral agents.[43] I do not propose to launch another volley in that game here. For it seems to me that even if his proposed instrumentalistic substitutes would protect the notion of personhood from the threat of being undermined by science, there is something patently disreputable about the move. In a clever and insightful paper Paul Churchland points out that the strategy Dennett recommends for saving folk psychology from falsification could have been marshaled, mutatis mutandis, by an alchemist seeking to protect his doctrine of "immaterial spirits" from the challenge posed by the materialistic elemental chemistry of Lavoisier and Dalton.[44] By construing his fundamental notions of "spirit" and "ensoulment" instrumentally, an alchemist could insist that atomic theory leaves alchemy unscathed. "Spirit" and "ensoulment" are "abstracta—calculation bound entities or logical constructs;" their role is that of "idealized fictions" in a reaction predicting calculus. A similar instrumentalistic defense could be mounted for the phlogiston theory of combustion. But, as Churchland properly notes, these defenses are "an outrage against reason and truth. . . . Alchemy is a terrible theory, well-deserving of its complete elimination, and the defense of it just explored is reactionary, obfuscatory, retrograde, and wrong."[45]

The instrumentalistic strategy Dennett recommends is reminiscent of Osiander's notorious though well-meaning attempt to take the sting out of Copernican theory by treating it as no more than a calculating tool—"sky geometry, without reference to physical reality."[46] In both cases we see an attempt to protect some cherished part of our world view by reconstruing a realistic theory as an instrumentalistic one. There is, however, no reason to think that Dennett's ploy will be any more successful than Osiander's. If the empirical presuppositions of folk psychology turn out to be false, as well they might, then we are in for hard times. Deprived of its empirical underpinnings, our age-old conception of the universe within will crumble just as certainly as the venerable conception of the external universe crumbled during the Renaissance. But that analogy ultimately suggests an optimistic conclusion. The picture of the external universe that has emerged from the rubble of the geocentric view is more beautiful, more powerful, and more satisfying than anything Aristotle or Dante could imagine. Moreover, the path from Copernicus to the present has been full of high intellectual adventure. The thrust of my argument is that we may be poised to begin a similar adventure. And that, surely, is an exciting place to be.

Notes

Chapter 1

1. Watson (1930, pp. 2–5). For a useful history of the beginnings of modern learning theory, see Hilgard and Bower (1975).
2. The terms 'manifest image' and 'scientific image' are borrowed from Sellars (1962), though, as Brand (forthcoming) notes, Sellars's distinction does not quite map onto the distinction between folk psychology and scientific psychology, since for Sellars the manifest image is restricted to the observable, while folk psychology is up to its ears in unobservable "theoretical" states.
3. See Schlick (1932), Carnap (1932), Stevenson (1937), Ayer (1946), Hempel (1965).
4. The magnum opus of philosophical behaviorism was Ryle (1949). For some other examples of the genre, see Gustafson (1964).
5. See, for example, Skinner (1974).
6. See Putnam (1962a, 1969), Fodor (1968), Dennett (1978b), and Erwin (1978).
7. Skinner (1971).
8. For reasoning see Wason and Johnson-Laird (1972), Wason (1977), Johnson-Laird and Wason (1970), and Johnson-Laird (1975). For problem solving see Newell and Simon (1972). For inference see Nisbett and Ross (1980), Kahneman and Tversky (1973), Tversky and Kahneman (1973, 1974), Ross (1977), Ross, Lepper, and Hubbard (1975), Kahneman, Slovic, and Tversky (1982). For perception see Gregory (1973, 1974), Eisenstadt and Kareev (1977). For imagery see Shepard (1978), Shepard and Metzler (1971), Simon (1972), Kosslyn (1975), Kosslyn, Pinker, Smith, and Swartz (1979), Dennett (1978c). For memory see Anderson and Bower (1973), Anderson (1976), Kintsch (1974).
9. Much to my surprise, some readers have taken this sentence to be an endorsement of functionalist theories of pain and sensations. No such endorsement is intended.

Chapter 2

1. Morton (1980).
2. See, for example, Armstrong (1968, p. 91).
3. Hempel (1935, sec. 4).
4. Carnap (1947, sec. 13).
5. See Putnam (1962a, 1963, 1969).
6. For an excellent survey of the literature on this theme, see Lycan (1971).
7. Lewis (1972, sec. 1).
8. For Lewis's account of the notion of typical cause, see Lewis (1966, p. 166).
9. Lewis (1972, sec. 3).

10. Lewis (1972, sec. 3), suggests that we take T to be a disjunction of all conjunctions of *most* of our platitudes. "That way it will not matter if a few are wrong."
11. Lewis (1972, sec. 3).
12. Though not Lewis; see Lewis (1980). For a critique of Lewis's view, see Block (1980b).
13. See the most recent quote from Lewis where he suggests that we assemble platitudes "regarding the causal relations of mental states, sensory stimuli and motor responses."
14. See Armstrong (1968, p. 39).
15. For an extended discussion see Block (1978).
16. See Lewis (1966, fn. 6).
17. Field (1978).

Chapter 3

1. See Fodor (1978b) and Field (1978).
2. Most of the items on my list are mentioned in Fodor (1978b), Field (1978), or Lycan (1981).
3. Vendler (1972).
4. Much of this paragraph is inspired by Dennett (1975).
5. Fodor (1978b, p. 517).
6. This is not to suggest that ascriptions of belief to animals and young children are free from problems. See chapter 5, section 5, and Stich (1979).
7. Harman (1970, 1973, 1975).
8. Field (1978).
9. Fodor (1975, 1978b).
10. Fodor (1978b, fn. 11).
11. Ibid., p. 515.
12. Ibid., p. 516.
13. See chapter 5, section 2.
14. Lycan (1981, p. 142).
15. Ibid.
16. Ibid.
17. Ibid., p. 143.
18. Ibid.
19. Field (1978, p. 96).
20. Fodor (1980a, p. 240).
21. Field (1978), Lycan (1981), Perry (1979, 1980a, 1980b), McDowell (1977).

Chapter 4

1. See, for example, Stich (1983).
2. See Nisbett and Wilson (1977).
3. See Fodor (1964).
4. See Lakatos (1970).
5. For a review of the literature, which is at once fascinating and deeply depressing, see Gardner (1974).
6. Most of the credit for this bit of fancy goes to Paul Churchland (1979, p. 112).
7. Philosophers, not surprisingly, have gone both ways on the issue. For a trenchant defense of the negative answer, see Feyerabend (1962). For the affirmative side, see Putnam (1973, 1975b).
8. See Donnellan (1966), Kaplan (1968), Kripke (1972), Putnam (1975b), Devitt (1981).
9. See chapter 3, section 5.

10. Perry (1977).
11. See Castaneda (1967), Perry (1977, 1979), Lewis (1979).
12. See Gregory (1966, p. 126).
13. Johnson-Laird and Wason (1970), Wason and Johnson-Laird (1972), Wason (1977).
14. See Armstrong (1973), Routley (1981), Dennett (forthcoming b).

Chapter 5

1. Fodor (1978b, p. 516); compare chapter 3, section 5.
2. Indeed a plausible case *has* been made in Fodor (1981c).
3. For an elaboration of the view that analytic philosophy at its best is continuous with cognitive simulation, see Todd (1977) and Sloman (1978). For examples of the sort of cognitive simulation I have in mind, see Schank and Abelson (1977), Minsky (1975), and Hayes (1971).
4. David Lewis's account of commonsense psychological concepts, sketched in chapter 2, adopts this viewpoint, though with some fancy logical footwork the sort of account Lewis develops can be turned into an explicit reductive definition. See Lewis (1970).
5. See chapter 3, section 4.
6. The notion of a prototype has received considerable attention in recent empirical work on the mental representation of concepts, and it will play a prominent role in my account of belief. For some references see notes 10–13. For quite a different view on our recognition of deviant causal chains, see Peacocke (1979).
7. Davidson (1968).
8. I should note that although I am borrowing Davidson's idea, I do not share his motivation. Davidson's analysis of *oratio obliqua* is offered with an eye toward providing Tarski-style semantic theories for natural language sentences. But this is a goal I take to be misguided. See Stich (1976) and Martin (1972).
9. Quine (1960, p. 219).
10. For an excellent survey see Smith and Medin (1981).
11. See Rips, Shoben, and Smith (1973) and Rosch (1973).
12. See Rosch (1973) and Mervis, Catlin, and Rosch (1976).
13. See Rosch and Mervis (1975).
14. See Tversky (1977).
15. See Kripke (1972), Putnam (1975b), Devitt (1981), McGinn (1982).
16. Burge (1979).
17. See Zemach (1976), Loar (1976), McGinn (1982), Fodor (1982).
18. See Stich (1982, pp. 201–203).
19. Haugeland (1979).
20. See Davidson (1974, 1975).
21. Evans-Prichard (1956, ch. 5).
22. See Horton (1967). I should note that this change in perspective is far from universal. Apparently Evans-Prichard himself retained the view that the Nuer were prerational.
23. See Pettit (1978).
24. There is an interesting analogy here with Kuhn's discussion of covert contradictions in premodern physics. See Kuhn (1964).
25. See Rokeach (1967).
26. Ibid.
27. Quine (1960, sec. 13).
28. Ibid., p. 59.
29. Davidson (1974). See also Stroud (1968).
30. Rorty (1972).

31. See chapter 4, section 2.
32. For an intersting discussion of some analogous cases, see Grandy (forthcoming).
33. See, for example, Routley (1981).
34. See, for example, Davidson (1975).
35. Stich (1979).
36. Fodor (1980a, p. 238).
37. Ibid., p. 240.
38. Ibid.
39. Fodor (1978a).
40. Ibid., p. 207.
41. See chapter 4, section 2.
42. Ibid.

Chapter 6

1. An ancestor of this chapter was a paper coauthored with D. C. Dennett and presented to a conference at Bristol University in November 1978. For Dennett's views on the topic, see Dennett (1982).
2. Quine (1956).
3. See Wallace (1972).
4. Among those who have pursued the former strategy are Hintikka (1962, 1967, 1970), Sellars (1968), Armstrong (1973), Kaplan (1968), and perhaps Sosa (1970). For a defense of the latter strategy, see Wallace (1972) whose goals are tentatively endorsed by Hornsby (1977).
5. Quine (1951, sec. 6).
6. Chastain (1975), G. Wilson (1978).
7. Chastain (1975, pp. 212–213).
8. Ibid., p. 224.

Chapter 7

1. Fodor (1981b, pp. 25–26). Emphasis is Fodor's.
2. Fodor (1978b, p. 505 and p. 506).
3. Fodor (1981b, p. 30).
4. See chapter 4, section 1.
5. Ross, Lepper, and Hubbard (1975), Ross (1977).
6. Fodor suggests this move in Fodor (1980b) in reply to Stich (1980b).
7. See chapter 4, section 1.
8. Morton (1980), p. 81.
9. See Burge (1979).
10. See Fodor (1982).
11. See the example of Dave^1, . . . , Dave^9 in chapter 4, section 3.

Chapter 8

1. This account of states is modeled on Kim's account of events. See Kim (1969, 1976).
2. Putnam (1975b).
3. Ibid., p. 137.
4. Ibid., p. 136.
5. Fodor (1980a, p. 226). For the remainder of this section, references to this paper will be given in parentheses in the text.

6. Fodor (1980b, p. 102).

7. Ibid., p. 103.

8. See Fodor (1974).

9. For a less rough-and-ready account of supervenience, see Kim (1978, 1982).

10. Stich (1978).

11. See Shapere (1982).

12. See Alston (1974).

13. Pylyshyn (1980, p. 161).

14. See Grice (1957) and Schiffer (1972).

15. See Heider (1972) and Rosch (1973).

16. For more on basic actions, see Danto (1965) and Goldman (1970).

17. Fodor (1981b, p. 24).

Chapter 9

1. But see chapter 11, section 1.

2. Fodor (1981b, p. 26). Emphasis added. N.B. This quote and quote (1) in chapter 7, section 1 are taken from the same page.

3. Fodor (forthcoming, ms p. 6).

4. Fodor (1978a, p. 223).

5. Fodor (1980a, p. 227).

6. Ibid., p. 240.

7. Fodor (1980c, p. 431).

8. Fodor (1978b, p. 517).

9. Ibid., p. 519.

10. Fodor (1975, p. 27).

11. Ibid., p. 31.

12. Ibid., p. 32.

13. Ibid., p. 39.

14. Fodor (forthcoming).

15. Pylyshyn (1980, p. 161).

16. See chapter 8, section 3.

17. Schiffer (1981). For the remainder of this section, references to this article will be given in parentheses in the text. For Field's version of the view, see Field (1978, sec. 5). For Loar's version, see Loar (1980) and (1982, ch. 8). Loar's discussion in this last reference is quite difficult, and it is not at all clear to me whether the sorts of objections I raise against Schiffer's paper can be mounted, mutatis mutandis, against Loar.

18. Fodor would agree. See Fodor (forthcoming).

Chapter 10

1. P. M. Churchland (1979, 1981), P. M. Churchland and P. S. Churchland (1981).

2. P. M. Churchland (1981, p. 75).

3. Ibid., p. 68.

4. Ibid.

5. Ibid., p. 67.

6. P. M. Churchland (1979, p. 114).

7. P. M. Churchland (1981, p. 73).

8. Ibid., p. 74.

9. Ibid.

10. Ibid., p. 75.

11. Ibid.
12. Ibid.
13. Ibid.
14. Ibid., p. 76.
15. For a fascinating, occasionally far-fetched reconstruction of the prehistory during which folk psychology was evolving and developing, see Jaynes (1976).
16. See Wilkes (1978, 1981).
17. Wilkes (1981, pp. 149–150).
18. Ibid., p. 149.
19. See P. M. Churchland (1970).
20. See Laudan (1977).
21. See P. S. Churchland (1980) and P. M. Churchland (1979, sec. 19).
22. P. M. Churchland (1979, p. 129).
23. Ibid.
24. Ibid., p. 130.
25. Ibid., p. 133.
26. Ibid.
27. Ibid., p. 134.
28. Ibid., p. 136.
29. Ibid.
30. Ibid., p. 128.
31. Hacking (1982, p. 44).
32. See Needham (1972).
33. Wilkes (1981, p. 152).
34. Ibid., p. 155.
35. Morton (1980, p. 95).

Chapter 11

1. See Quine (1948).
2. See Chomsky and Scheffler (1958).
3. See chapter 5, section 1.
4. Fodor (1983).
5. See chapter 9, section 2.
6. Dennett (1978d).
7. Needham (1972).
8. See Child, Bertholle, and Beck (1967, p. 88).
9. See Goldman (1978a, 1978b).
10. I have discussed this argument, on several occasions, with Paul and Patricia Churchland, though I have quite forgotten whether they suggested it to me or I suggested it to them. I also seem to recall Daniel Dennett suggesting or endorsing a similar argument in conversation.
11. See Bem (1972).
12. Storms and Nisbett (1970).
13. Zimbardo, Cohen, Weisenberg, Dworkin, and Firestone (1969).
14. Nisbett and Wilson (1977, p. 238).
15. Ibid. In this passage Nisbett and Wilson are quoting from a letter from Zimbardo.
16. Ibid., p. 248.
17. See, for example, Ericsson and Simon (1980).
18. Wilson (forthcoming).
19. Ibid., ms. pp. 21–22.

20. Ibid., ms. p. 1.
21. Wilson, Hull, and Johnson (1981).
22. Wilson (forthcoming, ms. p. 20).
23. I use this term with some reluctance, since it has recently been pressed into service by Jerry Fodor with a very different meaning. See Fodor (1983). Readers familiar with Fodor's essay are urged to keep the difference in mind.
24. See McCarthy (1959, 1977).
25. There are many variations on this theme. Among the more sophisticated are Anderson and Bower (1973) and Anderson (1976). See also Kintsch (1974), Norman and Rumelhart (1975), and Collins and Quillian (1972).
26. See Schank and Abelson (1977), Schank (1981), and Winograd (1981).
27. Winograd (1981, p. 233).
28. Ibid.
29. Ibid., p. 249.
30. Ibid., p. 250, emphasis added.
31. Dennett (1977, p. 107). For an important recent discussion of the use of explicit representations in psychological theories, see Stabler (forthcoming).
32. Minsky (1981a, p. 95). See also Minsky (1975).
33. Minsky (1981a, p. 127).
34. Minsky (1981b, p. 95).
35. Ibid., p. 100.
36. Ibid.
37. Dennett (1976, p. 277).
38. Dennett (1978a, p. 30).
39. Dennett (forthcoming a, ms. p. 13).
40. Ibid., ms. p. 20.
41. See Stich (1981, pp. 58 ff).
42. Dennett (1980, p. 73).
43. See Stich (1980a), Dennett (1980), Stich (1981), Dennett (1981).
44. P. M. Churchland (1981).
45. Ibid., p. 81.
46. See Koestler (1959, part 3). The quote is from p. 194.

References

(Note: When an article is listed as appearing in more than one place, page references in the notes refer to the version marked with an *.)

Alston, W. (1974). "Conceptual Prolegomena to a Psychological Theory of Intentional Action," in C. Brown, ed., *Philosophy of Psychology*, New York, Harper & Row.

Anderson, J. (1976). *Language, Memory and Thought*, Hillsdale, N.J., Lawrence Erlbaum.

Anderson, J., and Bower, G. (1973). *Human Associative Memory*, New York, John Wiley.

Armstrong, D. (1968). *A Materialist Theory of the Mind*, London, Routledge and Kegan Paul.

Armstrong, D. (1973). *Belief, Truth and Knowledge*, Cambridge, Cambridge University Press.

Ayer, A. (1946). *Language, Truth and Logic*, New York, Dover.

Bem, D. (1972). "Self-Perception Theory," in L. Berkowitz, ed., *Advances in Experimental Social Psychology*, vol. 6, New York, Academic Press.

Block, N. (1978). "Troubles with Functionalism," in W. Savage, ed., *Perception and Cognition. Issues in the Foundations of Psychology. Minnesota Studies in the Philosophy of Science*, vol. 9, Minneapolis, University Of Minnesota Press. Reprinted in Block (1980a).

Block, N., ed., (1980a). *Readings in the Philosophy of Psychology*, vol. 1, Cambridge, Mass., Harvard University Press.

Block, N. (1980b). "Introduction: What Is Functionalism?" in Block (1980a).

Block, N., ed., (1981). *Readings in the Philosophy of Psychology*, vol. 2, Cambridge, Mass., Harvard University Press.

Brand, M. (forthcoming). "Folk Psychology and Scientific Psychology: Friends or Enemies?" mimeo.

Burge, T. (1979). "Individualism and the Mental," in P. French, T. Uehling, and H. Wettstein, eds., *Midwest Studies in Philosophy, vol. 4, Studies in Epistemology*, Minneapolis, University of Minnesota Press.

Carnap, R. (1932). "The Elimination of Metaphysics Through the Logical Analysis of Language," reprinted in A. Ayer, ed., *Logical Positivism*, Glencoe, Ill. The Free Press, 1959.

Carnap, R. (1947). *Meaning and Necessity*, Chicago, University of Chicago Press.

Castaneda, H. (1967). "Indicators and Quasi-Indicators," *American Philosophical Quarterly*, 4.

Chastain, C. (1975). "Reference and Context," in K. Gunderson, ed., *Language, Mind and Knowledge: Minnesota Studies in the Philosophy of Science*, vol. 7, Minneapolis, University of Minnesota Press.

Child, J., Bertholle, L., and Beck, S. (1967). *Mastering the Art of French Cooking*, New York, Knopf.

Chomsky, N., and Scheffler, I. (1958). "What Is Said To Be," *Proceedings of the Aristotelian Society*, 59.

Churchland, P. M. (1970). "The Logical Character of Action Explanations," *Philosophical Review*, 79, 2.

Churchland, P. M. (1979). *Scientific Realism and the Plasticity of Mind*, Cambridge, England, Cambridge University Press.

Churchland, P. M. (1981). "Eliminative Materialism and Propositional Attitudes," *Journal of Philosophy*, 78, 2.

Churchland, P. M., and Churchland, P. S. (1981). "Functionalism, Qualia and Intentionality," *Philosophical Topics*, 12, 1.

Churchland, P. S. (1980). "A Perspective on Mind-Brain Research," *Journal of Philosophy*, 77, 4.

Collins, A., and Quillian, M. (1972). "Experiments on Semantic Memory and Language Comprehension," in L. Gregg, ed., *Cognition in Learning and Memory*, New York, Wiley.

Danto, A. (1965). "Basic Actions," *American Philosophical Quarterly*, 2.

Davidson, D. (1968). "On Saying That," *Synthese*, 17.

Davidson, D. (1974). "On the Very Idea of a Conceptual Scheme," *Proceedings and Addresses of the American Philosophical Association*, 47.

Davidson, D. (1975). "Thought and Talk," in S. Guttenplan, ed., *Mind and Language*, Oxford, Oxford University Press.

Dennett, D. (1971). "Intentional Systems," *Journal of Philosophy*, 68, 4. Reprinted in Dennett (1978a).

Dennett, D. (1975). "Brain Writing and Mind Reading," in K. Gunderson, ed., *Language, Mind and Knowledge, Minnesota Studies in the Philosophy of Science*, vol. 7, Minneapolis, University of Minnesota Press. Reprinted in Dennett (1978a).*

Dennett, D. (1976). "Conditions of Personhood," in A. Rorty, ed., *The Identities of Persons*, Berkeley, University of California Press. Reprinted in Dennett (1978a).

Dennett, D. (1977). "Critical Notice: *The Language of Thought* by Jerry Fodor," *Mind*, 86. Reprinted in Dennett (1978a) under the title "A Cure for the Common Code."*

Dennett, D. (1978a). *Brainstorms*, Cambridge, Mass.: MIT Press, Bradford.

Dennett, D. (1978b). "Skinner Skinned," in Dennett (1978a).

Dennett, D. (1978c). "Two Approaches to Mental Images," in Dennett (1978a).

Dennett, D. (1978d). "Current Issues in the Philosophy of Mind," *American Philosophical Quarterly*, 15, 4.

Dennett, D. (1980). "Reply to Professor Stich," *Philosophical Books*, 21, 2.

Dennett, D. (1981). "Making Sense of Ourselves," *Philosophical Topics*, 12, 1.

Dennett, D. (1982). "Beyond Belief," in A. Woodfield, ed., *Thought and Object*, Oxford, Oxford University Press.

Dennett, D. (forthcoming a). "Three Kinds of Intentional Psychology," to appear in a Thyssen Foundation Philosophy Group volume, ed. by Richard Healey.

Dennett, D. (forthcoming b). "Intentional Systems in Cognitive Ethology: The 'Panglossian Paradigm' Defended," to appear in *Behavorial and Brain Science*.

Devitt, M. (1981). *Designation*, New York, Columbia University Press.

Donnellan, K. (1966). "Reference and Definite Descriptions," *Philosophical Review*, 75.

Donnellan, K. (1972). "Proper Names and Identifying Descriptions," in D. Davidson and G. Harman, eds., *Semantics of Natural Language*, Dordrecht, Reidel.

Einstadt, M., and Kareev, Y. (1977). "Perception in Game Playing: Internal Representation and Scanning of Board Positions," in Johnson-Laird and Wason (1977).

Ericsson, K., and Simon, H. (1980). "Verbal Reports as Data," *Psychological Review*, 87, 3.

Erwin, E. (1978). *Behavior Therapy*, Cambridge, England, Cambridge University Press.

Evans-Prichard, E. (1956). *Nuer Religion*, Oxford, Oxford University Press.

Feyerabend, P. (1962). "Explanation, Reduction and Empiricism," in H. Feigl and G. Maxwell, eds., *Scientific Explanation, Space and Time: Minnesota Studies in the Philosophy of Science*, vol. 3, Minneapolis, University of Minnesota Press.

Field, H. (1978). "Mental Representation," *Erkenntnis*, 13, 1. Reprinted in Block (1981).*

Fodor, J. (1964). "On Knowing What We Would Say," *Philosophical Review*, 73, 2.

Fodor, J. (1968). *Psychological Explanation*, New York, Random House.

Fodor, J. (1974). "Special Sciences," *Synthese*, 28. Reprinted in Fodor (1981a).

Fodor, J. (1975). *The Language of Thought*, New York, Thomas Y. Crowell.

Fodor, J. (1978a). "Tom Swift and His Procedural Grandmother," *Cognition*, 6. Reprinted in Fodor (1981a).*

Fodor, J. (1978b). "Propositional Attitudes," *The Monist*, 61, 4.* Reprinted in Fodor (1981a).

Fodor, J. (1980a). "Methodological Solipsism Considered as a Research Strategy in Cognitive Psychology," *Behavorial and Brain Sciences*, 3, 1. Reprinted in Fodor (1981a).*

Fodor, J. (1980b). "Methodological Solipsism: Replies to Commentators," *Behavioral and Brain Sciences*, 3, 1.

Fodor, J. (1980c). "Searle on What Only Brains Can Do," *Behavioral and Brain Sciences*, 3, 3.

Fodor, J. (1981a). *Representations*, Cambridge, Mass., MIT Press.

Fodor, J. (1981b). "Introduction: Something on the State of the Art," in Fodor (1981a).

Fodor, J. (1981c). "The Present Status of the Innateness Controversy," in Fodor (1981a).

Fodor, J. (1982). "Cognitive Science and the Twin-Earth Problem," *Notre Dame Journal of Formal Logic*, 23.

Fodor, J. (1983). *The Modularity of Mind*, Cambridge, Mass., MIT Press.

Fodor, J. (forthcoming). "Psychosemantics or: Where Do Truth Conditions Come From?" mimeo.

Gardner, H. (1974). *The Shattered Mind*, New York, Vintage Books.

Goldman, A. (1970). *A Theory of Human Action*, Englewood Cliffs, N.J., Prentice-Hall.

Goldman, A. (1978a). "Epistemology and the Psychology of Belief," *The Monist*, 61, 4.

Goldman, A. (1978b). "Epistemics: The Regulative Theory of Cognition," *Journal of Philosophy*, 75, 10.

Grandy, R. (forthcoming). "Some Misconceptions about Belief," to appear in R. Grandy and R. Warner, eds., *Philosophical Ground of Rationality: Intentions, Categories, Ends*, Oxford, Oxford University Press.

Gregory, R. (1973). *Eye and Brain: The Psychology of Seeing*, 2nd ed., New York, McGraw-Hill.

Gregory, R. (1974). "Perception as Hypothesis," in C. Brown, ed., *Philosophy of Psychology*, New York, Harper & Row.

Grice, P. (1957). "Meaning," *Philosophical Review*, 66.

Grice, P. (1975). "Method in Philosophical Psychology (From the Banal to the Bizarre)," *Proceedings and Addresses of the American Philosophical Association*, 48.

Gustafson, D. (1964). *Essays in Philosophical Psychology*, New York, St. Martin's Press.

Hacking, I. (1982). "Wittgenstein the Psychologist," *New York Review of Books*, 29, 5, April 1, 1982.

Harman, G. (1970). "Language Learning," *Nous*, 4, 1.

Harman, G. (1973). *Thought*, Princeton, N.J., Princeton University Press.

Harman, G. (1975). "Language, Thought and Communication," in K. Gunderson, ed., *Language, Mind and Knowledge, Minnesota Studies in the Philosophy of Science*, vol. 7, Minneapolis, University of Minnesota Press.

Haugeland, J. (1979). "Understanding Natural Language," *Journal of Philosophy*, 76, 11.

Hayes, P. (1971). "A Logic of Actions," in B. Meltzer and D. Mitchie, eds., *Machine Intelligence, 6,* Edinburgh, Edinburgh University Press.

Heider, E. (1972). "Universals of Color Naming and Memory," *Journal of Experimental Psychology*, 93.

Hempel, C. (1935). "The Analysis of Psychology," in Block (1980a).

Hempel, C. (1965). "Empiricist Criteria of Cognitive Significance: Problems and Changes," in Hempel, C. G., *Aspects of Scientific Explanation*, New York, The Free Press.

Hilgard, E., and Bower, G. (1975). *Theories of Learning*, 4th ed., Englewood Cliffs, N.J., Prentice-Hall.

Hintikka, J. (1962). *Knowledge and Belief*, Ithaca, N.Y., Cornell University Press.

Hintikka, J. (1967). "Individuals, Possible Worlds and Epistemic Logic," *Nous*, 1.

Hintikka, J. (1970). "Objects of Knowledge and Belief: Acquaintances and Public Figures," *Journal of Philosophy*, 67.

Hornsby, J. (1977). "Singular Terms in Contexts of Propositional Attitude," *Mind*, 86.

Horton, R. (1967). "African Traditional Thought and Western Science," reprinted in B. Wilson, ed., *Rationality*, Oxford, Blackwell, 1979.

Jaynes, J. (1976). *The Origin of Consciousness in the Breakdown of the Bicameral Mind*, Boston, Houghton Mifflin.

Johnson-Laird, P. (1975). "Models of Deduction," in Falmange, R. C., ed., *Reasoning: Representation and Process*, Hillsdale, N.J., Lawrence Erlbaum Associates.

Johnson-Laird, P., and Wason, P. (1970). "A Theoretical Analysis into a Reasoning Task," *Cognitive Psychology*, 1:134–48. Also in Johnson-Laird and Wason (1975).

Johnson-Laird, P., and Wason, P., eds. (1977). *Thinking: Readings in Cognitive Science*, Cambridge, England, Cambridge University Press.

Kaplan, D. (1968). "Quantifying In," *Synthese*, 19.

Kahneman, D., and Tversky, A. (1973). "On the Psychology of Prediction," *Psychological Review*, 80.

Kahneman, D., Slovic, P., and Tversky, A. (1982). *Judgment under Uncertainty: Heuristics and Biases*, Cambridge, England, Cambridge University Press.

Kim, J. (1969). "Events and Their Descriptions: Some Considerations," in N. Rescher et al., eds., *Essays in Honor of C. G. Hempel*, Dordrecht, Reidel.

Kim, J. (1976). "Events and Property Exemplifications," in M. Brand and D. Walton, eds., *Action Theory*, Dordrecht, Reidel.

Kim, J. (1978). "Supervenience and Nomological Incommensurables," *American Philosophical Quarterly*, 15.

Kim, J. (1982). "Psychological Supervenience," *Philosophical Studies*, 41.

Kintsch, W. (1974). *The Representation of Meaning in Memory*, Hillsdale, N.J., Lawrence Erlbaum.

Koestler, A. (1959). *The Sleepwalkers*, New York, Grosset and Dunlap.

Kosslyn, S. (1975). "Information Representation in Visual Images," *Cognitive Psychology*, 7.

Kosslyn, S., Pinker, S., Smith, G., and Swartz, S. (1979). "On the Demystification of Mental Imagery," *Behavioral and Brain Sciences*, 2.

Kripke, S. (1972). "Naming and Necessity," in D. Davidson and G. Harman, eds., *Semantics of Natural Language*, Dordrecht, Reidel.

Kuhn, T. (1964). "A Function for Thought Experiments," in Johnson-Laird and Wason (1977).

Lakatos, I. (1970). "Falsification and the Methodology of Scientific Research Programmes," in I. Lakatos, *The Methodology of Scientific Research Programmes*, ed. by J. Worrall and G. Currie, Cambridge, England, Cambridge University Press.

Laudan, L. (1977). *Progress and Its Problems: Towards a Theory of Scientific Growth*, Berkeley, University of California Press.

Lewis, D. (1966). "An Argument for the Identity Theory," *Journal of Philosophy*, 63. Reprinted in Rosenthal (1971).*

Lewis, D. (1970). "How to Define Theoretical Terms," *Journal of Philosophy*, 67.

Lewis, D. (1972). "Psychophysical and Theoretical Identifications," *Australasian Journal of Philosophy*, 50. Reprinted in Block (1980a).

Lewis, D. (1979). "Attitudes De Dicto and De Se," *Philosophical Review*, 88.

Lewis, D. (1980). "Mad Pain and Martian Pain," in Block (1980a).

Loar, B. (1972). "Reference and Propositional Attitudes," *Philosophical Review*, 81, 1.

Loar, B. (1976). "The Semantics of Singular Terms," *Philosophical Studies*, 30.

Loar, B. (1980). "Syntax, Functional Semantics, and Referential Semantics," *Behavioral and Brain Sciences*, 3, 1.

Loar, B. (1981). *Mind and Meaning*, Cambridge, England, Cambridge University Press.

Lycan, W. (1971). "Noninductive Evidence: Recent Work on Wittgenstein's 'Criteria'," *American Philosophical Quarterly*, 8, 2.

Lycan, W. (1982). "Toward a Homuncular Theory of Believing," *Cognition and Brain Theory*, 4, 2.

Martin, E. (1972). "Truth and Translation," *Philosophical Studies*, 23.

McCarthy, J. (1959). "Programs with Common Sense," *Mechanisation of Thought Processes*, vol. 1, London, HMSO.

McCarthy, J. (1977). *First Order Theories of Individual Concepts*, Stanford Artificial Intelligence Laboratory.

McDowell, J. (1977). "On The Sense and Reference of a Proper Name," *Mind*, 86. Reprinted in M. Platts, ed. *Reference, Truth and Reality*, London, Routledge and Kegan Paul.

McGinn, C. (1982). "The Structure of Content," in A. Woodfield, ed., *Thought and Object*, Oxford University Press.

Mervis, C., Catlin, J., and Rosch, E. (1976). "Relationships among Goodness-of-Example, Category Norms, and Word Frequency," *Bulletin of the Psychonomic Society*, 7.

Minsky, M. (1975). "Frame-System Theory," in Johnson-Laird and Wason (1977).

Minsky, M. (1981a). "A Framework for Representing Knowledge," in J. Haugeland, *Mind Design*, Cambridge, Mass., MIT Press.

Minsky, M. (1981b). "K-Lines: A Theory of Memory," in D. Norman, ed., *Perspectives on Cognitive Science*, Norwood, N.J., Ablex.

Morton, A. (1980). *Frames of Mind*, Oxford, Oxford University Press.

Needham, R. (1972). *Belief, Language and Experience*, Chicago, University of Chicago Press.

Newell, A., and Simon, H. (1972). *Human Problem Solving*, Englewood Cliffs, N.J., Prentice-Hall.

Nisbett, R., and Ross, L. (1980). *Human Inference: Strategies and Shortcomings of Social Judgement*, Englewood Cliffs, N.J., Prentice-Hall.

Nisbett, R., and Wilson, T. (1977). "Telling More Than We Can Know: Verbal Reports on Mental Processes," *Psychological Review*, 84.

Norman, D., and Rumelhart, D. (1975). "Memory and Knowledge," in D. Norman, D. Rumelhart, and The LNR Research Group, eds., *Explorations in Cognition*, San Francisco, Freeman.

Peacocke, C. (1979). *Holistic Explanation*, Oxford, Oxford University Press.

Perry, J. (1977). "Frege on Demonstratives," *Philosophical Review*, 86, 4.

Perry, J. (1979). "The Problem of the Essential Indexical," *Nous*, 13.

Perry, J. (1980a). "Belief and Acceptance," in P. French, T. Uehling, and H. Wettstein, eds., *Midwest Studies in Philosophy, vol. 5, Studies in Epistemology*, Minneapolis, University of Minnesota Press.

Perry, J. (1980b). "A Problem about Continued Belief," *Pacific Philosophical Quarterly*, 61, 4.

Pettit, P. (1978). "Rational Man Theory," in C. Hookway and P. Pettit, eds., *Action and Interpretation*, Cambridge, England, Cambridge University Press.

Putnam, H. (1962a). "Dreaming and 'Depth Grammar,' " in R. Butler, ed., *Analytical Philosophy, First Series*, Oxford, Blackwell. Also in Putnam (1975a).

Putnam, H. (1962b). "The Analytic and the Synthetic," in H. Feigl and G. Maxwell, eds., *Scientific Explanation, Space, and Time: Minnesota Studies in the Philosophy of Science*, vol. 3, Minneapolis, University of Minnesota Press.

Putnam, H. (1963). "Brains and Behavior," in R. Butler, ed., *Analytical Philosophy, Second Series*, Oxford, Blackwell. Also in Putnam (1975a).

Putnam, H. (1969). "Logical Positivism and the Philosophy of Mind," in P. Achinstein and S. Barker, eds., *The Legacy of Logical Positivism*, Baltimore, Johns Hopkins Press. Also in Putnam (1975a).

Putnam, H. (1973). "Explanation and Reference," in G. Pearce and P. Maynard, eds., *Conceptual Change*, Dordrecht, Reidel. Also in Putnam (1975a).

Putnam, H. (1975a). *Mind, Language and Reality*, Cambridge, England, Cambridge University Press.

Putnam, H. (1975b). "The Meaning of 'Meaning'," in K. Gunderson, ed., *Language, Mind and Knowledge, Minnesota Studies in the Philosophy of Science*, 7, Minneapolis, University of Minnesota Press.* Also in Putnam (1975a).

Pylyshyn, Z. (1980). "Cognitive Representation and the Process-Architecture Distinction," *Behavioral and Brain Sciences*, 3, 1.

Quine, W. (1948). "On What There Is," *Review of Metaphysics*, 2. Reprinted in W. Quine, *From A Logical Point of View*, Cambridge, Mass., Harvard University Press, 1953.

Quine, W. (1951). *Mathematical Logic*, rev. ed., New York, Harper & Row.

Quine, W. (1956). "Quantifiers and Propositional Attitudes," *Journal of Philosophy*, 53. Reprinted in W. Quine, *The Ways of Paradox*, New York, Random House, 1966.

Quine, W. (1960). *Word and Object*, Cambridge, Mass., MIT Press.

Rips, L., Shoben, E., and Smith, E. (1973). "Semantic Distance and the Verification of Semantic Relations," *Journal of Verbal Learning and Verbal Behavior*, 12.

Rokeach, M. (1967). *The Three Christs of Ypsilanti*, New York, Vintage Books.

Rorty, R. (1972). "The World Well Lost," *Journal of Philosophy*, 69, 19.

Rosch, E. (1973). "On the Internal Structure of Perceptual and Semantic Categories," in T. Moore, ed., *Cognitive Development and the Acquisition of Language*, New York, Academic Press.

Rosch, E., and Mervis, C. (1975). "Family Resemblance Studies in the Internal Structure of Categories," *Cognitive Psychology*, 7.

Rosenthal, D. (1971). *Materialism and the Mind-Body Problem*, Englewood Cliffs, N.J., Prentice-Hall.

Ross, L. (1977). "The Intuitive Psychologist and His Shortcomings," in L. Berkowitz, ed., *Advances in Experimental Social Psychology*, vol. 10, New York, Academic Press.

Ross, L., Lepper, M., and Hubbard, M. (1975). "Perseverance in Self-Perception and Social Perception: Biased Attributional Processes in the Debriefing Paradigm," *Journal of Personality and Social Psychology*, 32.

Routley, R. (1981). "Alleged Problems in Attributing Beliefs, and Intentionality, to Animals," *Inquiry*, 24.

Ryle, G. (1949). *The Concept of Mind*, London, Hutchinson.

Schank, R. (1981). "Language and Memory," in D. Norman, ed., *Perspectives on Cognitive Science*, Norwood, N.J., Ablex.

Schank, R., and Abelson, R. (1977). *Scripts, Plans, Goals and Understanding*, Hillsdale, N.J., John Wiley and Sons.

Schiffer, S. (1972). *Meaning*, Oxford, Oxford University Press.

Schiffer, S. (1981). "Truth and The Theory of Content," in H. Parret and J. Bouverese, eds., *Meaning and Understanding*, Berlin, Walter de Gruyter.

Schlick, M. (1932). "Positivism and Realism," reprinted in A. Ayer, ed., *Logical Positivism*, Glencoe, Ill., The Free Press 1959.

Sellars, W. (1962). "Philosophy and the Scientific Image of Man," in R. Colodny, ed., *Frontiers of Science and Philosophy*, Pittsburgh, University of Pittsburgh Press. Also in Sellars (1963).

Sellars, W. (1963). *Science, Perception and Reality*, New York, Humanities Press.

Sellars, W. (1968). "Some Problems about Belief," *Synthese*, 19.

Shapere, D. (1982). "The Concept of Observation in Science and Philosophy," *Philosophy of Science*, 49.

Shepard, R. N. (1978). "The Mental Image," *American Psychologist*, 33.

Shepard, R. N., and Metzler, J. (1971). "Mental Representation of Three Dimensional Objects," *Science*, 171.

Simon, H. A. (1972). "What Is Visual Imagery? An Information Processing Interpretation," in L. W. Gregg, ed., *Cognition in Learning and Memory*, New York, John Wiley.

Skinner, B. F. (1971). *Beyond Freedom and Dignity*, London, Jonathan Cape.

Skinner, B. F. (1974). *About Behaviorism*, New York, Vintage Books.

Sloman, A. (1978). *The Computer Revolution in Philosophy: Philosophy, Science and Models of Mind*, Atlantic Highlands, N.J., Humanities Press.

Smith, E., and Medin, D. (1981). *Concepts and Categories*, Cambridge, Mass., Harvard University Press.

Sosa, E. (1970). "Propositional Attitudes de Dictu and de Re," *Journal of Philosophy*, 67, 21.

Stabler, E. (forthcoming). "How Are Grammars Represented?" to appear in *Behavioral and Brain Sciences*.

Stevenson, C. (1937). "The Emotive Meaning of Ethical Terms," *Mind*, 46. Reprinted in A. Ayer, ed., *Logical Positivism*, Glencoe, Ill., The Free Press (1959).

Stich, S. (1976). "Davidson's Semantic Program," *Canadian Journal of Philosophy*, 4.

Stich, S. (1978). "Autonomous Psychology and The Belief-Desire Thesis," *The Monist*, 61.

Stich, S. (1979). "Do Animals Have Beliefs?" *Australasian Journal of Philosophy*, 57, 1.

Stich, S. (1980a). "Headaches," *Philosophical Books*, 21, 2.

Stich, S. (1980b). "Paying the Price for Methodological Solipsism," *Behavioral and Brain Sciences*, 3, 1.

Stich, S. (1981). "Dennett on Intentional Systems," *Philosophical Topics*, 12, 1.

Stich, S. (1982). "On The Ascription of Content," in A. Woodfield, ed., *Thought and Object*, Oxford, Oxford University Press.

Stich, S. (1983). "Armstrong on Belief," in R. Bogdan, ed., *Profile: David Armstrong*, Dordrecht, D. Reidel.

Storms, M., and Nisbett, R. (1970). "Insomnia and the Attribution Process," *Journal of Personality and Social Psychology*, 2.

Stroud, B. (1968). "Conventionalism and the Indeterminacy of Translation," *Synthese*, 19, 1&2.

Todd, W. (1977). "The Use of Simulations in Analytic Philosophy," *Metaphilosophy*, 8, 4.

Tversky, A. (1977). "Features of Similarity," *Psychological Review*, 84, 4.

Tversky, A., and Kahneman, D. (1973). "Availability: A Heuristic for Judging Frequency and Probability," *Cognitive Psychology*, 5.

Tversky, A., and Kahneman, D. (1974). "Judgments under Uncertainty: Heuristics and Biases," *Science*, 185.

Vendler, Z. (1972). *Res Cogitans*, New York, Cornell University Press.

Wallace, J. (1972). "Belief and Satisfaction," *Nous*, 4, 2.

Wason, P. (1977). "Self-Contradiction," in Johnson-Laird and Wason (1977).

Wason, P., and Evans, J. (1975). "Dual Processes in Reasoning," *Cognition*, 3.

Wason, P., and Johnson-Laird, P. (1972). *Psychology of Reasoning: Structure and Content*, London, B. T. Batsford.

Watson, J. (1930). *Behaviorism*, Chicago, University of Chicago Press.

Wilkes, K. (1978). *Physicalism*, London, Routledge and Kegan Paul.

Wilkes, K. (1981). "Functionalism, Psychology and the Philosophy of Mind," *Philosophical Topics*, 12, 1.

Wilson, G. (1978). "On Definite and Indefinite Descriptions," *Philosophical Review*, 87, 1.

Wilson, T. (forthcoming). "Strangers to Ourselves: The Origins and Accuracy of Beliefs about One's Own Mental States," mimeo.

Wilson, T., Hull, J., and Johnson, J. (1981). "Awareness and Self-Perception: Verbal Reports on Internal States," *Journal of Personality and Social Psychology*, 40.

Winograd, T. (1981). "What Does It Mean to Understand Language?" in D. Norman, ed., *Perspectives on Cognitive Science*, Norwood, N.J., Ablex.

Zemach, E. (1976). "Putnam's Theory on the Reference of Substance Terms," *Journal of Philosophy*, 73, 5.

Zimbardo, P., Cohen, A., Weisenberg, M., Dworkin, L., and Firestone, I. (1969). "The Control of Experimental Pain," in P. Zimbardo, *The Cognitive Control of Motivation*, Glenview, Ill., Scott Foresman.

Index